# ALGA
# e SOUT
# PORTUGAL

# *ALGARVE & SOUTHERN PORTUGAL*

Brian and Eileen Anderson

A & C Black · London

Published by
A & C Black (Publishers) Limited,
35 Bedford Row, London WC1R 4JH

Photographs © B. and E. Anderson

Maps and plans by Robert Smith,
© A & C Black (Publishers) Limited

ISBN 0–7136–4148–7

A CIP catalogue record for this book is
available from the British Library

The authors and the publishers have done
their best to ensure the accuracy of all the
information in this guide. They can accept
no responsibility for any loss, injury or
inconvenience sustained by any traveller as
a result of information or advice contained
in this book.

The publishers invite readers to write in
with comments, suggestions and corrections
for the next edition of the guide. Writers of
the most informative letters will be awarded
a free Regional Guide of their choice.

Typeset in 9 on 11 pt Optima

Printed in Singapore by Imago

To good friends Rosie Pires and Jack Thornton who shared with us some of the delights of southern Portugal

## Acknowledgements

Considerable help was received from Tourist Office staff throughout the whole of southern Portugal, but in particular we would like to thank Mária Elizabeta Máximo of the Faro Office and João Andrade Santos and Terésa Chicou of the Évora office. There is no disguising the fact that we fell in love with Mértola and it is due in no small part to the enthusiasm of the archaeologist Waldemar Miguel who gave so freely of his time in showing us around. Two residents of Algarve who we must mention for their hospitality and help are John and Madge Measures, authors of *Southern Portugal — its people, traditions and wildlife.*

# CONTENTS

## *Maps and plans*

# 1. INTRODUCTION

Algarve has been so heavily promoted as a tourist destination that some visitors cease to think of it as part of Portugal but simply as a region to spend a holiday. There are good reasons for this and not least is its unique character. Here is a touch of Europe which enjoys 3000 hours annually of Mediterranean-bright sun, some of the most beautiful and scenic beaches imaginable and a flavour of Africa after centuries of Moorish occupation. The beaches alone are such a draw that the wealth of interest in the inland towns and villages of Algarve is greatly overlooked and Alentejo, the neighbouring region, almost totally neglected. It takes a little over two hours to drive the length of Algarve, which many visitors happily undertake, whilst a drive northwards of the same duration is more than enough to penetrate Alentejo, to visit, perhaps, the walled town of Mértola, on the banks of the Guadiana River, which was nourished by the Romans and sustained by the Visigoths and the Moors, all of whom have left rich traces. Algarve is not an island, just a region of Portugal which is convenient to reach and which makes a particularly good staging post to explore the very best of the southern part of the country.

Volumes of space, long straight roads through undulating plains, achingly blue skies, pigs snuffling in the fields, Alentejo could not be more different from Algarve. The elemental beauty of its landscapes alone is enough to satisfy but there is a rich topping in ancient walled towns, castles and layers of history from the Romans through to the Moors. This little known and little visited region of the country describes itself, with real justification, as the hidden treasure of Portugal. Alentejo is a very large province occupying a third of the country but only the area south of Lisbon is explored here.

## Geography and Geology

Occupying the most southern part of the country, the province of Algarve is cut off from the north by a series of low hills which straggle from east to west. Insignificant in height, these mountains probably contributed more to its sense of isolation in the days before the introduction of motorised transport. Algarve is not an especially large province. From the Guadiana River, which forms its eastern boundary with Spain, the distance to the west coast is around 100 miles (132km) while the depth from north to south is some 20–25

1

miles (30–40km). The restless Atlantic Ocean, which has provided boundless energy over aeons of time to grind away the sandstone cliffs into superb beaches, forms the southern and western boundaries.

Algarve has areas of sharply contrasting geology which have effectively influenced land use and economic development. The Serras which make up the north of the region are composed of schists which yield extremely poor stony soils, acid in nature and low in nutrients which sustain little in the way of agriculture. Much of these highly folded hills is covered with the dark sticky-leaved, *Cistus ladanifer*, which adds its own drabness to the hillsides for much of the year. Cork oaks grow well under these conditions and cork is probably the most important product of this region although it is small compared to the production in Alentejo. The geology is not entirely uniform in this area and the granite Serra de Monchique is distinctly different. Here good soil depths and water for irrigation have encouraged farming to the point where even the steep mountain sides have been terraced to bring more land under cultivation. A major product from this area is the blue granite itself which is quarried extensively.

Occupying an irregular lens-shaped area across virtually the whole of the central region is the Barrocal, a zone of limestone, which forms the garden of Algarve. Here the rich terra-rosa soils support endless orchards of oranges, almond, figs, olives, carobs and, not least, vines. South of the Barrocal is the littoral zone which constitutes the third distinctive geological area. Sedimentary rocks, alluviums and sand make up this highly heterogeneous region which has been claimed in the main by touristic development. A surprising number of small farms still exist between the high rise developments.

Alentejo shares the acid, schistose Serras which divide it from Algarve but north of those the countryside opens into vast undulating plains lying mostly below 1300ft (400m). The whole of the province is free of significant mountain ranges but it still shows remarkable diversity. There are regions of granite, seen particularly in the rich megalithic remains around Évora, areas of marble which is mined extensively around Estremoz, fertile plains and river valleys as well as mineral deposits which were rich enough to attract attention two millennia ago. Its plains support extensive grain crops and the province is known as the granary of Portugal.

## Climate

Algarve enjoys largely a Mediterranean climate with hot dry summers and mild wet winters. Winter rain falls largely between October and March often in heavy showers over several days but these periods are usually separated by good spells of sunshine. Coastal areas average around 400mm of rain annually and are appreciably drier than the inland mountains with Serra de Monchique, reaching an altitude of 902m (2960ft), enjoying the highest rainfall. The pattern of winter weather is by no means reliable and average figures do not tell the whole story. Not infrequently, there are exceptionally dry winters and occasionally some with unusually high rainfall. Although cold spells are possible, there is warmth in the sun and most days are mild with temperatures up to 20°C possible as early as February.

March, with increasing day length and rising temperatures announces spring. Showers are still possible as they are in April, but by May the steady transition towards summer becomes obvious as the herbage at lower levels turns steadily browner.

Only the Atlantic breezes moderate the long, hot and sunny days of summer to bring relief from the oppressive heat. The breezes are not necessarily uniform across the region and are most strongly felt in the west, particularly so on the promontories of Sagres and Cape St Vincent which often suffer the full force of the south-westerlies. For this reason the western part of the province is termed the Barlavento (windward) and the eastern side the Sotovento (leeward) and these terms are still in common use. The transition between the two areas is gradual and the influence of the Barlavento starts somewhere west of Loulé but becomes more obvious travelling westward, particularly beyond Lagos. The winds are so strong at times here that it limits the use of the land for agriculture and the wind cut trees in the extreme west tell their own story. Two other terms sometimes used in Algarve to indicate east and west are *Nascente* (sunrise) and *Poente* (sunset).

Autumn stays warm virtually to the end of the year but there is a steadily increasing risk of rain as early as October.

The climate in Alentejo is less kind in winter with lower temperatures and a greater risk of rain. Conversely, the summers are long and hot with inland temperatures frequently rising into the 40's C.

## When to Go

Algarve is very much an all-the-year-round resort and especially popular with long stay visitors taking advantage of the mild winter months. There is no more invigorating season than spring with the weather fine, easily warm enough to air the shorts, and with the flowers in bloom, the countryside is at its most beautiful. Relatively few visitors take advantage of this season which means that the beaches are quieter and it is easy and comfortable to get around.

Summer is unquestionably the most popular period, especially July and August. If it can be avoided, it is not the best time to go. The beaches are full, the roads are busy and the services often stretched beyond capacity with the more popular restaurants operating a booking system.

Even autumn remains busy and there are plenty of visitors around, declining only after October, although Algarve remains fairly alive right through until Christmas.

# Flora and Fauna

## *Flora*

Algarve has a rich flora which, typical of Mediterranean species, is fully adapted to survive the long, hot dry summers. Geophytes, bulbous plants, which retire to below ground to rest throughout the hot summers and annuals which flower in spring and drop their seed to propagate the next generation are common. Native trees and shrubs are predominantly evergreen often with inbuilt protection to reduce loss of water by evaporation, rolled leaves to reduce the leaf area or a thick felting of hairs to protect from water loss.

The greater majority of the species are found in the coastal zone and in the Barrocal with the northern serras providing much less interest. Dominating these northern serras, often generating an extensive cover, is the dull looking *Cistus ladanifer* which grows to around 1.5m (5ft) in places. Its large white flowers, usually with a red blotch at the base of each petal but sometimes plain white, are pretty but, like most Cistus, they survive only a day or two. This Cistus has not been without its commercial interest and was used as a source of resin for perfumes and fumigants for a time. More widespread was its use as a fuel to fire outdoor ovens for breadmaking, a practice which still continues in some small villages. It burns especially well when dry, produces a fierce heat and leaves little ash.

Erica species, especially *Erica arborea* and *E. australis* also grow here as does lavender, including green lavender, *Lavendula viridis*. Ground flora is not exactly profuse below the shrub layer in these northern serras, but there are a surprising number of species which can be found, including the crocus-like *Romulea bulbocodium* and the champagne orchid, *Orchis morio ssp champagneuxii*.

The Barrocal is especially rich in flowers and is where a great many of the regions twenty or so orchids can be found. Visitors need to be early to see them for March and April are the main months. Apart from the already mentioned species, the list includes (in the order in which they come into flower):

| | |
|---|---|
| *Ophyrs fusca* | *O. morio* |
| *Orchis lactea* | *Anacamptis pyramidalis* |
| *Aceras anthropophorum* | *Neotinea maculata* |
| *Ophrys bombyliflora* | *Cephalanthera longifolia* |
| *O. tenthredinifera* | *Ophrys scolopax* |
| *O. vernixia* | *O. apifera* |
| *O. lutea* | *Serapius lingua* |
| *Orchis mascula* | *S. parviflora* |
| *O. italica* | *Epipactis helleborine* |

Other species which are a delight to find include the bright yellow *Anemone palmata*, *Tulipa sylvestris ssp australis*, *Fritillaria lusitanica*, the electric blue *Scilla peruviana* and a trio of narcissus, *N. papyraceus*, the paper white narcissus which is fairly widespread and often in damp locations, *N. bulbocodium*, the hoop petticoat narcissus which is also widespread found on a range of substrates and the truly diminutive *N. gaditanus* which is the perfect miniature growing to around 10–15cm (4–6in). The pink flowered *Paeonia broteroi* is found in the Barrocal and again on the granites of Monchique.

In the shrub layer, known as the matos in Portugal but commonly called the phrygana in other Mediterranean countries, Cistus species are common, and there are about eight throughout the region. *Rosmarinus officinalis, Pistacia lentiscus, Thymus species, Lithospermum prostrata, Quercus coccifera* and the wild olive, *Olea europaea* are all easily observed.

Amongst the forest trees, the stone pine, *Pinus pinea*, with its umbrella shaped crown, is easily recognised and there are large stands of it around the Vilamoura area. Eucalyptus, especially *E. globulus*, is common as an introduced species for timber production, an action not now without regret. Eucalyptus on a large scale brings problems. It ignites and burns easily, increasing the risk of fires; it is water grasping, denatures the soil and its leaf litter is slow to decompose so diminishing the number of other species found on the forest floor. Some of the earlier plantations are being rooted out and replaced with pine.

The cork oak, *Quercus suber*, is easily recognised by its wine red trunk which forms after its cork layer has been stripped. It is seen throughout the region but more commonly in the northern serras. Chestnut trees, *Castanea sativa*, grow in the Monchique area, on the slopes of both Foia and Picota.

## *Fauna*

Most of the fauna now remaining comprises small mammals like rabbit, fox and genet but, surprisingly, there are still plenty of wild boar around and its foraging marks are frequently seen in the countryside and on the golf courses. It is a nocturnal creature so countryside walkers are unlikely to encounter it during the daytime. Lizards abound, with the Moorish gecko prominent in the lowland coastal areas. Snakes are around too, with the harmless grass snake, *Natrix natrix*, most common; it is also believed that a species of viper is present although it is rarely encountered.

If flowers lovers are well catered for in Algarve, it is an absolute feast for bird-spotters with something in the order of 300 species to focus on throughout the year, either residents or migrants. With all the river estuaries, old salinas and marshes, there are a number of areas rich in bird life which have been protected as reserves. Included in these are the Castro Marim reserve, the Ria Formosa Natural Park, and the Quinta do Lago reserve which comes under the umbrella of the Ria Formosa but on a separate location. Details of the bird life on each of these reserves are featured separately in the appropriate chapters (see pages 56, 68, 89). Some of the species which excite particular interest include white storks, *Ciconia ciconia*, which can frequently be seen nesting on tall chimneys, church tops or even on telegraph poles, black-winged stilts, *Himantopus himantopus*, the ubiquitous egrets, both little and cattle, *Egretta garzetta* and *Bubulcus ibis*, avocets, *Recurvirostra avosetta* and the hoopoe, *Upapa epops*, which is migratory although a small population overwinters in the region.

## Green Issues

There is a growing awareness of green issues and the need for conservation which is reflected by the measures taken to protect the avifauna. However, in every day life there is practically no awareness, although unleaded petrol is now freely available throughout the region except for small rural stations. Expect to see burning rubbish tips whilst touring around and plenty of unauthorised rubbish dumping. With increasing wealth over the last decade, the number of old cars for disposal is growing and the number littering the countryside is on the increase, a rare sight just a few years ago.

# 2. HISTORY

Portugal came together as a nation in 1297 with the Treaty of Alcanices which was signed only after Algarve had been liberated from the Moors. Prior to this, the history of southern Portugal followed a different course, which was certainly less violent and traumatic than those in the north. Little is known in detail about the very early history of the region but, from megalithic monuments which are particularly abundant in Alentejo, there is plenty of evidence of settlers from the neolithic period, around 3000 BC, who survived on food which could be gathered, fished and farmed.

In c 700–600 BC the north of the country was invaded by warrior-like Celts, but few filtered down to the extreme south leaving the peaceful Phoenicians resident there to trade undisturbed. The Phoenicians, skilled mariners from the eastern Mediterranean, founded trading colonies throughout virtually the whole of the Mediterranean. By the early part of the 1st millennium BC the Phoenicians were busy in Algarve searching inland for metals and establishing trade in tin, copper and salted fish. Greek traders joined them by the 6th century but within a short time, with the rise of Carthage, the Carthaginians eclipsed the Phoenicians and remained until their war with Rome.

## Under the Romans

As a consequence of the Second Punic War (218–202 BC) the peninsula as a whole passed to the control of the Romans and Portugal as it is known today simply became part of Hispania Ulterior. It was not an easy war for the Romans. Attacking from the south they had little trouble in colonising coastal areas but met serious resistance when attempting to capture the interior. Major resistance came from the Lusitani who lived north of the Tagus. Portugal's first legendary hero, **Viriathus**, emerged from the bitter fighting which continued for almost two centuries. He led resistance cleverly and held up the Roman advance until he was finally assassinated in 139 BC by three of his followers who had been bribed by the Romans. Within two years the legions of Decimus Junius Brutus had swept through and taken control.

Using Olisbo (Lisbon) as his capital, it was **Julius Caesar** in 60 BC who set about integrating the peninsula into the Roman Empire. Colonies were established at Ebora (Évora), Scallabis (Santarém), Pax Julia (Beja) Myrtilis (Mértola)

*Milreu, the Roman ladies' bath*

and Bracara Augusta (Braga), although, with a few exceptions, little remains to excite the present day visitor. This page of history is still not entirely closed since their 400 year rule has left lasting legacies in the Romance language, the legal system, roads and bridges, large scale farming in the crops of wheat, barley and the now ubiquitous vine.

Christianity was established towards the twilight of their rule with important bishoprics at Évora and Braga. Early in the 5th century, with the Romans in decline, waves of barbarians swept through Spain and Portugal from beyond the Pyrenees. First the Vandals settled in Galicia and the Alani in Lusitani, with the Suevi taking up the region between the Minho and the Douro. The **Visigoths**, arriving in 507, were amongst the early invaders and they eventually established a tenuous rule over most of the peninsula which they managed to maintain until the beginning of the 7th century. Their art and architecture was inspired by the Romans and, although their presence in southern Portugal is not marked by too many artefacts, the museum in Beja's Igreja de Santa Amaro has some of the finest exhibits of that period.

## The Moors

In 711, the arrival in the south of the Moors from Africa seriously challenged the Visigoth rule. They overran Spain quickly and moved steadily northwards into Portugal pushing Christianity north of the Douro, an area which was never really conquered by the Muslims. Southern of Portugal became part of Spain and was known by the Moors as **Al-Garb** (the West) which evolved eventually into the modern name of Algarve. They established a capital at Shelb, now Silves, and their rule was characterised by tolerance; for example they respected the rights of the Christians and the Jews to practise their own religions. Social order brought considerable advances, with the Moors allowing smallholders to rent land owned by the state and encouraging work to improve irrigation techniques introduced by the Romans. New crops were introduced including oranges, lemons and cotton. Centuries of harmony and prosperity gradually decayed with the decentralisation of rule and with the arrival, at the end of the 11th century, of more militant Muslim groups like the Almoravids.

## The Birth of a Nation

The victory of the Christians at the **battle of Covadonga** in the Asturias in 718 is regarded as the start of the long struggle for liberation from the Moors. From that small start the Muslims were pushed back slowly but steadily from León and Galicia southwards. Porto was taken in 868, Coimbra in 878 and raids were mounted against Lisbon by 955. South of the Douro there was no real consolidation of territory throughout this period and the land remained a fluctuating battle ground. Towards the end of the 9th century, the country that was to become Portugal started to emerge with the consolidation of the lands between the Lima and the Minho. This territory was called Portucale after its capital city. Although under the command of the kingdom of León, the region was stabilised by a dynasty of *duces* beginning with Gonçalo Mendes, but the incipient nation suffered control by division before its status as a country was finally accepted in the 11th century.

## Towards a Kingdom

**Alfonso VI** succeeded his father, Ferdinand I of León, in 1065 and by 1073 he had declared himself emperor of the kingdoms of León, Castile, Galicia and Portucale. His call for crusaders to help fight the Almovarids brought, amongst others, Raymond of Burgundy and his cousin Henry who both married daughters of Alfonso, Henry marrying the illegitimate Teresa. Henry took charge of the County of Portucale and worked steadily towards confirming the autonomy of the state of Portugal, work carried on by Teresa after Henry's death around 1112 when she became regent for her son, Afonso Henriques.

After the death of Alfonso VI a war of succession broke out and the mantle of Emperor was assumed by **Alfonso VII**, son of Raymond and Urraca. Teresa's attempts to maintain Portugal's independence eventually failed when her armies fell and she accepted dominance by Alfonso VII in 1127. This inspired Teresa's 18 year old son, **Afonso Henriques** (1128/39–85), to rebellion and over the next decade and a half he constantly vied with his cousin for control of Portugal. The Treaty of Zamora, signed between them in 1143, made Afonso Henriques the first King of Portugal. Not feeling entirely secure, Afonso sought recognition from Pope Lucius II but it was not forthcoming since the Pope favoured a policy of supporting Iberian union as the best hope of holding back the Muslim tide. Later, in 1179, Pope Alexander III finally granted recognition to the 70 year old Afonso Henriques in exchange for a yearly tribute and other privileges.

## The First Dynasty, House of Burgundy

| | |
|---|---|
| Afonso Henriques I, o Conquistador (the Conqueror) | 1128/39–1185 |
| Sancho I, o Pavoador (the Resettler) | 1185–1211 |
| Afonso II, o Gordo (the Fat) | 1211–1223 |
| Sancho II | 1223–1248 |
| Afonso III | 1248–1279 |
| Dinis, o Lavrador (the Husbandman) | 1279–1325 |
| Afonso IV, a Bravo (the Brave) | 1325–1357 |
| Pedro I, o Justiceiro (the Justicer) | 1357–1367 |
| Fernando, o Formoso (the Beautiful) | 1367–1383 |

## Evicting the Moors

In his determination to establish Portugal and his kingdom, Afonso Henriques also enlisted the help of crusaders to fight against the Moors. Santarém and Lisbon were both taken in 1147 and joined with his emerging nation. Lisbon was taken by siege with the help of the English, French, Flemish and German crusaders who were passing through on their way to the Holy Land. Fighting for Christianity alone proved not persuasive enough, but the offer of loot and land grants secured their services. The Reconquista was eventually backed by the Church, convinced by the argument that chasing out the Muslims here was just as important as fighting the infidel in the Holy Land. The Knights Templar and the Hospitallers lent their support and became extremely wealthy and powerful as a consequence of land grants.

Afonso Henriques fought his last battle in 1170 at Badajoz. Fernando II of León, concerned that land retaken from the Moors was in effect expanding Portugal instead of his own kingdom, joined forces with the powerful Almohads. Afonso Henriques broke a leg in the midst of the battle and was captured. He secured his release only by yielding land and castles to his enemy.

The final victory was still over a century away. Again with the help of passing crusaders, Sancho I invaded western Algarve and captured the capital Silves in 1189 but lost it together with much of the area south of the Tagus the following year in what proved to be the last great campaign of the Moors led by al-Mansur. Steady expansion under Sancho II and his successor Afonso III led to the recapture of territory in Alentejo and eastern Algarve until, in 1249, western Algarve too had been recovered and the Portuguese kingdom, endorsed by the Treaty of Alcanices in 1297, took its ultimate shape.

## Organising a New Kingdom

New territories were divided between the Church, the Templars and other Holy Orders, and the most powerful nobles. Most of the population of 400,000 lived in the north so some internal recolonisation programmes were introduced to protect the new areas. There were problems of a social order too; the northerners with their Celtic genes had the arrogance of conquering invaders whilst the southerners had learnt gentler ways from a more settled existence under the rule of the Moors. An increase in social mobility amongst the lower classes did much to weld the divergent cultures but never completely so, not even to this day.

Some moves towards democracy started when the kings of the Burgundian line recognised the need for popular and financial support and began to consult with the nobles and clergy and later the wealthy merchants and townsmen. This was formalised into the *Cortes* (parliament), the first of which was held in Coimbra in 1211. In the 1254 *Cortes* at Leira, the king conceded the right of municipal representation in fiscal matters, an important concession since the king only called a *Cortes* when he needed to raise taxes. The Church was doing well with its extensive lands, freedom from taxation and the right to collect its own taxes from the population; rather too well in fact and its increasing power was soon felt as a threat by the monarchy. Afonso II generally failed in his attempts to curb their power as did Sancho II who was ultimately excommunicated and dethroned in 1245.

The reign of **Dom Dinis** (1279–1325) proved significant in consolidating Portugal's independence and putting the monarchy firmly in control. Dinis was far-sighted in his reforms which were extensive and affected all walks of life. For security he financed the building of 50 castles along the frontier and started negotiations with Spain which eventually led to the 1294 Treaty of Alcanices by which Spain acknowledged Portugal's borders. He introduced agricultural reforms to produce export quantities of wine, olive oil, grain and dried fruit, and afforestation schemes. He encouraged music and poetry and gave Lisbon a university in 1290 which was transferred to Coimbra in 1308. The Templars, in decline in Europe, were reorganised as the Order of Christ (of which Henry the Navigator was later to become a Grand Master) responsible to the King and not the Pope so the church was forced to accept a larger degree of state control.

**Afonso IV** (1325–57), who succeeded Dinis, had a much less happy reign. The Black Plague struck in 1348–49 and decimated the population, especially in the urban centres. It became a burden throughout his reign, indeed over the next century, as the pestilence returned again and again. Labour problems arose through migration to urban cities leaving insufficient agricultural workers to fill the nation's breadbasket, creating inflationary pressures and stagnation. Fears of Castilian domination persisted, not helped by continual intermarriage between the two royal families. But Portugal was bent on independence. Fear of a Castilian heir through his son's love affair with Inês de Castro, first a mistress and later his wife, was enough for Afonso to arrange her brutal murder.

Just two years later, in 1357, **Pedro I** came to the throne after the death of his father and one of his first acts was to seek out the murderers of Inês to extract his revenge. Peaceful coexistence with Castile continued throughout his reign as the country started to recover from the ravages of the plague, but the growing power of the nobles and the emerging bourgeoisie was to create social unrest in the reign of his son, **Fernando I** (1367–83). Alienating his subjects with an unpopular marriage to Leonor Teles and engaging the country in a series of unpopular wars against the Castilians, Fernando failed to produce a male heir and in 1383 the House of Burgundy came to an untidy end. Power passed to his wife Leonor but not for long as their daughter Beatriz, at the age of 12, married the widowed Juan I, King of Castile. By the terms of the marriage contract Beatriz, with her husband, would succeed to rule Portugal. Following the death of her father, Juan insisted that Beatriz be proclaimed queen and entered Portugal to take authority from Leonor. Although this move received support from the nobles, it incited the middle classes to riot and throw their weight behind the claims of João, the Grand Master of the Order of Avis and illegitimate son of King Pedro, who became regent. It started two years of war with Castile which was finally settled with the battle of Aljubarrota (1385) which resulted in a decisive victory for João, backed by a force of English archers, against overwhelming odds. Later that year João was crowned at Coimbra to become **João I**, the first king of the House of Avis, and the great abbey of Batalha was ordered to commemorate the victory. Relations with England were sealed through the Treaty of Windsor of 1386 and by João's marriage to Phillipa of Lancaster, daughter of John of Gaunt, the following year.

## Second Dynasty: House of Avis

| | |
|---|---|
| João I, de Boa Memoria (of Good Memory) | 1385–1433 |
| Duarte, o Eloquente (the Eloquent) | 1433–1438 |
| Afonso V, o Africano (the African) | 1438–1481 |
| João II, o Principe Perfeito (the Perfect Prince) | 1481–1495 |
| Manuel I, o Venturoso (the Fortunate) | 1495–1521 |
| João III, o Piedoso (the Merciful) | 1521–1557 |
| Sebastião, o Desejado (the Awaited) | 1557–1578 |
| Henrique, o Casto (the Pure) | 1578–1580 |

The new dynasty was much like the old, except the mercantile classes gained political representation, and skirmishes with Castile continued until peace was finally made in 1411. It was during this reign that Portugal started to look overseas to solve problems at home and the proximity of North Africa made it a natural target for overseas expansion.

# Building an Empire

João's main contribution to building a new empire was in fathering some brilliant children, including Pedro, who travelled widely sending home maps and works of geography, and **Henry the Navigator** (1394–1460) who played a very significant early role. Henry founded a school of navigation at Sagres in Algarve and used his power and wealth to staff it with the cream of Europe's cartographers, astronomers and navigators. During his lifetime Madeira (1419), the Azores (1427) and the Cape Verde Islands (1457) were all discovered and colonised and the west coast of Africa explored. Following the death of Henry the Navigator, who is also featured on p 121, there was a lull in the process of exploration.

**Duarte** (1433–38) succeeded João I but died in 1438 after only five years on the throne, some say from grief over the fate of his younger brother delivered as a hostage to the Muslims following an ill-fated expedition against Tangier in 1437. His son, **Afonso V** (1438–81), was too young to rule without a regent so Pedro stepped forward with the support of the ordinary people to press his claim over that of Queen Leonor, Duarte's widow. Events took a dramatic turn when Afonso came of age and turned to the parties who opposed Pedro. Pedro fought the king in the battle of Alfarobeira in 1449 and lost his life. Two uncles who had proved trusted advisers, Fernão, the Duke of Bragança, and Henry the Navigator, were both rewarded with a large share of independent power. Afonso is remembered most for his crusading in North Africa which gave him his epithet of *o Africano*.

Overseas exploration became important again under **João II** (1481–95) especially when, in 1487, Bartolomeu Dias finally made it around the southern tip of Africa which he christened `the Cape of Good Hope'. He started to assert more royal power over the nobles, particularly over the problem of land. A conspiracy gathered against the king but the perpetrators were quickly discovered and rapidly dispatched. In 1483 the Duke of Bragança, head of a family whose estate covered a third of the kingdom, was executed and his lands recovered by the crown, and the following year the queen's brother, the Duke of Viseu, was similarly treated.

**Dom Manuel I** (1495–1521) succeeded João and pursued similar policies to centralise power in the crown but appeased the nobles by restoring their estates although not their political power. It was an enlightened reign in which a postal service was instituted, the taxation of the districts was regulated and exercise of justice brought under royal control. He presided over Portugal's greatest period of exploration and enjoyed the wealth flowing from it. The exuberance of this age lead to the development of a new architectural style involving twisted forms in the columns, ribs and corbels which later became known as Manueline (featured on p 164).

However, Portugal's hitherto lenient attitude with its Jewish minority was gathering resentment.

# The Age of Discovery

Portugal's explorations started haphazardly and were curiously motivated. Outflanking the Muslims and spreading the Christian faith lent a crusading element and respectability to their excursions but there were other issues like the need for gold, which was short throughout Europe, and the need to stabilise currency and support commerce. Maritime trade was of growing importance too and there was the unending search to discover the earthly paradise of **Prester John**. Prester John was known as a king and leader of a vast Christian empire somewhere in the middle of Africa. This deeply held belief stretched all the way back to Rome. The Pope granted Portugal the sole right to explore and colonise Africa except for those parts ruled by Prester John.

However faltering or motivated in the beginning, Portuguese sailors developed skills of seamanship superior to any in Europe and rapidly became intrepid explorers. A number of epic voyages took place around the dawning of the 16th century. Vasco da Gama (1497–99) sailed to India and back again, Pedro Alvares Cabral (1500) discovered Brazil and, from 1519–22, Ferdinand Magellan, ignoring pleas from his Portuguese masters led the first navigation of the globe under the sponsorship of the Spanish. At this time the Spanish were also taking to the seas, creating fresh dispute between these two nations; but, with Papal intervention, the Treaty of Tordesillas (1494) divided the world between them at an imaginary line 370 leagues west of the Cape Verdes. This gave Portugal the, as yet, undiscovered Orient and the key to great wealth.

Opening new trade routes brought with it enormous wealth and not just in gold. Spices from the east, cinnamon, cloves and peppers, grain, sugar and dyestuffs from Morocco, and slaves from Africa activated the merchants and stimulated the development of key overseas trading posts not always achieved without battles. On a more humble scale, one product from their discovery of Newfoundland, *bacalhau* (dried, salted cod) became virtually part of the staple diet and remains so even today.

This period of Portugal's history produced some epic heroes and a stable economy but no lasting wealth. Only the monarchy, taking a royal fifth from all trade revenues, benefited but even its wealth had no permanency.

# The Jews and the Inquisition

As physicians, astronomers, bankers, money lenders and tax collectors, the Jews had lived in Portugal for a thousand years or more without gathering any great resentment. Their influence was growing and it was the Jews who opened Portugal's first presses with their first eleven books all in Hebrew. Complaints against the Jews raised in the *Cortes* in 1490 indicated changing attitudes and events in Spain were to compound their difficulties further.

Some 60,000 Jews expelled from Spain in 1462 were allowed to settle peacefully in Portugal. Unfortunately for the Jews, Dom Manuel was forced to take a hardened attitude against them as a condition of his marriage to Princess Isabela of Spain just four years later. There was a considerable reluctance in ordering the expulsion of such a valuable sector of the community so he offered the option of baptism to expulsion. Some did leave for the Netherlands but many were baptised as `New Christians', accepting assurances that there would be a 20 year period of grace before their new faith was tested. New Christians and Old Christians intermarried freely but it was to offer no protection for the Jewish heritage.

Dom João III in 1536 eventually persuaded the Pope of the need to introduce the Inquisition, in spite of the fact that there was no disunity threatening the faith in Portugal. Intended as a tool of the monarchy, it quickly took on a life and force of its own with the inquisitor-generals responding directly to the Pope. The main target was the New Christians and thousands were tortured, left to rot in prison cells or burnt at the stake as the Inquisition became nothing more than a reign of terror until it was finally suppressed in 1820.

Small Jewish communities still exist in Portugal and there are traces of Jewish quarters in the towns where they first settled, including Viana do Castelo, Bragança, Lamego, Guarda and Castelo de Vide. The latter houses the oldest synagogue in Portugal, founded in the 13th century, hidden away down a small side street. In Tomar, too, there is a 14th century synagogue which now contains a museum named after Abraham Zacuto. A brilliant astronomer and mathematician, it was Zacuto who first published *Almanac Perpetuum*, in Hebrew, which enabled mariners to calculate latitude at sea by declination of the sun. He was amongst those who declined to convert at the bidding of Dom Manuel and left the country.

# An Age of Decline

**João III** (1481–95) continued Manuel's policies of establishing royal authority and expanding trade. Literature was flowing from the printing presses and the humanistic influences of Europe were making a noticeable impression. Colleges were established and the university at Lisbon was moved permanently to Coimbra in 1537. Permitting the establishment of the Inquisition was a turning point that led Portugal into decline. Slowly and steadily a whole entrepreneurial class was snubbed out robbing the country of the engine to drive the huge commercial empire it had striven so hard to build. Humanism and the Inquisition proved incompatible bedfellows and it was the Inquisition which gathered force.

Stability still held with the ascension of the young **Dom Sebastião** in 1557 and it was during his reign (1572) that Luís de Camões published his epic *The Lusiads* which was to achieve lasting fame. Strains in the economy were showing which became overpowering around the 1570s when increasing competition, falling prices, foreign debts and a drop in productivity signalled a serious decline.

Sebastião, an unstable and idealistic king, yearned for a crusade against the Moors in North Africa and when he sensed the time was right he emptied his coffers to equip an 18,000 strong force. It sailed to Morocco from Algarve in 1578 but met a superior force at Alcacer-Quiber and was effectively annihilated. Around 8000 were left dead on the battlefield including the king and many young nobles, and most of the rest were taken prisoner, with only a 100 or so escaping capture.

Cardinal Henrique, an elderly uncle, assumed control and further weakened the country by paying ruinous ransoms for the release of prisoners. He died after only two years in power leaving no male heirs. King Philip II of Spain invaded and was installed as **King Filipe I** of Portugal in 1581.

# The Castilian Usurpers

Although this rule was initially unpopular, the union with Spain brought short term advantages to the economy. Spanish wheat helped to feed the people and the Spanish helped to guard the Portuguese empire. Filipe started well by observing Portuguese autonomy and leaving control of the *Cortes* and the judicial system entirely with the Portuguese while promising that the Portuguese language would remain and that their empire overseas would still be ruled by Portugal. Apart from the first two years, the whole of the Castilian reign was conducted from Spain.

The balance of power was tilting from Spain to Europe around this period. 1588 witnessed the failure of the Spanish Armada which was supported by boats built in Lisbon and crewed by Portuguese. Portugal assumed the enemies of Spain. Portuguese ports were closed to English ships and the seizure of 50 Dutch ships in Lisbon by Filipe in 1594 brought a Dutch retaliation aimed at the Portuguese in India. By 1602, with both the English and the Dutch established in India, the Portuguese monopoly was broken. Much of their maritime empire was under threat with the country no longer powerful enough to mount a robust defence.

---

## Third Dynasty: the Hapsburgs

| | |
|---|---|
| Filipe I, o Prudente (the Prudent) | 1581–1598 |
| Filipe II, o Pio (the Pious) | 1598–1621 |
| Filipe III, o Grande (the Grand) | 1621–1640 |

---

**Filipe II**, not as diplomatic as his father, started to advance the power of Spain by appointing Spaniards to the Council of Portugal in Madrid. Although he still retained favour with the *Cortes*, seeds of resistance were sown amongst the populace. In 1621 Filipe III succeeded to the throne but his reign continued to erode and undermine the union. Portugal was drawn into Spain's 30 year war with France and its troops were pressed into battle to quell an uprising in Catalonia. 1 December 1640 dawned as any other but on this day Spanish rule was effectively overthrown creating a landmark in Portuguese history remembered to this day as a national holiday. A group of conspirators stormed the palace in Lisbon to depose the Duchess of Mantua, governor of Portugal, and install the Duke of Bragança, head of one of the oldest families in Portugal and reluctant leader of the uprising, as king.

### The House of Bragança

The Duke of Bragança was crowned **João IV** (1640–56) in 1640 and with Spain seriously distracted on other fronts there was no immediate opposition. Dom João focused his efforts on rebuilding the country, placing its independence beyond doubt and gaining recognition abroad. England agreed to renew the old alliance of 1386 and treaties were signed with Charles I (1642) and Oliver Cromwell (1654). Later, in 1661, the alliance was strengthened by the marriage of Charles II to Catherine of Bragança. Although skirmishes with Spain had waxed and waned and taxes had been raised to fairly high levels, it was a quietly successful reign which had also seen the emphasis in trade swing from India to Brazil.

Consolidation continued under Luisa, the Spanish wife of João IV, acting as regent for her son, Afonso IV, and a peace treaty was signed with Holland. Young Afonso, just 13 years old, was a problematic child associating with street gangs and criminal elements. His mother was deposed as regent by the Count of Costelho Melhor who promptly married off Afonso to a French princess, Marie-Françoise. The count himself became subject of a conspiracy and fled whereupon Marie-Françoise immediately entered a convent and asked for an annulment of the marriage on the grounds that it had never been consummated. This was agreed by *Cortes* and the Princess promptly married Afonso's younger brother who assumed the role of regent.

Luisa's third child, Catherine, was married to Charles II in 1662 to give Portugal another treaty of alliance with England which provided forces to help fight off the Spanish at Évora. The treaty gave England a handsome dowry and trading rights in all Portuguese territories, Tangiers and Bombay. Spain, on the other hand, now seriously weakened, finally agreed peace in the Treaty of Lisbon of 1668.

Remarkably, all Luisa's three children ascended to a throne, Afonso and Pedro as kings of Portugal and Catherine as queen of England.

Pedro acted as regent for his brother from 1668 until he was crowned King **Pedro II** in 1683. Economic problems beset the country throughout this period reflecting a decline in maritime commerce, the loss of the spice trade and greater competition in the sugar trade. Agriculture at home was not so productive and wheat shortages continued so efforts were directed towards increasing manufacturing output to solve the difficulties. Tariff-protected glass and textile industries were developed, exports boosted and the import of luxury goods was controlled, and this together with concessions from the English for Portuguese wines (Methuen Treaty) did much to stabilise the economy. The discovery of gold in Brazil poured in a new wealth and the growing new industries instantly faltered.

When **João V** succeeded Pedro II in 1706 he had Brazilian gold to spend. The Crown's revenues soared as it took one fifth of the gold and the money was spent on building palaces, churches and monasteries including the monastery-church at Mafra which virtually bankrupted the monarchy.

---

## Fourth Dynasty: House of Bragança

| | |
|---|---:|
| João IV, o Restaurador (the Restorer) | 1640–1656 |
| Afonso VI, o Vitrioso (the Victorious) | 1656–1683 |
| Pedro II, o Pacifico (regent from 1668) (the Peace-keeper) | 1683–1706 |
| João V, o Magnanimo (the Magnanimous) | 1706–1750 |
| José, o Reformador (the Reformer) | 1750–1777 |
| Maria I, a Piedosa (the Merciful) | 1777–1816 |
| João VI, o Clemente (the Merciful) | 1816–1826 |
| Pedro IV, o Libertador (the Liberator) | 1826 (abdicated) |
| Miguel, o Usurpador (the Usurper) | 1828–1834 |
| Maria II, a Educadora (the Educator) | 1834–1853 |
| Pedro V, o Esperancoso (the Hopeful) | 1853–1861 |
| Luís, o Popular (the Popular) | 1861–1889 |
| Carlos, o Martirizado (the Martyr) | 1889–1908 |
| Manuel II, o Desventuroso (the Unfortunate) | 1908–1910 |

Scholarship flourished under his patronage and with his concern also for the poor João became known as the *Magnanimo*. Palaces were also built to house João's bastard sons, three from nuns.

**José** (1750–77), Dom João's successor, was genial and easy going. He shared his father's love of the arts, particularly opera, and was happy to leave the affairs of state in the capable hands of his minister, the **Marquês de Pombal**. Pombal was to go down in history as one of Portugal's greatest statesmen, admired by some but reviled and hated by others. His was an oppressive dictatorial rule exercised by using the royal prerogative rather than his own personal power.

It was church as usual for the people of Lisbon on All Saints' Day, 1 November 1755, when a terrifying and furious **earthquake** suddenly hit the town. Buildings collapsed everywhere and fires from the many church candles added further devastation. After nine days of raging fires the heart of the city was reduced to ashes. Much of the surrounding country was also seriously affected as shock waves spread as far as France in the north and Algarve to the south yet the north of the country escaped serious damage. The Jesuits laid the blame for this divine retribution entirely on Pombal. After surviving an assassination attempt, Pombal declared the Jesuits and certain nobles as responsible and took his revenge with executions and by disbanding the Jesuit movement in 1759. Granted emergency powers by the king, Pombal set about building Lisbon in a simple grid fashion with houses in neo-classical style.

Oppressive though his regime was, his policies helped to reform Portugal's economy and lay the foundation of the modern Portuguese state. Towards the end of King José's life, Pombal plotted to force Maria to renounce her rights to the throne in favour of her son, José, who was a disciple of Pombal. It failed and, on her succession, **Maria** (1777–1816) tried Pombal for crimes against the state and confined him to his estates.

A pious woman, Maria revived many of the religious elements of government but left Pombal's economic reforms undisturbed. Roads and canals were built, agricultural methods improved and industry again supported including the textile industry. Slowly and steadily Portugal started to make economic progress until the French Revolution of 1789 reverberated around Europe. Maria, deeply disturbed by the loss of loved ones, including her eldest son to smallpox after she had forbidden vaccination, and other events, suffered hallucinations and slipped towards insanity. In 1791 she was declared insane and her son, João, took over as regent until his mother died in 1816, when he was ultimately crowned **King João VI** (1816–26).

# The Era of Napoleon

In 1807 Napoleon delivered an ultimatum that Portugal declare war on Britain and close its ports to British shipping. Since Portugal was dependent for half her trade on Britain and on British sea power to protect her trade routes there was little option but to reject Napoleon and face the inevitable war. The monarchy immediately slipped off to Brazil to set up court there as the French, under General Junot, entered Lisbon. The Portuguese invoked the alliance with Britain and an expeditionary force commanded by the brilliant tactician Sir Arthur Wellesley (later the Duke of Wellington) quickly defeated the French. In all there were three waves of French attacks in the Peninsular War, all repelled, but it left the country fatally weakened. The French failed to pay the agreed compensation and another Anglo-Portuguese treaty, this one in 1810, gave Britain the right to trade freely with Brazil eliminating Portugal's lucrative middle-man's role. Brazil itself was proclaimed a kingdom in 1815.

From 1808 to 1821, Portugal effectively became a British protectorate governed by **Marshal William Beresford**. He ruled with a heavy hand which brought about bitter resentment. Liberal ideas introduced from France were spread by secret societies including the Masonic order of which Lisbon had 13 groups. A plot was hatched to dispose of Beresford but it was discovered and 12 conspirators were executed in October 1817. In 1820, Beresford, alarmed at the growing strength of the liberals in Spain and the support spilling over the border, went to Brazil to request more powers from the king. In his absence the liberals rose to seize power and João VI was forced to return from Brazil, but he was too late to resist the new liberal ideologies.

# Constitutional Wrangles

A new constitution was adopted in 1822 which assured the establishment of broad voting rights, no special prerogatives for nobles or clergy, a liberal *Cortes* more truly representing the people and the end of the Inquisition. On a divergent course from the King, the Queen remained firmly against its adoption and used ill health as an excuse to avoid becoming a signatory.

In the same year, Crown Prince Pedro, who had remained in Brazil, was stirred by attempts at home to restrict Brazilian autonomy and promptly declared Brazil independent. Portugal had troubles enough on home ground with an uprising to restore absolute monarchy by the anti-liberals headed by Miguel, the Queen's youngest son, and backed by the Queen. They won a victory and the constitution was suspended in 1824. This almost destabilised the monarchy which left the King no option but to send his son Miguel into exile.

By 1825 Portugal had conceded and recognised Brazil as an independent empire with Pedro as Emperor of Brazil. On João's death the following year, the Regency council declared **Pedro IV** king. He hardly knew Portugal or his younger brother Miguel but he had conceived a plan to settle all the problems. He proposed a new compromise constitution in which a chamber of deputies was partly elected and partly nominated with an upper house of hereditary peers. Pedro IV then abdicated on condition that **Miguel** marry Maria, his seven year old daughter, and rule as her regent under the new constitution. Miguel happily agreed, returned to Portugal, swore his oath of loyalty and promptly abolished the constitution. He recalled the old *Cortes* and, in 1828, proclaimed himself king. Maria, still in transit when the news reached her, diverted to England. The Azores, out in the Atlantic, were not in favour of accepting Miguel so declared Pedro regent in the name of his daughter. Pedro abdicated his Brazilian empire to establish his daughter's claim to the throne and promptly set sail for the Azores where he made his base. The `War of Two Brothers' led to capitulation by Miguel and in 1834 he was back in exile. Pedro died in the same year and his 15 year old daughter took the throne as **Maria II**.

# The Decline of a Monarchy

At 16, Maria married the Duke of Leuchtenburg but he died soon after his arrival in Lisbon. A year later she married the German Duke Ferdinand of Saxe-Coburg-Gotha, had 11 children and died, still only 36, giving birth to her twelfth. Her reign was to witness the birth of political parties.

Disputes still continued over the constitution. Some favoured the charter introduced by Pedro II, strongly supported by Maria herself, whilst the liberals wanted a return to the constitution of 1822. The liberals themselves failed to present a unified view and soon divided into conservatives and progressives, the latter calling themselves the **Septembrists** after their revolutionary victory of September 1836 brought them to power. Their first demand was the restoration of the 1822 constitution but in 1838 they adopted a more moderate version. The **Chartists** made a return in 1842 and, under Costa Cabral, restored the Charter of 1826. It proved a firm government which re-established free trade and set Portugal on a track back towards prosperity. Cabral foundered on a relatively minor issue but one which struck at the very heart of age old custom. He declared that burials inside church were unhygienic and must stop. Devout women from the north were outraged and one in particular, Maria da Fonte, became the symbol of unrest which grew into a national rebellion in 1846. Feeling personally threatened, Cabral fled in disguise to Spain. On the edge of a civil war, English and French intervention steadied the unrest and restored Costa Cabral. In 1851 Cabral was ousted for good by another Chartist, Saldanha.

Maria II died in childbirth in 1853 and her husband, Duke Ferdinand of Saxe-Coburg-Gotha, ruled as regent for the next two years until their son, **Pedro V**, came of age. It was a brief reign and he died in 1861. He was succeeded by his brother Luís who became king at 23. **Dom Luís** (1861–89) was generally judged a popular king but then he left politics to the politicians and concentrated on things he did best, like translating Shakespeare and playing the cello. Two sons were born from his marriage to Maria Pia, daughter of Victor Emmanuel of Savoy who later became king of Italy.

Although it was a popular and peaceful reign, Portugal continued to lag behind the rest of Europe. An improved infrastructure encouraged foreign investment but the growth of industry was slow. It was tenacious on holding on to its colonial claims and territories in Africa but these too were a burden on the country's finances.

**Carlos** succeeded Luís in 1889 and inherited a crisis. In 1887 the Portuguese announced their intention to bring all the lands between the Angolan and Mozambican coasts under their control. This brought them into conflict with British interests and in 1890 Lord Salisbury issued an ultimatum: Portugal was to withdraw from that territory. There was no compromise on offer and the old alliance was at stake so Portugal had little option but to concede. The Progressist government fell, the Regenerators formed a government and fell, and a coalition government failed. Crisis followed crisis but Portugal was broke and forced to declare itself bankrupt.

The real threat to the establishment of the monarchy came from Republicanism, a radical and nationalist movement arising from the middle and lower classes. This movement attacked the government for its corruption and inefficiency but the pendulum of power started to swing in their favour with the collapse of the governing parties in the crisis of the 1890s.

Carlos, still dreaming of restoring the empire, could do little about growing Republicanism, socialism and trade unionism. Struggling to maintain some sort of control he appointed João Franco as Prime Minister in 1906 and endowed him with dictatorial powers. He promptly dismissed the *Cortes* and ruled by decree, but it had the effect of driving more liberals over to the Republican movement. Demonstrations against his dictatorship frequently ended in violence. An attempted Republican revolt in 1908 was followed by the assassination of the King and the Crown Prince. The Republicans denied involvement yet it benefited their cause.

Portugal's last king, **Manuel II** ascended the throne in 1908. His attempts to appease the Republicans also proved futile and the monarchy was violently overthrown on 5 October 1910. Dom Manuel, the Unfortunate, went into exile in England where he died in 1932.

## The Republic

It can hardly be said that the Republicans grasped their opportunity with both hands. It is true that they won an overwhelming victory in 1911 with strong support from the urban and rural poor but they promptly disenfranchised much of their support by introducing electoral laws based on literacy. Unrealistically high hopes of the Republican supporters never materialised and there were further measures which alienated support, like the Law of Separation passed by parliament in an attempt to divide the Church from the State and gain control of the Catholic Church. Weak economic factors, cyclical revival of the monarchists and general political turmoil brought about 45 changes of government in the years up to 1926.

# The Salazar Dictatorship

A bloodless coup on 28 May 1926 overthrew the Democratic party and put the military in control. Portugal's first Republic was at an end. There was an instant jostling for power but General Carmona emerged finally and became president.

One of Carmona's first acts was to invite the well-known professor of economics from Coimbra University, **António de Oliveira Salazar**, to take the post of finance minister, but he quickly resigned when he realised his control was too limited. In 1928, with the country's finances in an even worse mess, Salazar was re-appointed, this time with full powers, to put the economy in order. Now he had complete control over government and departmental expenses and by using strict monetarist policies he brought the budget into balance for the first time in many years. In 1932 he was appointed Prime Minister and held that position until an accident with a deck chair in 1968 brought on a stroke.

In 1933 a new political constitution converted the military dictatorship into an authoritarian, nationalistic and pro-Catholic regime. A special police force kept vigilant guard against subversive activities and censorship was rigid, especially over journalism. Salazar had no appetite for party politics so he permitted just one, the National Union, but it was without power. Numerous coup attempts were put down but Salazar's leadership was never seriously threatened and he continued to govern virtually as a dictator. Improvements in the infrastructure included bridges over the Tejo, Douro and other important waterways, new roads and hospitals, while the economy in general grew steadily.

Portugal remained formally neutral throughout the Spanish Civil War but sent an unofficial army of some magnitude to aid Franco's Nationalistic forces. Although Salazar and his ministers were admirers of Germany, Portugal remained neutral again in World War II. Under pressure to sell the metal wolfram to the Germans, a balancing act was achieved by allowing Britain the use of a base on the Azores and in giving generous credit. Refugees flooded into neutral Portugal including the rich and the famous, and also spies of all nationalities. There was no doubt where the sympathies of the ordinary people lay and the allied victory was widely celebrated throughout the country.

Following the end of the war Salazar called free elections allowing a role for a newly formed liberal party, the Movement of Democratic Unity. It was the first legal opposition party permitted under Salazar's rule. Some election-eering was permitted in the month preceding elections but the disenchant-ment of the new party was immediate when they were listed by the police as dissidents. Portugal's strategic location proved more important than their record on democracy when membership of the North Atlantic Treaty Organisation was mooted and they joined in 1949.

By 1960, events in the colonies were causing concern to Portugal, especially the violent uprising in Angola in 1961. It proved the spark to ignite war across all of Portugal's African colonies. Portugal reacted by crushing the revolts and, without offering concessions, tried to appease them by speeding up economic reforms. India, too, seized Goa in 1961. Greater military involvement in the colonies, now renamed `Overseas Provinces', was draining the country's finances. Salazar's tight control of the nation's purse strings had ensured the country was free from national debt but, equally, had no foreign investment. With the tasteful conversion of some of the country's historic buildings into *pousadas*, tourism was playing a more important role and bringing in a new source of wealth but not enough and, by 1965, Salazar, on his 76th birthday, agreed to allow foreign investment.

# Revolution

A deck chair accident in 1968 brought Salazar's active term in office to a close. Acting Prime Minister Marcelo Caetano had the vision but not the strength to reform the New State at home and solve the colonial problems overseas. His limited liberal changes only stimulated demand for further democratisation. The clandestine Communist party, which had been in existence for around 20 years, gained ground and military unrest led to the formation of the Armed Forces Movement (MFA) in 1973. In February 1974, the ageing **General António de Spínola**, a member of government but dismissed, published *Portugal and the Future* which was a comprehensive critique of the country and its problems. The solution proffered was a military coup. After a couple of abortive attempts, it happened bloodlessly on 25 April 1974. The populace was euphoric sensing the end of a long nightmare.

The following day Spínola announced a **Junta of National Salvation** comprising seven military officers, co-ordinating committees and a council of state. Censorship was immediately abolished and elections promised. On 15 May, Spínola was inaugurated as president and a provisional government formed from a coalition of Communists, Socialists and Centrists led by Adelino da Palma Carlos with socialist Mário Soares as foreign secretary. Discontent festered with waves of strikes, shortages and general unrest which brought Carlos' resignation. Colonel Vasco Gonçalves, military governor of Lisbon, took over. Spínola himself, opposed to early decolonisation, consented to the independence of Guinea in 1974 but was reluctant to hand over Angola. He was pushed aside as president in 1974 and succeeded by General Costa Gomes who lasted for two years. Decolonisation did continue with Mozambique and the Cape Verde islands going peacefully but Angola and East Timor only after civil wars.

# Towards Democracy

Elections for a constituent assembly on 25 April attracted almost 92 per cent of the registered voters and was won by the Socialists and Centrists, but it did not bring stability. In the two years after the revolution Portugal had six governments and in the following two years, between July 1976 and July 1978, they elected ten. By 1976 the economy was in poor shape, banks and insurance companies had been nationalised and giant monopolies taken over by the workers. A new constitution attempted to uphold democracy and socialism while giving greater powers to the president. Elections of 1976 favoured General Eanes as president who appointed **Mário Soares** as Prime Minister.

The next decade brought no greater stability since elections invariably failed to give any party overall majority, at least until 1987. Mário Soares held office as prime minister for three times in that politically volatile period. In 1986 the presidential elections were narrowly won on the second round by Mário Soares who became the first civilian head of state in 60 years.

In 1986 Portugal entered the European Community which initiated changes greater than at any time since the revolution. Funds poured in to help modernise the infrastructure and, with increased foreign investment, the country enjoyed a sustained period of economic growth. Today, there is a new wealth about, with many now enjoying a good standard of living, but it masks a deep poverty still experienced in parts of the countryside.

# 3. TOURING THE REGION

## National Tourist Offices

Useful information leaflets are usually available on just about all areas of Portugal, as are brochures on the *Pousadas*. Enquiries should be made to:

**UK**
Portuguese National Tourist Office, 22/25A Sackville Street, London W1X 1DE. Tel: 0171 494 1441

**USA**
Portuguese National Tourist Office, 590 Fifth Avenue, New York, NY 10036–4704. Tel: 212 354 4403/4/5/6/7/8

**Canada**
Portuguese National Tourist Office, 60 Bloor Street West, Suite 1005, Toronto, Ontario M4W 3B8. Tel: 416 921 7376

Other enquiries not directly connected with the promotion of tourism, such as visa applications, should be directed to the Embassy or consulate.

## Passport Requirements

A valid passport allows entry for EU nationals for a period of 90 days and for North American citizens for a period of 60 days. To extend this period it is necessary to apply before the time expires to the Foreigners' Registration Service, Rua Conselheiro José Silvestre Ribeiro, 22, 1600 Lisbon.

## Embassies and Consulates

Consular help is available in emergency situations and is largely advisory. The following indicates some areas in which they can help but it does not fully define the powers of the office:

- in the event of a lost or stolen passport they can issue an emergency one if necessary
- help with problems over lost or stolen money or tickets but only by contacting relatives or friends at your request to ask for financial assistance
- advise on details of transfering funds
- encash a cheque supported by a banker's card but only in an emergency
- make a loan to cover repatriation expenses but only as a last resort
- arrange for the next of kin to be informed following an accident or death and advise on procedures
- act for nationals arrested or imprisoned to inform relatives
- provide a list of local interpreters, English speaking doctors and solicitors
- give guidance on organisations experienced in tracing missing people.

Useful addresses in this context are:

British Embassy,
35–37 Rua São Domingos à Lapa,
Lisbon.
Tel: 01 661 191

British Consulate,
3072 Avenida da Boa Vista,
Porto.
Tel: 02 684 789

British Consulate,
21 Rua de Santa Isabel,
Portimão,
Algarve.
Tel: 082 23 071

British Consulate,
4 Rua General Humberto Delgardo,
Vila Real de Santo António,
Algarve.
Tel: 081 43 729

British Consulate,
Quinta de Santa Maria,
Estrada de Tavereve 3080,
Figueira da Foz.
Tel: 033 22 235

United States Embassy,
Avenida das Forças Armadas,
Lisbon.
Tel: 01 726 6600

United States Consulate,
826–3° Rua do Júlio Dinis,
Porto.
Tel: 02 63 094

Canadian Embassy,
2 Rua de Rosa Araújo,
Lisbon.
Tel: 01 562 547 or 563 821

## Getting There

Faro is well served by charter flights throughout the year and a fly-drive is the easiest way to explore the southern region. Many motorists journey down from Britain, especially in winter when there is virtually an armada of camper vans. Ferry services are available to both Santander and Bilbao and there is a wide choice of routes from there, either through Portugal or Spain. Lisbon, also well served by charter flights, is a good entry point for Alto Alentejo.

## By Air

*TAP*, the Portuguese National airline runs scheduled flights between London Heathrow and Porto, Lisbon and Faro; similar services are also offered by *British Airways*. In North America *TAP* operates services to Lisbon from New York, Boston, Los Angeles and Toronto. Some American carriers also offer direct flights to Portugal and other Spanish cities which may be equally convenient on a fly-drive holiday.

Charter flights from the UK especially to Faro and Lisbon, vastly outnumber scheduled services and offer the most economical way to travel. If a seat only is required then these can be booked through a travel agent. *TAP* and some tour operators sometimes offer fly-drive holidays but it is just as convenient, and often more economical, to book a car in the UK before departure. All the major car hire companies are present in Portugal and can arrange car hire before departure but the most competitive of these is *Transhire* (Tel: 0171 978 1922, Fax: 0171 978 1797) which operate through *Auto Jardim*, a leading car hire company in Portugal with offices at all airports. Portugal is one of the cheaper countries in Europe for car hire.

Charter flights including a package holiday offer such good value that visitors from North America sometimes find it more economical to fly to Britain to take advantage of them. There are many tour operators listing holidays in Portugal, especially Algarve, but one of the first and one which has remained small offering destinations and special interest holidays in Algarve is the highly respected London based *Travel Club of Upminster* (direct bookings only), Station Road, Upminster, Essex RM14 2TT, Tel: 01708 225 000. Travel agents mostly deal with a limited number of tour operators and may not be able to offer the destination required. All of them have directories and, on request, will check which operators do offer the preferred destination although it may be necessary to book elsewhere.

## By Ferry

Car ferries link the south coast of England with ports in northern Spain which are convenient for Portugal. There are no services directly to Portugal itself. *Brittany Ferries* offer services between Plymouth and Santander in northern Spain while *P&O* operate ferries from Southampton to Bilbão. The choice of which route to motor down from Spain into Portugal will be dictated by the intended destination. Since the borders are now open, crossing between Spain and Portugal offers no problems. Facilities for money exchange and refreshments exist only at major crossing points. *Brittany Ferries* also offer inclusive holidays which can be booked through travel agents.

# Travel in Portugal

## By Car

The Portuguese drive on the right. Main roads are generally well surfaced and there is an increasing network of motorways, some of which are toll roads. Minor roads are mostly reasonable but potholes can be a danger. Road markings have improved considerably in recent years making driving much safer but there is a need to keep a watchful eye on the local drivers who lack awareness of others and have a compulsion to overtake any vehicle in front without necessarily waiting for an opportune moment. Warning signs, especially temporary ones, are not necessarily in English so words to look out for are *perigo* = danger; *desvio* = diversion, *obras* = road works and *lombas* which is a ridge in the road to calm traffic flow. As far as road maps are concerned, *Hildebrand's Travel Map*, 1:400,000 series, is reasonably accurate (few maps are particularly accurate for the web of minor roads) and, available in Portugal, the *Turinta* maps are fairly good.

Drivers must be over the age of 18, seat belts are compulsory and speed limits for cars without trailers are 60kph (37mph) in built up areas, 90kph (55mph) in rural areas and 120kph (75mph) on motorways. Certain items of equipment are obligatory and these include a fire extinguisher, a warning trainagle in case of breakdown or accident, a spare set of light bulbs and a small first aid kit. If the car is a right-hand drive then headlight deflectors must also be fitted.

Police checks are frequent and drivers must be able to produce their passport, driver's licence and papers relevant to the vehicle or face a heavy fine.

In the event of an accident it is essential to call the police before the vehicle is moved. Emergency SOS telephones (orange coloured) are available along main roads for reporting accidents and emergencies. Otherwise the emergency telephone number nationwide is 151.

Petrol stations are plentiful along main routes, although it pays to fill before leaving if a route is chosen following minor roads. Unleaded petrol (*sem chumbro*) is freely available and major credit cards are accepted at main petrol stations although a small surcharge is sometimes levied.

The most useful road in Algarve is the EN125 which runs parallel to the coast for the whole length of the region. It once had some notoriety for high traffic density and accidents but improvements have been made steadily over the years with clearer road markings, overtaking lanes on the hills and traffic systems in general. In addition there is a new motorway, the IP1, to relieve traffic, which takes a more inland route from Spain, via Castro Marim, to Albufeira where it joins the main Lisbon road, also the IP1, but not of the same standard. Although the line of the new road is now shown on most maps, the motorway junctions are not always marked which limits the usefulness of the road to visitors. They are, however, shown on the maps accompanying the appropriate chapters in this guide. For longer distances it is much quicker than the EN125 and very useful for travelling around the eastern half of Algarve. Plans are afoot to extend the IP1 further west in the fullness of time.

The network of minor roads in Algarve and the countless hamlets is too challenging for most road map publishers who tend to settle for the easier option of showing just the more important roads. Many of the smaller roads are well surfaced, good to drive and lead through rustic areas which are often more interesting than the main road routes. Even with a good map a compass is handy for these roads as they wind and twist so much that it is easy to lose orientation.

## By Train

There is an extensive rail network in Portugal connecting most of the major towns. Long-distance services by *rapido* trains are excellent. They are fast and comfortable usually offering restaurant and refreshment facilities. The *directo* trains stop rather more frequently whilst the *tranvia* service is primarily local and stops at every lamppost. Main services are listed in the Thomas Cook Continental timetable, available both in the UK and USA, and other time-tables can be picked up locally. Tickets must be purchased before boarding.

## By Bus

Comfortable express buses, some with toilet and refreshment facilities, connect most major towns to Lisbon and Porto. Until recently they carried the RN logo but privatising has replaced Rodoviária Nacional by at least nine new companies so the operating company varies with the region. In spite of this division, it remains an integrated nationwide service and the various regions work in harmony. Timetables are available locally and tickets must be obtained before boarding. Otherwise there is a good network of local buses which operate reliably to timetable.

# Accommodation

Algarve is teeming with hotels, apartments and villas of all standards but many of these are taken up by major tour operators. Out of the main season, there is plenty of spare capacity and finding suitable accommodation is not normally problematic. The situation is very different in high season, from July through until September, when the independent traveller is best advised to make prior bookings. Alentejo has far, far less accommodation and only a fraction of the visitors but the same advice applies, especially for Beja and Évora.

Other forms of accommodation, like *pousadas* and manor houses, now called *solares*, which predominate in the north of the country, have a smaller presence in the south.

State run *pousadas* are mostly located in outstanding beauty spots and often in buildings of great historical interest, like a converted castle or monastery. They are the equivalent of the Spanish *paradores* and represent the flagship of luxury accommodation. Unfortunately, these state run establishments do not always meet the high standards intended and the warm welcome and personalised service not always evident but, as always, some succeed more than others. They are priced according to three categories from B, lowest, through C to CH which are the most expensive. Bookings are made through ENATUR, a central agency, on Av. Santa Joana a Princesa, 10–1700 Lisbon, telephone 01 848 1221. There are 12 in the southern region but only two in Algarve.

### Solares de Portugal
These houses are classified into three distinct groups: *casa antigas, quintas* and *herdades* and *casa rusticas.*

**Casa Antigas** are elegant manor houses and country estates mostly originating from the 17th and 18th centuries. They are furnished with period furniture and may contain valued works of art.

**Quintas and Herdades** are agricultural farms and estates with a rural setting and atmosphere. These often have their own distinctive architectural style which is rather grand and their estates are enclosed by tall walls.

**Casa Rusticas** are generally of a simpler architectural style and located in the heart of the country or within a farm.

Very few are in town locations, most are well off the beaten track and personal transport is essential. Booking conditions specify a minimum of three nights and there is no high and low season, prices for January and August are exactly the same. There are around ten of these establishments scattered throughout Algarve but many more in Alentejo.

Bookings can be made directly or through ANTER, Região de Turismo de Évora, Rua 24 de Julho 1, telephone 066 742 535, who specialise in rural tourism, and TURIHAB, Praça da Republica, 4900 Ponte de Lima, telephone 058 741672.

Apart from hotels, there are **albergarias** and **estalagems**, both of which are described as inns. *Albergarias* offer a four star comfort whereas the Estalagems may be four or five star. Both seem indistinguishable from hotels. A **residencial** slots in somewhere between a hotel and a *pensão* and offers one to four star accommodation. Some hotels prefer to operate as *residencials* as do some pensions. **Pension**s form the lowest stratum and can be a mixed bag best sorted out by actual inspection.

# Crime and Theft

Portugal is normally a safe destination and a relatively crime free country but recently there has been a rise in non violent crime, particularly involving theft from car boots. Motorists are strongly advised to leave nothing on display in the car nor to leave valuables locked in the boot and not to let their car out of sight if it is loaded with luggage. Some areas are worse in this respect than others and the Lisbon region is one of the worst.

Otherwise, it is wise to protect valuables, including camera, with as much care as at home and not make it easy for any casual thief. All losses must be reported to the police, especially if an insurance claim is anticipated. In towns seek out the PSP (Policia de Segurança Pública) who deal with tourist incidents but in rural areas this function is taken over by the GNR (Guarda National. Rebulicana) who normally carry out traffic responsibilities and police the motorways. The chances of finding an English speaking policeman are only fair. Old fashioned courtesy and respect goes a long way in Portugal in all walks of life and is particularly recommended in dealing with the police.

## Disabled Travellers

Portugal is only slowly coming to terms with the needs of the disabled and only the more recently built hotels offer anything like good facilities. Airports and main stations have generally adapted toilet facilities and there are specially reserved spaces in most towns for disabled motorists. Local tourist offices (addresses at the end of each chapter) can sometimes supply a list of wheelchair accessible hotels and campsites but the Institute for the Promotion of Tourism, Rua Alexandre Herculano 51, 1200 Lisbon publishes a list of hotels which are more suitable to wheelchair users. Ramps for crossing roads are still in short supply as are pavements outside main towns.

## Money Matters

Most towns of any size have a bank where money can be changed, either from bank notes, travellers cheques or eurocheques. Bank hours are from 8.30am to 3.00pm during weekdays. Exchange bureaux can also be found in popular tourist areas. In addition there is a growing network of automatic teller machines called Multibanco which dispense cash 24 hours a day and can be used with a wide selection of cards including Visa, Eurocheque, Eurocard and American Express. There is a daily limit of 40,000 *escudos*.

## Museums and Galleries

In general, museums are closed on a Monday and, like the rest of Portugal, closed for a couple of hours midday. Although not closing officially until 12.30pm, last entry is usually 12noon and is strictly enforced.

# Public Holidays

Since virtually every town has one or more religious festivals it sometimes seems that the country is on permanent holiday but the list of National Holidays celebrated nationwide is appreciably shorter. Easter is consistent with the rest of Europe and the holidays associated with it include Shrove Tuesday and Good Friday. Corpus Christi, late May or early June, is another variable holiday but the remainder are fixed as follows:

| | | | |
|---|---|---|---|
| 1 January | New Year's Day | 5 October | Republic Day |
| 25 April | Liberation Day | 1 November | All Saints |
| 1 May | May Day | 1 December | Independence Day |
| 10 June | Camões Day | 8 December | Immaculate Conception |
| 15 August | Assumption | 25 December | Christmas Day |

# Restaurant Closing Days

Most eating places close on at least one day each week. Rather surprisingly, popular closing days are clustered around weekend, especially Friday, Saturday and Sunday and in some places there is a very limited selection on these days. The closing day is usually posted on the door and it pays to take note of this at favoured restaurants.

# Sport

Portugal is a haven for golfers, especially Algarve which is well endowed with courses and where the climate allows the sport to be enjoyed the whole year around, although new courses seem to be opening steadily in other parts. The latest of these is near Ponte de Lima. Tennis facilities are mostly associated with hotels, some of which allow public access, but also there are clubs which open their courts to non members. Similarly horse riding stables are usually to be found in centres of tourism. There is plenty of opportunity for walking but no officially marked trails. Some holiday companies lead organised walks, but the best guides are three books published by Sunflower books, *Landscapes of Algarve, Landscapes of Costa Verde* and *Landscapes of Sintra, Estoril & Cascais*, all by the authors of this book, which detail long and short walks.

Hunting mainly for wild boar, partridge and pheasant, is a new growth area and reserves and lodges are on the steady increase. Further details can be obtained from the Federação Portuguesa de Tiro com Armas de Caça, Avenida Júlio Dinis, 10–4° Esq°, 1200 Lisboa.

There are plenty of opportunities for water sports in the main resort areas, conditions for surfing are often good, especially on the west coast, but there are also good spots for wind surfing. Sailing too is popular with marinas spread around the coast, the majority in the south.

Particular details of facilities are listed at the end of each chapter, as appropriate.

## Tax Free Shopping

Visitors from outside the European Union can take advantage of the tax free system by shopping at any of the 1500 shops which display the tax free logo. A receipt must be obtained for which a reimbursement of tax will be made at the airport on departure, either in cash or by credit if a credit card was used in the first instance.

# 4. FOOD AND WINE

Some of the huge kitchens in the older manor houses tell how the Portuguese discovered the art of good eating and lavish entertainment many centuries ago. As a nation of explorers, their great seafarers brought back more than gold and metals, they brought back pepper and spices of which cinnamon was the real prize. It is often said one boatload of cinnamon raised enough money to pay for an entire expedition to India. Vasco da Gama brought curry powder for the kitchen which continues to find frequent use but rarely in overpowering quantities, more to add a background oriental flavour to a wide range of soups and stews. The hot chilli pepper so successfully cultivated in Angola is another favourite of Portuguese chefs but it turns up under its African name of *piri-piri,* and is frequently used as a sauce mixed in oil and vinegar. It is these hints of other cultures, the taste of Africa, the smell of the Orient, which brings a uniqueness to the Portuguese cuisine.

Like the French, the Portuguese are devoted to their food and will happily drive long distances to their favourite restaurant or to try out a friend's recommendation. On the whole, they have farmer-size appetites which is reflected in massive portions and some restaurants list half portions (*meia dose*) on the menu which are more or less half price. Where there is an option, the half *dose* is normally adequate and, in any case, there is always the opportunity of ordering another portion, or even something different, if it is not enough. The size of the portions do vary and tend to be smaller — actually not so much smaller as normal size — in regions like Algarve which cater more for tourists.

## *Soup*

A meal starts invariably with soup and, for the Portuguese, may also end with a soup. One of the specialities of the north but equally popular throughout the country is **caldo verde**, a jade-green soup rich with potatoes, garlic, shreds of green cabbage and olive oil with a slice of a spicy sausage lurking at the bottom. Although it originated in the Minho, just about every region of Portugal is prepared to call this soup its own and it does vary around the country. The cabbage used is a non-heading variety with tender leaves which are taken from the plant as desired leaving a progressively longer bare stalk, rather like a sprout plant with all the sprouts removed. Cutting the cabbage is the secret to calde verde soup. A stack of cabbage leaves are rolled into a cigar shape and then cut from the end into extremely fine shreds, the finer the

# Coffee and Cakes

The Portuguese are renowned for genteel afternoon tea, a custom which Catherine of Bragança introduced to the English. Visitors are unlikely to see any evidence of this but are certain to witness the Portuguese calling in to a local café during the morning for a quick coffee and cake. This is a national pastime. The larger shops act as a gathering place for those happy to wile away the hours, morning, noon or night. The coffee is always excellent which is perhaps not too surprising for acountry which once ranked some of the great coffee producing countries, like Brazil, Angola and Timor, amongst its colonies. **Coffee** is served in a bewildering variety of ways. The Portuguese mainly prefer a *bica*, a small strong coffee, which is good for a quick fix of caffeine but hardly slakes a thirst. Worse still, the small cup is only half full, so for a full cup ask for a *cheio* which simply means full. Milk lovers can ask for a *pingo* which will bring a small strong coffee with a drop (*pingo*) of milk but for a larger coffee ask for a *meia de leite* which is usually a normal cup size, half of strong coffee filled up with hot frothed up milk. In tourist areas *café com leite* is well understood and it usually produces a white coffee, but if less milk is preferred then *só pouco leite* added to the order should result in a less milky coffee. To be sure to get a large cup the word *grande* can be added to the order. Terms for coffee tend to be very local and do not always apply in other parts of the country. On one occasion, a request for *meia de leite*, literally half of milk, which works well in the north, produced a cup of milk and a cup of coffee in a part of the country where *café com leite* is more normally used. Two more coffees which are invariably on the list are *galão*, weak, milky coffee served in a glass and *galão direita*, which is half milk, half coffee served in a glass. Other descriptions of coffee may appear on the menu but these are mainly alternative names of the types described.

Tea drinkers should beware that many of the shops make tea very badly often trying to brew it from hot rather than boiling water. If there is an opportunity, head for a tea shop for the best brew where herbal teas may also be available. *Chá* will bring tea, *chá com leite* will bring tea with milk and *chá com limão* a refreshing tea with lemon.

Few coffee shops sell coffee without selling **cakes** (*bolos*). Almonds figure strongly in the cakes from Algarve, sometimes with figs. Rice cakes (*arroz*) offer a light sponge which is not usually so sweet, *bolo da rocha* is a delicious bun with a coconut top and filled with custard, whilst coconut cakes, *cocos*, are also good. *Donuts* are mostly filled with custard; but for something plainer try the *palmier* which look like butterfly wings. Visitors to Reguengos and districts around can try their *Bolo Rançoso* which is a larger cake sold in slices.

shreds the better the colour of the soup, and these shreds are added at the last minute with minimum cooking before the soup is served. There is another soup frequently on the menu which has achieved widespread popularity, **açorda à Alentejana** or Alentejo bread soup. It is more than a soup, it is a meal in itself. Coriander, salt and garlic are ground to a paste, let down with olive oil and poured into boiling water. Bread is added, sometimes in pieces or sometimes whole slices, and one or two eggs are dropped in. Even the Portuguese may struggle to start and finish a meal with this soup. Most commonly served in tourist regions is the simple but delicious vegetable soup, *sopa de legumes* and fish soup, *sopa de peixe*.

## Bacalhau

Fish and meat dishes appear on the menu in almost equal ratio. Surrounded by sea, fresh fish is constantly available, but it is the dried salted cod, **bacalhau**, which has become the national dish. Looking more like pieces of board, it is distinctly unappetising and smelly in the dry state and it advertises itself strongly on passing one of the shops. As early as the 16th century sailors learnt to salt cod at sea and sun dry it for the long journey home. It dries down to thin, stiff slabs which can be safely kept for months and quickly reconstituted by soaking in water. Almost since Columbus discovered America, Newfoundland's Grand Banks have been the traditional fishing ground for cod, and it has provided catches enough to be a source of cheap food which has served the tables of the poor particularly well. The over fished Grand Banks no longer yield enough to meet the nation's demands and it has become necessary to import *bacalhau* from Norway at a price which the poor can now hardly afford.

The Portuguese claim at least 365 ways to prepare *bacalhau*, one for every day of the year. All the recipes start by soaking the cod in water for 24 to 48 hours with frequent changes of water to remove the salt. Afterwards the cod is usually boiled gently until soft then mixed with potatoes in some form, covered with a cheese sauce and baked in the oven. Only the more popular recipes appear on restaurant menus which include *bacalhau à bràs*, with egg, onion and thinly sliced fried potatoes, and *bacalhau à gomes de sá* which is a casserole dish with onions and sliced potatoes then garnished with black olives and hard boiled eggs. Restaurants boasting regional cuisine in Algarve usually list a *bacalhau* dish but it normally does not find too much favour with tourists and it is absent from most menus. In Alentejo it remains very popular.

Some fish items on the menu are easily recognised like *truta* and *sardinhas* but others are less obvious:

| | | | |
|---|---|---|---|
| *robalo* | bass | *salmão* | salmon |
| *pargo* | bream | *salmonete* | red mullet |
| *eirós* | eels | *linguado* | sole |
| *pescada* | hake | *espadarte* | sword fish |
| *carapau* | mackerel | *atum* | tuna |
| *solha* | plaice | *lampreia* | lamprey |

## Bacalhau à Algarvia

The recipe is as follows: take 600g of *bacalhau*, cut into two inch squares (5cm), and soak in water for 24 hours then remove all scales and bones and allow to drain. Cover the squares of cod in flour and brown in a frying pan in hot olive oil. Remove the cod to a serving dish and in the same oil fry chopped garlic (3 cloves) and onions (150g) cut into rings and place around the cod. In the meantime, boil clean potatoes (800g) in salted water and peel them when cooked. Warm the potatoes in the same olive oil and place around the cod.

## Sardines

One speciality above all others which has to be tried in Algarve is sardines and Portimão is the place. They are grilled over charcoal, sometimes in the street outside the restaurant, and traditionally served with boiled potatoes. Local sardines are in season from June to October, which is the best time to buy them, but they are available all year round although the Portuguese claim they are too bony to eat between November and April. They are barbecued at just about every outdoor fair or celebration throughout the country.

## The Cataplana

A speciality introduced by the Arabs and particularly popular in Algarve is the *cataplana*. This traditional seafood dish has a place on menus throughout the country, particularly in the larger restaurants. The cataplana is a hinged metal pan with a long handle which can be thrust into the fire. A close fitting heavy lid retains the steam so that the pan behaves a little like a pressure cooker which can be safely shaken and turned over whilst cooking. In the modern version, the cataplana is without a handle. There are various recipes in which clams feature prominently but one of the most popular uses clams, pork, onions, herbs and white wine. Often the cataplana is brought to the table so that diners can enjoy the rich aroma released when opened.

## Pork

Pork figures strongly on the meat menu and with good reason, the meat is truly tender and succulent. Pigs in Portugal live the high life on a diet of acorns and chestnuts, with probably a few truffles thrown in, and are highly prized for the production of *presunto*, smoked ham. Pork is also used in endless garlicky sausages which are popular with the locals. *Chouriço* is a dark sausage, around six or seven inches long and an inch thick, which is made from cured pork and spiced with garlic and paprika. *Murcela* is a blood

*Grilling sardines at Portimão*

sausage and one commonly used to add to *calde verde* soup. *Linguica* is like chouriço but slimmer, while *alheira* is a fresh sausage made from pork. Thin slices of ham are used in a number of recipes in which they may be used to wrap around fish or chicken. *Alentejo* and pork are virtually synonymous and it features strongly on menus, often running to several dishes.

## Other Meat Dishes

Steak turns up mostly as *bife à Portuguesa* which is either grilled or cooked with a port wine sauce. *Cabrito*, kid, is also very popular with the Portuguese and finds its way onto most menus in some dish or other and is usually excellent. Recipes for roast kid often read like Mrs Beeton ...kill the kid, cleanse and hang it in the cellar, while still warm wash well with water and salt... this is followed by frequent painting with a garlicky seasoning while still hanging before it reaches the oven two days later. Both chicken (*frango*) and turkey (*peru*) appear on the menu but are mostly served simply, although the locals prefer chicken with piri-piri sauce. Turkey is usually served as steaks.

## Vegetables

Vegetables abound on local markets and they are good quality vegetables too. There is just about everything imaginable from carrots, through cauliflower to turnips, leeks or whatever is in season. None of this shows up on the dinner plate in the restaurant, unless *cozido* is ordered. The recipe featured here shows how the vegetables are used and the quantities that the Portuguese eat.

## Portuguese Cozido

These quantities are for six people! Boil 500g of beef in water using a large pan and, a little while later, add half a chicken and season with salt. Cook in a separate pan, 300g ham, 500g salted pigs ears, 500g fresh bacon, 500g salted pork ribs, one meat sausage and one blood sausage. Add no salt since the meat is already salted. To the beef pan add now the vegetables comprising two good green cabbages, one white cabbage and three large carrots but tie the vegetables with white thread so that they can easily be removed. After 30 minutes, boil six halved potatoes separately until partly cooked and transfer to the beef pan followed by all the meat, now cooked, from the other pan. The *cozido* is ready as soon as the potatoes have finished cooking. Carefully remove the vegetables, place all the meat suitably cut onto a serving dish and decorate with the vegetables after removing all the threads.

The stock from the large pan can later be used to make soup by adding cooked small white beans and small noodles.

Salads are sometimes served with the meal in place of vegetables and rice is rarely absent from the plate in restaurants where the Portuguese eat.

### Desserts

The Portuguese have a sweet tooth so there is certain to be a sweet trolley hovering at the end of the main course or a *sobremesa* list on the menu. Eggs and sugar are used in abundance to produce the fantasies so loved by the Portuguese. Fantasies they are too judging by some of the descriptive and colourful names, like *barriga de freiras* (nun's belly) and *papos de anjo* (angel's breasts). Two sweets ever present on the menu are *arroz doce*, a cold rice pudding liberally sprinkled with cinnamon and usually very sweet, and the ubiquitous *pudim de flan* which is none other than crème caramel of which the Portuguese are extraordinarily fond. The calorie count is so high for most sweets that the energy released is best measured on the Richter scale; check out some of the recipes featured here.

### Cheese

If the puddings are all too sweet there is always the cheese which is some-times put on the table with olives to provide nibbles at the start of a meal. The pick of Portugal's limited cheeses, which are mostly expensive to buy in the shops, is the brie-like *queijo da serra* made strictly from the milk of sheep

# Nun's Thighs and All That

There is an endless selection of recipes for sweets but they have two things in common, a huge quantity of sugar and countless eggs in some form.

## *Leite Pudim (Custard Cream)*

Beat eight egg yolks with 250g sugar and the rind of one lemon for 20 minutes. Blend two tablespoons of cornflour into one litre of milk, beat well and add to the egg yolk mixture. Heat to bring to the boil while stirring constantly, remove the lemon rind and pour into a dish. Before serving, sprinkle the surface with sugar and place under a grill to caramelise the surface.

## *Viana Pie*

A fairly large tray is needed for this Swiss roll type sweet. Beat ten egg yolks with 200g sugar and add grated lemon (or orange rind). Beat the whites stiffly and add to the dough and sift in 170g flour. Beat lightly and bake on a tray lined with paper. Do not over bake otherwise it becomes difficult to roll. To make the filling, boil 100g sugar to a soft syrup, add the whisked yolks of four eggs and heat until the mixture comes to the boil.

Take the cake from the tray and place on a sugared surface, spread the egg filling and roll carefully.

## *Rabanadas Minhotas*

These are essentially cooked bread slices which can be eaten for breakfast or at any time of the day.

Boil a little red Vinho Verde wine with sugar and cinnamon and dip slices of bread into the mixture until well soaked. Dip the bread next into beaten egg and fry in olive oil. Sprinkle with sugar and cinnamon before eating.

## *Egg cigars (speciality from Arcos de Valdevez)*

Make the filling by boiling 250g sugar with a little water until the syrup reaches the thread stage and adding 250g ground almonds, eight egg yolks, a tablespoon of butter and the rind of a lemon.

Dampen some round filo pastry sheets with egg white, add the filling and roll into cigar shapes. Deep fry and coat with sugar before eating.

*Washing intestines (for sausage skins) in river*

grazing on the mountains of Serra da Estrela. *Serpa*, cured in caves and brushed regularly with an olive oil/paprika mixture, is from Alentejo and is equally delicious but much stronger after ageing. Tangy and creamy *azeitão*, from the Arrábida peninsula across the Tagus south of Lisbon is another of the more famous cheeses as is *beja*, a semi hard cheese again from Alentejo. For the calorie counters there is always *queijos frescos* which is an uncured soft cheese rather like cottage cheese.

# Wines

## *Port*

Port wine is Portugal's most eminent ambassador. It has had a place on the dinner tables of Europe and beyond for more than three centuries, and is a household name. But there is no better place to drink port than in Portugal. The full range of styles is quite bewildering but the chief variables are the ageing process and the age. All ports start in casks for two years but after that they are either matured in wood or in bottles and may be a single vintage or a blend of different years. Some of the major styles are:

**Ruby port**: this is made for drinking as soon as it is bottled which is usually after about three years in wood. This full-bodied fruity wine of good ruby colour is still the biggest selling port wine. More sophisticated `Reserve' and `Vintage Character' rubies are also made. Both of these are aged longer in the casks, usually to around four or more years, and the Vintage Character may be from selected harvests from different years but it will not continue to improve in the bottle.

**White port**: made and fortified in exactly the same way as ruby but made from white grapes. It may be sweet or dry but the modern tendency is for dry or extra dry. Taylors produced the first white port, Chip Dry, in 1935 and it is still one of the best and great as an apéritif, chilled.

**Crusted**: it starts life earmarked as vintage but it does not meet the standards so it is blended and aged for at least three years in a cask and two years in a bottle. During bottle storage it throws a deposit, or crust, and needs to be decanted before drinking.

**Tawny**: usually made from grapes from the lower Douro which are less heavily pigmented. It is matured in wood for much longer than the ruby so that the wine loses its red colour and acquires a brownish tawny colour. Smooth and mellow, the tawnies are very popular, especially the older ones. There are strict regulations controlling the labelling of port wines and a date on the label is not permitted except for exceptional wines of a single harvest under certain conditions. Even though they start life as blends, good quality tawnies can, with special approval from the Port Wine Institute, show their age as 10, 20, 30 or over 40 years old.

All the above wines are blends of several years but the following are only from single years and sometimes from particular *quintas*. The wines are allowed to carry the date on the label.

**Single Quinta**: this is an unblended wine usually from a single harvest. It is vintage in character but without the full depth and character and it usually requires long ageing in the bottle to reach perfection.

**Vintage**: this is the flagship of the port wine industry. Hopes are raised for a vintage in years when the climate has been favourable and the harvest good but they remain no more than hopes at that stage. Only after two years in the cask is a decision made and, if declared a vintage, it is bottled straight away. When mature it has a different quality to the cask aged ports. Vintage declarations are not taken lightly and reflect the individuality of each of the port houses. The Douro has such a multitude of vineyard sites with different grape varieties and different micro-climates that declared vintages are not universal but mostly quite specific to a particular manufacturer. The larger port houses which have a wider variety of farms have more chance of producing a vintage than the smaller firms. Vintage ports take some years to reach their optimum and they do not all mature at the same rate. Cockburn's declare their 1963 vintage as drinking well and one of their finest vintages of recent times, the 1970 vintage, as ready soon and the 1975 vintage as light but of good quality and just ready.

**Late Bottled Vintage**: is port of a single year, aged in wood for 4–6 years and filtered before bottling to prevent crusting.

The Port Wine Institute is the controlling body which guarantees that standards are maintained. The Institute has a bar in Porto where port wines can be tried by the glass. Every port wine made from all the manufacturers is on the menu listed by style and by manufacturer so it is a great place to sample the various ports (except the expensive vintages) without having to buy full bottles.

Something like 83 million litres of port are consumed annually and most of it in Europe with France drinking the lion's share. The UK has fallen down the league table of port consumption to be overtaken by Portugal itself. The USA is a low market taking only around 1.5 per cent of the annual production but it is strongly biased to premium styles.

## Vinho Verde and Douro Wines

Apart from port, Portugal has many very fine wines to offer apart from the well known Mateus rosé, and some very ordinary ones too. There are some excellent labels which have only a very local and limited distribution. *Quinta da Pacheca*, in Alto Douro, is an excellent red Douro wine but only rarely can it be found in shops or in restaurants away from the region where it is made. At least there is a sense of adventure in trying different wines with a chance of some rewarding discoveries.

The country has a number of regions of demarcation, two in the northern area, Vinho Verde and the Douro. Although Vinho Verde translates to green wine it really means young or fresh wine and is usually listed separately on the wine list in restaurants, the other wines are listed under *Vinhos maduros*, or mature wines, which means everything other than the Vinho Verdes. *Garrafeira* on the wine label means that the wine has been aged for a minimum of two years in the barrel and one in the bottle, but often much longer, whilst *Reservas* spend even longer in the wood.

**Douro wines** arise from grapes grown in the Alto Douro in areas generally away from the river. The land close to the River Douro is prized for the port wine grapes. Even away from the river it is the same impossibly dry and impoverished stony soil which looks as though it will not sustain any sort of plant growth. This region produces some very fine and exciting wines including one of the country's best red wines, *Barca Velha*, made in limited quantity. Some of the best years which are still around are 81, 82, 83 and 84. *Quinta do Cotto* produces dense fruity wines which are well worth searching out and laying down.

The area of demarcation for **Vinho Verde** is quite extensive and covers much of the region outside the Douro. In fact the only region north of the Douro which is not dedicated to vineyards is the higher part of Trás-os-Montes. White Vinho Verdes are stimulatingly acidic and refreshing—ideal for picnics. With so many small producers in the north, the list of labels is endless but the *Ponte de Lima* whites have a good reputation. The white made from a single grape variety, the loureiro grape, and called by that name is especially worth trying. *Casa de Sezim*, which is one of the more comfortable manor houses in the Solares scheme, is another small producer with a good reputation.

## Bairrada and Dão Wines

Two demarcated areas south of the River Douro produce good wine, these are the Bairrada wines which come from an area south of Porto and the Dão wines from the region south of the Alto Douro. The mountainous Dão region is served by a river of the same name which filters down to the sea through Coimbra. The **Dão wines** built up a good reputation in the past but they have not advanced in quality in recent years as other regions have, notably Alentejo. With considerable capital investment in new stainless steel plant and new technology, wine making in Portugal is in a mobile phase which is advancing some of the newer wines over old favourites. A new high-tech Sogrape plant in Viseu is producing some worthwhile *Grão Vasco* wines, both white and red.

**Bairrada wines** are made in the area south of Porto stretching all the way down to Coimbra. Although wine manufacture has been in hand here as long as most other areas in Portugal, it was recognised as a demarcated region only as recently as 1979. Vineyards are dominated by the *baga* grape and make good red wines which take some years to reach maturity. It pays to buy the garrafeiras and the older the better. The last years of the 1970s from '75 onwards are all worth buying. Guests at the Palace Hotel in Buçaco Forest have the opportunity to try their legendary red wine, *Buçaco*, which is unavailable outside their chain of hotels. Much of the white wine of this region is converted to a sparkling wine by the champagne method.

## Colares, Carcavelos, Bucelos and Setúbal Wines

Nearer to Lisbon there are four small demarcated areas: Colares (see feature) and Carcavelos, both very small, with the slightly larger Bucelos all on the north side of the Tagus and the Setúbal vineyards on the south. With the expansion of the holiday resorts of Estoril and Cascais south of Lisbon, the **Carcavelos** area is under threat — small and getting smaller. It produces a Madeira style sweet aperitif or dessert wine of around 19 per cent strength, but it is difficult to find. Look for the *Quinta do Barão* label. Some 15 miles (24km) north of Lisbon lies the **Bucelos** wine area centred around the Trancão river. Predominantly two white grape varieties, *arinto* and *esgana cão*, are grown on the clay slopes and floor of the river valley. These produce reliable wines of moderate strength, 11–12 per cent, which are clean and dry with a slight acidity. As in the other small areas here, production is in the hands of one main producer, Camillio Alves, and the label to look for is *Caves Velhas*.

South of the Tagus is **Setúbal** which produces another of Portugal's distinctive and famous wines. This is the sweet and perfumed *Moscatel de Setúbal*. The vines are grown around the villages of Palmela and Azeitão and Setúbal muscles in on the name only because it is the nearest port. The crushed grapes are fermented in cement vats and arrested by the addition of grape brandy at the required sugar level, the same technique as used in the production of port wine. The secret of this wine lies in the next stage when it is transferred to fresh cement vats and lightly crushed grapes and skins are added to impart to the wine the signature of the moscatel grape with its delightful aroma. After pressing again, the wine is held in casks until ready for bottling. This highly aromatic dessert wine is usually available in two ages, six and 20 year old. First one to try is Fonseca's *Muscatel de Setúbal*.

## Colares Wines

Colares, near Sintra, produces one of the best and most distinctive wines in Portugal from vineyards which are not just unique, they defy belief. The practice is by no means new, it can be traced back as far as 1154. Vines are planted into clay but to reach the clay it is first necessary to dig through a depth of sand which may be as much as 10m (33ft). Digging a trench so deep through sand is not without danger and it was commonplace for workers to cover their heads with a wicker basket while excavating to give them protection and air to breath should the trench collapse. Once planted, the vines are encouraged to produce lateral shoots which are pegged down at intervals and allowed to root thus producing a whole row of seemingly individual vines. As the vines start to grow the sand is slowly replaced until, eventually, the vines reach normal surface level. Once above ground, the vines are grown along wire strainers without achieving any great height and the vineyards are protected by high fences of fine netting to prevent the Atlantic winds from disturbing the sand. One unexpected and invaluable advantage of this method was that the depth and density of the sand gave protection to the vine roots from the ravages of the phylloxera beetle which decimated the vineyards of Europe last century. This beetle operates by burrowing through the soil and feeding from the rootstock which eventually sickens the vine. It was introduced from the United States during viticultural exchanges and, oddly enough, the solution to the problem also came from the States in the form of more rugged root stocks which had proved immune to the scourge. European vines were then universally grafted onto these rootstocks. Colares still uses the original pre-phylloxera vines. The red wines are generally better than the whites but must be matured in oak casks for several years, at least ten, before reaching their best. The one to try is the award winning *Colares Chita* which is a very quaffable, aromatic and fruity red wine.

## Algarve and Alentejo Wines

The final area of demarcation is in Algarve which has been growing vines since the time of the Romans but its wines have no great reputation. Some 31 new areas throughout Portugal are seeking recognition and were accepted in 1990 as IPRs (*Indicacões de Proveniência Regulamentada*) on  six years probation for official wine region status (DOC). Both Lagos and Lagoa in Algarve are amongst the new applicants.

Alentejo is currently the rising star in the wine world. Although it has only IPR regions, there has been considerable investment in new plant and it is already producing some of the country's most exciting wines which are eclipsing better known names. Areas worth trying include Redondo, Reguengos and Vidigueira.

## Brandy

To accompany coffee at the end of a meal there is always the local brandy-like *aguardente* made from distilled wine or the *bagaceira* distilled from the alcoholic left-overs from the wine making. Two brandies which are popularly found on the shelves are *Macieira* and *Croft's*, neither of which is particularly expensive making them rather good value for money.

## Water

Water usually has a place on the dining table and bottled water may be offered as carbonated (*com gas*) or natural (*sem gas*). One of the really outstanding bottled waters is from Carvalhelhos.

# 5. THE SOTAVENTO:
# Faro to Vila Real

The Algarvian coast east of Faro contrasts sharply with its more familiar rugged counterpart to the west. Its beaches may not display the same character but the sweeping strands of fine sand create their own special landscape. At least there is no need to clamber up and down numerous steps to the beach which makes access easier. The coastline is protected by an endless stretch of sandy barrier islands which still harbour small fishing communities. Here tourism is low key when compared with developments along the central coastal area, with Monte Gordo providing the largest concentration. The nature reserves of Ria Formosa (Parque Natural da Ria Formosa) at Faro and Castro Marim on the Spanish border are protected areas and a mecca for bird watchers and botanists. Of the towns in this part, Tavira is the most interesting with a lively market which oozes local ambience. The barrier islands are popular too, even though they are usually accessed by ferry or, in one case, a narrow gauge railway. No need to search further for desert island solitude, where the only sounds might be the crashing of waves and the distant chug of a fishing boat. These faces of Algarve are perhaps the least known but contain their own brand of hidden charm.

Although many visitors arrive in their own transport, especially over the winter months, the majority fly into Faro airport. When coming in to land, the views down onto the Ria Formosa Reserve lagoon make an intriguing introduction to this part of Portugal. The reserve, a pattern of irregular shapes edged by golden spits of pure sand, lies clearly mapped out from this aerial vantage point. A lighthouse at Cabo de Santa Maria marks the southernmost point of Portugal. Faro pushes into the nose of land which juts into the lagoon whilst the long straggle of buildings along a spit of sand facing the open sea is Faro's seaside, Praia de Faro.

# Faro

Faro's present image as a bustling town which has casually embraced a more recent tourist invasion masks a more chequered and turbulent history. A fishing community was already flourishing here long before the Phoenicians and Greeks arrived to set up trading posts. It took the arrival of the Romans, who gave it the name Ossonoba, to transform it into an important port and administrative centre. When the Visigoths ousted the Romans in 418 the town became the centre of a cult to the Virgin and was renamed Santa Maria, until they too were evicted by the Moors 300 years later. By the time Dom Afonso III finally defeated the Moors in 1249 Faro was known as Santa Maria de Hárune, the name Hárune taken from one of the 11th century Moorish governors. Over the ensuing years, it is believed Hárune became transmuted to Faarom and thus to Faro.

Commercial activity flourished, mainly due to a large incumbent Jewish community, and in 1487 one of their number, Samuel Gacon, printed the first book in Portugal. It contained the first five books of the Old Testament, known collectively as the Pentateuch. Although the Jews have long since gone, their now derelict cemetery and museum can be found on the outskirts of town, between the hospital and stadium, on Rua Leão Penedo. Faro's fortunes might have wavered with the break up of the Jewish community but it was elevated to city status (1540) and declared capital of Algarve 16 years later. Its position was further strengthened in 1577 when the Bishopric of Algarve was transferred from Silves to Faro where it remains to this day. The Spanish occupation of the Portuguese throne, only three years later, provided the English with a legitimate excuse to mount the occasional raid along the Algarve coast. Faro escaped any devastating raids until 1596 when the Earl of Essex, en route home from sacking and burning Cadiz, put in at the undefended city with a force of 3000 troops. Whilst his troops sacked Loulé and Faro, Essex ensconced himself in the bishop's palace where he discovered some 200 leather bound volumes. These were the theological works of Bishop Jeronimo Ossorio, known as the `Portuguese Cicero', who had been the incumbent at the time the see was moved from Silves to Faro. For reasons known only to himself, Essex saved them from the devouring flames of the city he left behind despite their having been defaced at the hands of the Inquisition. The text must have proved none too riveting as, two years later, he off-loaded them onto his friend Sir Thomas Bodley who had just founded a library at Oxford (Bodleian).

Like the mythical phoenix, Faro rose out of the ashes and continued to prosper but could do little to avert the effects of the earthquakes of 1722 and particularly that of 1755 which razed it to the ground yet again. Faro dusted itself down and got on with a programme of rebuilding only to find itself occupied once more in 1808 by Napoleonic forces when, fortunately for the citizens, their stay was short-lived. A further period of unrest, during the final stages of the wrestle for power between the royal brothers Pedro and Miguel in 1834, preceded a long period when Portugal was more bound up in its own internal politics.

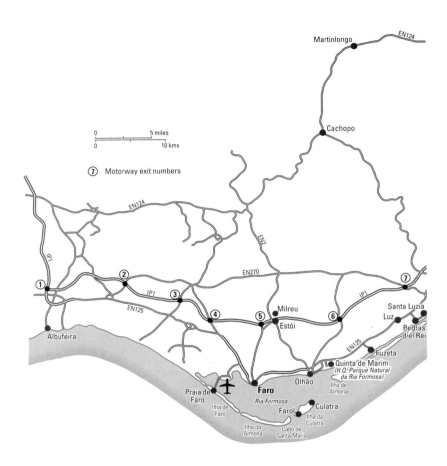

Wealth from tourism has triggered a sprawl of new building which fans outwards from the nucleus of the original city. Faro's waterfront and old walled town provide the focal point of interest and there are pleasant pedestrianised shopping streets to stroll along. Excellent beaches are but a boat ride away on the sand bars but Praia de Faro, being accessible by car, can become very congested in summer.

Faro is not really a resort as such and not a relaxing place to stay for those seeking a slower pace of life. The sights can be visited in the space of one visit

but it does have hotels and makes a convenient base for a few days before moving on. In Faro itself *Hotels Eva* and *Faro* have choice positions on the waterfront whilst a more recent addition, *Hotel Dom Bernardo*, lies a short walk away. A further option, *Hotel Ibis*, makes a comfortable base closer to the airport.

Car parking is a problem in Faro at busy times, early arrivals are more likely to find space close to the centre around the bus station and marina. An early start also allows time to fit in visits to churches and museums before the interminable midday lock out. Traffic buzzes through Praça Dom Francisco Gomes by the harbour named after the bishop (1739–1816) who did much to restore earthquake shattered Faro and whose statue stands close to the cathedral. Jardim Manuel Bivar close by provides a shaded retreat with its café a local focal point. Historic Faro (Vila-a-Dentro) is the most interesting part to visit but pockets of old Faro lie tucked amongst the press of buildings outside this small enclave. Rua D. Francisco Gomes leads to the heart of the pedestrianised shopping area with a choice of pavement cafés along the way, which includes the popular *Café Aliança*. The visitor with some time to spare could search out the churches of Carmo, São Pedro (St Peter) and Pé da Cruz along with the Ethnographical and Maritime Museums. Extensive views over the city and surrounds are the reward for those willing to hike up Avenida 5 de Outubro to Capela de Santo António, now a museum of iconography, built on the site of a former watch tower.

## Old Faro

Old Faro sits on a small mound close to the harbour facing across the lagoon to the open sea. Much of the old wall remains to bind the cluster of small houses and grand buildings which cling tenaciously together. Narrow cobbled streets and grand squares now exude a peace and tranquillity far removed from its more turbulent past. Everything of note to see in Faro is in, or within easy reach of, the old walled town. Entrance is gained through the 18th century **Arco da Vila**, next to Turismo and opposite Igreja Misericórdia.

LISBON, LAGOS

A castle gate before the 1755 earthquake, the imposing arch was constructed afterwards complete with niche for a statue of Saint Thomas Aquinas. He was adopted as the patron saint of Faro after being petitioned to save its inhabitants from plague a century earlier. Rua do Município soon leads up past the Câmara (Town Hall) into expansive Largo da Sé lined with orange trees. Not far from here, behind the Sé, is hidden the small *Restaurante Cidade Velha*, an ideal rendezvous for a special dining experience. Opposite the main door to the **Sé** (cathedral) lies the 18th century Episcopal Palace. Beneath the Sé, the remains of the Roman forum have been discovered which was built in all probability on an earlier settlement. Later, the Visigoths used the same site for their church of Santa Maria over which the Moors later erected a mosque. The present church was founded during the 13th century but subsequent reconstruction has left the building a mishmash of early Romanesque-Gothic, clearly discernible in the tower which lost its top section in the earthquake,

Renaissance and Baroque. A hint of a Moorish element can be seen in the mosque-like dome and external architecture of one of the side chapels. Entrance to the Sé is limited to two hours, on weekdays only from 10am, except for services at weekend. A more consistent style of decoration greets the visitor who manages to get through the door, as most of the internal decoration dates from after the earthquake of 1755; this includes blue *azulejos*, gilded carving and an eye-catching red and gilt chinoiserie-painted organ.

A short stroll away behind the Sé, in Praça Dom Afonso III, is the former 16th century Convento de Nossa Senhora da Assunção. Founded by Dona Leonor, third wife of Dom Manuel I, the building is now used to house the **Museu Arqueológico Lapidar Infante Dom Henrique** (Archaeological Museum). Treasures of the Roman era from Faro, Milreu and other sites in Algarve, are displayed in rooms off the attractive two storey cloister along with a range of *azulejos* and other interesting exhibits. Also in the museum, is the private collection of artefacts which belonged to a local dignitary, Doctor Ferreira de Almeida.

Flower decked streets and poky alleyways invite further exploration of this small but unexpected haven. The remains of the **city walls**, reconstructed by the Christians in the 13th century, can best be inspected by following down the narrow cobbled street at the far side of the Episcopal Palace, in a south-westerly direction towards the sea. This leads past an atmospheric antique shop to the small medieval gate of **Arco da Porta Nova**, giving direct access to the sea and the seasonal ferry to Praia de Faro. A further medieval gate, the **Arco do Repouso** (Arch of Rest), opens inland and is reached by heading down right on leaving the Archaeological Museum, or by skirting round to the left on exiting through the Arco da Porta Nova. One story relates that Arco do Repouso is where Dom Afonso III relaxed after vanquishing the Moors from Faro, hence its name.

To the right of the Arco do Repouso is **Largo de São Francisco**, where local festas and fairs are held. On the far side stands the 17th century church of **São Francisco** which contains elaborate gilded wood carvings and *azulejos* depicting the life of St Francis. Its adjoining Franciscan monastery has gone the way of most since 1834, and been commandeered for military use. **Igreja do Pé da Cruz**, located in the Largo of the same name at the far end of Rua do Bocage, contains unusual paintings of the Creation and equally unusual *azulejos* and frescoes. This 17th century church is thought to have been built on the site of a synagogue by New Christians, who were Jews forced to convert to Christianity. For an insight into the traditional Algarvian way of life before tourism, the Rua do Pé da Cruz connects the short distance from here to Praça da Liberdade and the **Museu Etnográfico**. Exhibits are well presented in the museum, located in the District Assembly building, and consist of handicrafts, costumes, old photographs and models depicting home life. Next port of call is across Praça da Liberdade, along pedestrianised Rua Vasco da Gama to **Praça Ferreira de Almeida**. The area around this square harbours some typical Algarvian fish restaurants. A curiosity only a short distance from the square, along Rua do Lethes, is the 19th century **Teatro Lethes** which is housed in the church of a former Jesuit college. Continue along Rua José Estêvão to Largo de São Pedro.

**Igreja de São Pedro**, usually open except for two hours midday, started life as a humble fishermen's chapel in 1518 and was elevated to an edifice of some stature during the 1570s. Apparently, it escaped the destructive flames of the Earl of Essex's foray into Faro some 20 years later only to succumb to the earthquakes of the 18th century. The 16th century porch remains whilst the façade was subjected to rebuilding after the earthquake of 1755. Inside, the combination of gilding and *azulejos* make a pleasing combination around the central altar. Of paintings worth seeking out are *The Last Supper* and a 16th century painting on wood of *The Descent from the Cross*.

Behind and adjacent to São Pedro, in Largo do Carmo, is the 18th century church most people come to see. The imposing Baroque façade of the **Igreja do Carmo**, with its twin bell towers, must have been an impressive sight before the surrounding tower blocks intruded. Despite this, the interior glistens with gilded carving, shown off to advantage by a backdrop of plain white walls, and is regarded as one of the finest examples of such workmanship in the area. In the sacristy is a collection of sacred art but the main draw is the adjoining macabre Capela dos Ossos (Chapel of Bones). Ghoulish portent is further implied by the inscription above the doorway to the chapel which translates — `Stop here and think of the fate that will befall you' — similarities here to the even larger Capela dos Ossos in Igreja de São Francisco at Évora. The walls and ceiling of the chapel are covered with around 1250 skulls and bones of monks from the Third Order of the Carmo, and probably others, whose remains were removed from an adjacent cemetery in 1816.

Return to the harbour via Rua de São Pedro to the **Museu Maritimo** (Maritime Museum) situated in the harbourmaster's office close to Hotel Eva. Along with models of ships and fishing paraphernalia, this fascinating museum is a mine of information about fishing practices and in particular the old tuna fishing trade. An added bonus is labelling in English.

## Beaches

Beaches in this part of the world are the superb strips of sand on the barrier islands. **Ilha de Faro** is easily the most accessible, being 9km from Faro via the airport road, but not the best place for solitude. Tourist accommodation, restaurants, summer houses and the *Estalagem Aeromar* (by the bridge) jostle for space in this confined area. As parking is very limited, it makes sense to bus out or take the seasonal ferry which plies between Faro and the Praia and also quieter **Ilha da Barreta**.

# Olhão

A short distance eastwards along the EN125 from Faro lies one of Algarve's newest cities (1985) and important fishing port, Olhão. It was little more than

*Alcatruz: pots for catching octopus*

a hamlet of simple fishermen's huts on the sand until the late 1700s when more permanent housing began to be constructed. In 1808, the inhabitants rose up and dispatched a French garrison billeted in the town. This action prompted 17 of its fishermen to sail across the Atlantic in a small boat, without navigational charts, to inform the exiled Dom João VI in Rio de Janeiro that Portugal was rid of Napoleon's troops. As a reward for their endeavour, the King granted Olhão a town charter with the title Olhão da Restauração (Olhão of the Restoration) but the latter name was subsequently dropped. The town prospered and developed on fishing and canning during the 19th century and even today it remains a working town which makes little concession to tourism.

Intrepid explorers, who probe beneath the uninspiring crush of Olhão's modern sprawl might be surprised to find the original fishing village. An even bigger surprise is the strong Moorish element found in the architecture of the white cubic houses with their flat roofs, outside stairways and plain, squat `balloon chimneys'. Not a legacy of Moorish occupation as might at first be thought, the inspiration for their design coming from trade with North Africa.

Fish is the hub around which Olhão revolves, so early morning visitors catch the fish market in full swing, especially Tuesday to Saturday. This is also the starting point for exploration of the old town and close to ferries out to the barrier islands. Follow signs to *Mercados* (markets) on Avenida 5 de Outubro or Port (Porto de Pesca), which is just around the corner to the east on Avenida das Forças Armadas. The two **covered markets** with unusual silver domed turrets, one for food and vegetables (on the port side) the other for fish, are flanked by gardens on what passes as a promenade along the edge of the Ria Formosa. Ferries run all year out to the **Ilhas of Armona** and **Culatra** from the front close to the port, to service small fishing communities facing the mainland. The warm sheltered waters of the lagoon are enticing but the long sandy strands facing the open sea offer the best chance of solitude, especially on Armona. On the Ilha da Culatra, the village of Culatra holds little appeal; it is better to move on to Farol at the far end. An unusual sailing trip from Olhão along the Ria Formosa is offered in the last of the original tuna fishing boats (Barca do Atum).

The main centre of interest in Olhão lies inland, from the open square between the markets. Apart from the fishing quarter up to the right, with its narrow winding cobbled streets, a few steps further on leads to the centre of town and the 1698 **Igreja Matrix** (parish church). Ascend the belfry for a good view over the town, then visit the Capela da Nossa Senhora dos Aflitos (Chapel of our Lady of the Suffering) behind. Here is where local women come to pray for the safe return of their men when there are storms at sea.

Return to the EN125 and continue in the direction of Vila Real. In just under 1km from the road signposted Port, on the outskirts of Olhão, watch for the road off right to Parque Natural and Campismo. A fraction over 1km up this road leads to the extensive grounds and office of the Parque Natural da Ria Formosa. Open to the public Monday to Friday, a visit to the informative visitors' centre and café in the main office building situated in the grounds, and a wander through the park pass a pleasant and interesting couple of hours or so.

---

## Parque Natural Ria Formosa

Visitors arriving by air into Faro airport get an absorbing bird's-eye view down over an extensive maze of salt marshes, waterways, mud flats, interlinked islands and lagoons which make up the Parque Natural Ria Formosa. Its boundaries are extensive: it covers the coastal area from Quinta do Lago in the west to Manta Rosa, beyond Tavira, in the east. Formosa means beautiful but it is hard to appreciate its beauty without exploring the reserve on foot or by boat. It is more than just a reserve for countless plants and animals, it actually provides work of a very traditional nature, as it has since Roman times, for many thousands of people over the years whose homes lie within the park boundaries.

Shellfish farming, especially of bivalve molluscs, and harvesting clams and razor clams is an important economic activity which contributes significantly to the country's production of shellfish. Salt production from salinas at Ludo, Olhão, Tavira and Fuzeta account for half the country's salt output and old salinas are being put to a new use; bass, sea bream, sole and whitebream are being successfully farmed there. Dredging to keep the inlets clear produces good quality sand for the building trade and the latest industry allowed to join the ranks is tourism. All the outer barrier islands are virtually sand banks and, although access is often only by boat, leisure activities are growing thanks to regular ferry services from Faro, Olhão, and Fuzeta.

The outer barrier islands absorb all the battering from the winds and the sea and afford considerable protection to the inner salt marshes which are in effect platforms for vegetation which themselves are sometimes covered by tidal movements. All this provides an ideal habitat for fish, more than 50 species recorded, and an ideal feeding ground for wading birds. Since Algarve is a resting place for birds migrating between northern Europe and Africa, these feeding grounds are particularly important and attract a lot of species. Apart from the salt marsh vegetation, there are also many plant species which inhabit the dunes and the more stable areas behind.

A large part of the park, located just east of Olhão, is open to visitors on an organised basis as an education centre. A map showing the routes around the reserve and indicating points of interest can be obtained at the information centre where there is also an exhibition featuring the activities within the reserve.

It is known that the Romans were active in this area, busy salting fish for export and there are remains of a Roman villa in the east of the reserve. It awaits excavation which is not likely to happen until funds are available. Apart from salting fish, the Romans also made the condiment garum from the maceration and fermentation of fish to which herbs were then added. Packed in amphorae, this paste was also exported. Just behind the Roman area is a reed lake with a hide for bird watching.

Part of the conservation work of the park involves a breeding programme to preserve the **Cão de Água**, the **Portuguese water dog**. These curly haired, over-large poodles have membraned paws, swim extremely well and have been assisting fishermen for centuries. Just how they helped is not clear but they were certainly used for retrieving gear and carrying ropes from boat to boat; it is also said that they can dive and steer shoals of fish towards the nets. With changes in fishing methods these dogs are no longer used and are in danger of becoming extinct, although there are still thought to be around 1000 throughout the country. Fortunately, these sturdy dogs are good tempered and make excellent pets. The kennels lie to the north of the park where several breeding pairs are housed.

At one time there were as many as 30 **tide mills** in use throughout Algarve but the only one in operation today lies on the southern edge of the reserve. These mills simply took advantage of the tidal flow and used the energy of the returning water to drive the mill. Mechanisation and modern forms of energy destroyed these mills just as they did windmills.

Spring and early summer are the best times to find most of the **plants** in flower and many species can be seen by just walking around the reserve. A comprehensive list can be purchased at the information centre which is so extensive (693 species) that just to pick out highlights fails to do it justice. Nevertheless, particularly attractive are many of the bulbous species including the crocus-like *Romulea bulbocodium* and the smaller *R. ramiflora*. Two narcissus are seen in spring, *N. papyraceus* and *N. bulbocodium*, but late summer and autumn offers two gems of the same family in the sea daffodil, *Pancratium maritimum* and the autumn snowflake, *Leucojum autumnale*. Amongst the bulbs, there is one diminutive Scilla found here which is hard to find elsewhere, *S. oderata*, but the other Scilla, *S. monophyllus* is common also on the high ground of Serra de Monchique. *Fritillaria lusitanica* also grows on the reserve but may rest and not appear if the season is too dry. Seven species of wild orchids grow within the reserve area including the yellow bee orchid, *Ophrys lutea* and the mirror orchid, *O. vernixia*. The borage family is well represented with the bright blue *Borago officinalis* and *Cerinthe major* amongst others; one plant of interest is the scrambling shrub *Lithodora prostrata* which never seems to be without a flower. Geraniums, campanula, poppies, thymes all abound but one eye-catching bright blue pimpernel, *Anagallis monelli*, is worth looking out for.

Bird watchers no doubt will head for the hide by the pond. Information available at the centre lists **214 birds** for the wider area of the reserve. These include summer visitors, migrants and occasionals as well as the usual residents. The secretive and purple gallinule, *Porphyrio porphyrio*, takes pride of place and is used as the symbol of the park, but Ludo, west of Faro, is the best place to see it. A much shortened list shows the diversity of the avifauna:

grey heron (*Ardea cinerea*)
purple heron (*Ardea purpurea*)
cormorant (*Phalcrocorax carbo*)
white stork (*Ciconia ciconia*)
marsh harrier (*Circus aeruginosus*)
hen harrier (*Circus cyaneus*)
spoonbill (*Platalea leucorodia*)

booted eagle (*Hieraaetus pennatus*)
marsh sandpiper (*Tringa stagnatalis*)
redshank (*Tringa totanus*)
green sandpiper (*Tringa ochropus*)
short-eared owl (*Asio flammeus*)
barn owl (*Tyto alba*)
black-winged stilt (*Himantopus himantopus*)

*Santa Luzia*

## Fuzeta

The large fishing village of Fuzeta lies next along the coast where salt production is very much in evidence. Accommodation is limited to a camp-site and rooms mainly to cater for summer visitors who use the village as a base to hop over to the nearby **Ilha de Armona**. Its older fishermen, known as `lobos do mar' (sea wolves), once sailed off to the Newfoundland cod banks for a few months each year to replenish stocks of foul smelling dried salted cod (*bacalhau*). An arduous journey, undertaken in four-masted trawlers aptly named *bacalhoeiros*. History buffs might be interested in the medieval watch-tower, **Torre de Ares**, lying a little further along the coast. This is also the area where Roman ruins, thought to be Balsa, have been found.

## Ilha de Tavira

There is not much to stop for in **Luz de Tavira**, except perhaps to admire the much remarked Manueline portal of its church, found on the side close to the main road. Press on for around 2km and turn right off the main road to Pedras d'el Rei and Santa Luzia. The road makes its way through countryside and an upmarket holiday complex before eventually reaching the shore by a small car park. As this is the starting point for a novel jaunt out to **Barril** on the Ilha de Tavira, parking may have spilled out along the nearby track. This is Parque Natural territory and, except for the beach itself, visitors are requested to keep to the designated walkways, and dogs, music, motor bikes and casual camping are not allowed. A pontoon footbridge, over a channel in the mud flats, connects with the narrow, single gauge railway which chuffs merrily across the sand barrier to the superb beach on the far side. Walkers who prefer the 20 minute tramp on the paved path alongside the line, may be rewarded by sight of fiddler crabs (*Uca tangeri*) scurrying into holes in the mud flats — they quickly abandon their sunbathing at the slightest sound. These decapod crustaceans have one claw larger than the other, part of the mating ritual, and can only be found on the southern Iberian peninsula in Europe. The train stops at a small beach settlement of some sophistication, with chalet accommodation, a surfing school and tennis courts.

## Santa Luzia

No need to return to the N125 as the onward route keeps close beside the lagoon. A wide, palm-lined promenade lends an exotic touch to the fishing village of Santa Luzia. The cafés and restaurants overlooking the lagoon are a relaxing place to watch the world go by. Colourful fishing boats bob at anchor, whilst fishermen potter around on the jetty amidst stacks of crustacean covered pots (*alcatruzes*). These pots are the answer to Santa Luzia's special line in fishing, octopus. See feature on page 104. A cosier ambience can be sought amongst the narrow cobbled streets and traditional houses of the village, behind the promenade. Try sampling the fare on offer at *Restaurant Á do Abade* in the main square near the church.

# Tavira

Santa Luzia soon gives way to the environs of Tavira, which rates as one of the most appealing towns in Algarve. The Rio Gilão, becoming Rio Ségua upstream from the old bridge, flows between palm trees and classical façades with `Pombaline' terracotta tiled rooftops which lend a tropical air of elegance still unblemished by unsightly development. This oriental style of four-pitch roof was used extensively in the rebuilding programme instigated by Pombal after the 1755 earthquake and is particularly noteworthy here. It also boasts over 20 churches but most are kept locked. Of accommodation in Tavira itself, *Residential Marés* is centrally placed on the quay from where a ferry connects with the beach in season. More peacefully situated on the outskirts are the traditional apartments of *Quinta do Caracol*.

Tavira's foundation is rather vague and probably dates back to a prehistoric farming and fishing settlement. Evidence has been unearthed that the Greeks were present about 400 BC, which supports the theory that someone was around with whom to trade, and the Romans definitely left their mark on the area. A Roman bridge once straddled the river, part of the route linking Faro with Mértola, on whose foundations the present medieval structure was built. Tavira was thought to have once been Roman Balsa, but this claim appears to have been refuted in favour of a site further west, near Luz. The Arab conquest led to a period of growth and development until they were expelled by Paio Peres Correia in 1242. Its development continued and Tavira grew into an important port, exporting almonds, carobs, figs and the scarlet kermes dye, obtained from the kermes oak (*Quercus coccifera*), and was awarded city status in 1520. A series of catastrophes — the silting up of the river, plague in 1645 and then the earthquake of 1755 — led to a decline in economic growth. Tuna fishing and canning were more recent big business until the gory nature of their slaughter, discontinued in 1972, and over-fishing caused the industry to slump. This annual carnage entailed netting tuna shoals in the estuary and harpooning the fish, a practice christened the `bullfight of the sea'. See feature page 104. Nesting storks on derelict chimneys, abandoned boats and gear are the only reminders of this once flourishing industry. Tourism has been instrumental in an upturn of fortune but is still relatively low-key.

## *The Town*

A modern bridge in Tavira, nearer the estuary, makes for easier crossing of the river and access to the EN125. A congested centre and tricky one-way system do not add up to easy parking, but there is usually space by the river on the seaward side of the market hall. Activity centres around the **Praça da Republica** by the old bridge and market, the latter reached by walking

*Tavira*

through the palm shaded **riverside gardens**. These gardens offer a welcome retreat from the bustle of the lively covered market with its choice selection of local produce and fresh fish. When refreshment calls, open air cafés and fish restaurants are never too far away.

The old walled town is approached off Praça da República, up cobbled Rua da Galeria past the Turismo office. This attractive alley passes beneath the Arco da Misericórdia, with its granite crest and armillary spheres, directly to the locked **Igreja da Misericórdia**, now used for concerts. Admire the church's fine 16th century portal, with statues of Saints Peter and Paul, and move on up to the scant ruins of the castle and **Igreja da Santa Maria do Castelo**. The church was built on the site of a mosque in the 13th century, about the same time Dom Dinis was busy strengthening the defensive walls. Rebuilt after the 1755 earthquake, the decoration of the light and airy interior hints at Classical rather than the more ornate Baroque prevalent at the time. Fortunately, some of the original Gothic elements remain including the main doorway. In the chancel is the tomb of Paio Peres Correia who liberated Tavira from the Moors in 1242. An inscription here commemorates the `Sete Caçadores', seven Christian knights, whose massacre by Moors at a time of truce was a spur to Correia's final and terrible assault on the town. The church also witnessed the knighting of Henry the Navigator and his brothers by their father Dom João I, on their return from conquering Ceuta in North Africa. Not much remains of the castle, but the views out over Tavira with its distinctive rooftops are best appreciated from the ruined ramparts through the garden.

A stroll across the river, over the medieval bridge, to the east bank unfolds a wider viewpoint back over the walled town. A plaque on the side of the bridge commemorates brave locals, who repelled a Castilian invasion force in the 14th century. Those in search of Baroque splendour will find it in the 18th century **Igreja do Carmo**, sited above the old residential area which flanks the riverside. Ask for the key at number 22 opposite if the church is locked, but respect the lunchtime break.

To reach the long sandy strip of beach at **Ilha da Tavira**, follow the road out through the salt pans, beyond the new bridge, to reach the seasonal ferry in 2km (1¼ miles). A bus connects with Tavira in summer and there is a camp-site with full facilities on the Ilha.

## Cabanas

Moving further along the EN125, pass the large complex of Quinta das Oliveiras with its villas, apartments and Eurotel hotel before turning right down to Cabanas at Conceição. Tourist accommodation crowds the area behind Cabanas but the snuggle of old village houses shrug off this encroaching tide. Fishing boats collect within sight of Tavira across the estuary and a sand spit protects from the open sea. Cabanas is still relatively new to tourism, so retains the flavour of a more relaxed backwater. Beyond the end of the promenade to the east, behind the pine backed sands which line the lagoon, it comes as a surprise to stumble upon a complete dry-moated fort. The fort is little mentioned and its locked entrance faces inland but the presence of bastions for cannons suggest a later defensive design, probably 17/18th century. Locals dig for shellfish in the lagoon at low tide when it is possible to wade over to the sand spit which stretches all the way to Manta Rosa to meet the coast. Alternatively a local fisherman will act as ferry at high tide.

## Cacela Velha

Just before Manta Rosa is delightfully atmospheric Cacela Velha, a small hamlet with a miniature 18th century fortress and dazzling white church. The whole village hugs closely together on a perch above a lagoon, which is accessed by steps down an easy tree-lined slope. Thought to date from the time of the Romans and known as Qastalla to the Moors, it was briefly the centre of attention during the War of the Two Brothers when a force landed here in 1833. Vila Nova de Cacela lies inland of the N125, nearer the Manta Rota turn-off.

## Manta Rota and nearby centres

Manta Rota marks the end of the lagoons and the start of an uninterrupted dune-backed beach as far as Vila Real. This seemingly endless stretch of sand is easily accessible with facilities, of varying sophistication, scattered along the shore. Manta Rota itself is becoming hemmed in by low-rise development but remains a small resort. Nearby *Estalagem Oásis* is well situated for the beach, edging onto the dunes. **Altura** and **Alagoa** merge into a mushrooming tourist development, with all the attendant trappings of tourism, but building is kept well back behind the dunes. A low cliff marks **Praia Verde**, approached between umbrella pines, where a track leads down to the café/restaurant on the beach and **Praia da Cabaço** is yet more sand and a restaurant.

## Monte Gordo

A clutch of high-rise building greets the visitor to Monte Gordo. This purpose-built resort has sprung up around a much older fishing village and fishing is still a major occupation of the locals, as the number of boats and shacks to store their gear testify. In sharp contrast, a casino adds an international touch to the wide promenade and vast expanse of beach. Surprisingly, Monte Gordo has not yet developed into the swamping sprawl typical of resorts west of Faro and remains fairly compact; but things are changing. A popular stop for a decent sized cup of coffee is the pavement café/pastelaria *Dom Fernando*, close to *Hotel Vasco da Gama* with its plum position right on the seashore.

The onward road (EN511) to Vila Real leads quickly past an extensive pine covered picnic area behind the shore and campsite inland. When the road reaches the river, turn left to park along the riverside near the centre of Vila Real. Parking restrictions and one-way systems make life difficult for the unsuspecting motorist within the narrow streets of the grid.

## Vila Real de Santo António

Vila Real de Santo António, shortened to Vila Real for most purposes (not to be confused with Vila Real in the north), was the brainchild of the Marquês de Pombal (see feature page 65) and part of his grand plan to control the commerce of the country. Earmarked as the headquarters of the General Company of Royal Fishing in the Region of Algarve, building began in earnest in 1774 near the site of an ancient settlement, Santo António de Arenilha, slowly submerged by the sea sometime at the beginning of the 17th century. The nucleus of the new town was built in five months on the much vaunted grid plan used for Lisbon's Baixo district, with the project as a whole taking two years to complete. Inhabitants of the earlier settlement had moved to safer ground at Monte Gordo and Pombal now wanted them to populate his new town. Pombal's bullying threats to burn Monte Gordo encouraged but a few, many preferring exile in Spain. Despite Pombal's efforts to create a major centre for fishing at Vila Real, it was not until 1865 that it achieved an upturn in fortune with the building of the country's first tuna canning factory in the town. The past 20 or more years have witnessed a downturn in the fishing industry whilst tourism has developed. In no way can Vila Real be classed as a resort but it has flourished as a major crossing point from Spain. This trade has recently diminished with the opening of a new bridge further up-river but ferries still ply between Vila Real and Ayamonte across the river, the 15 minute crossing bringing a daily horde of Spaniards in search of Portugal's bargain buys in textiles. Boats once navigated the River Guadiana as far inland as Serpa and there are remains of a Roman port at Mértola. Vila Real was used as a port for boats servicing the copper mines of São Domingos which sailed as far as Pomarão from where the first railway in Portugal connected with the mine (see Chapter 11). Today, there are summer boat trips up-river to Alcoutim and sometimes as far as Mértola.

There is not much to excite the visitor to Vila Real but **Praça Marquês de Pombal** has charm. The large square is laid out in geometric style with black and white rays of *calçada* paving radiating out from a central obelisk, dedicated to Dom José I. Orange trees soften the uniformity of the surrounding buildings, whose heady blossom in spring is excuse enough to linger at one of the outdoor cafés. A small museum of pictures on wood, Museu Manuel Cabanas, is located in the square along with the Igreja Matriz. Continue by following the road along the riverside and round left before a right turn at the EN122 to Castro Marim.

## The Marquês de Pombal

Sebastião José de Carvalho e Melo, was born into the lower aristocracy in 1699. Better remembered as the Marquês de Pombal, he firmly established himself in Portugal's history during his lifetime. The combination of a clear, calculating mind and powerful physical presence — he stood at over six feet tall — were no doubt instrumental in his meteoric rise to fame. Dom João V, disliking the man but respecting his ability, dispatched him off to London as envoy to the Court of St James.

Pombal made a timely return to Portugal just before the death of Dom João in 1750. Untutored in the affairs of state, the affable new king, José, preferred the delights of the opera, card table and horse-riding. He made Pombal secretary of state and later chief minister, being quite happy to let him control the everyday running of the country, which included putting his signature to any document Pombal produced.

A man of vision and brilliance, Pombal nevertheless exerted a dictatorial rule which brought him many enemies, particularly amongst the nobility and the Church. Matters came to a head after the 1755 earthquake when much of Portugal lay in ruins. Pombal was granted emergency powers by the king, not rescinded for 20 years, and took control. Plans were drawn up to rebuild Lisbon in neo-classical style to a geometric plan and bring piecemeal commercial activity, at home and in the colonies, under central control. Chartered companies were created for tobacco, fishing, whaling and port wine, the latter business in particular being in a state of chaos and set on a course of self destruction.

The formation of the General Company for the Cultivation of the Vineyards of the Upper Douro, in 1756, caused great bitterness. Demarcated areas were created for wine growing and anyone outside those areas had their vines destroyed. With despotic determination opponents were ruthlessly weeded out, some hanged others deported, only those who adapted survived and prospered. An assassination attempt on his life only served to provide Pombal with the excuse he needed to move against the Jesuits, although it was never really known who was responsible. A reign of terror followed in January 1759 when nobles known to oppose Pombal and Jesuits were subjected to an orgy of torture, beheading and burning. Eight months later the Jesuits were expelled from Portugal and in the same year Pombal became Count of Oeiras.

All opposition squashed, Pombal now bulldozed through more, much needed, change. Reforms at Coimbra University weakened religious influence, which had caused serious students to seek a broader education outside Portugal, and grammar schools were created. An observatory, botanical gardens and laboratories were established, slavery banned and distinctions between Christians and new Christians (converted Jews) abolished as was discrimination by colour in the eastern colonies.

Pombal was created Marquês in 1770 but fell from grace on the death of Dom José. In an attempt to keep his position of power, Pombal plotted to force José's daughter Maria to renounce the throne in favour of her son José, an admirer of his. The plan backfired and Pombal found himself being tried for crimes against the state. In his defence, none of his actions was shown to have been undertaken without the king's signature on the appropriate document. A new regime under an anti-Pombal queen sealed his fate, he was banished to serve out the rest of his life on his estate, but his economic and administrative reforms remained in place.

Loathed by many during his lifetime, Pombal's foresight and draconian methods of achieving his objective only served to improve an otherwise stagnating country. His implacable will might have swept aside all that stood in his way but, despite personal ambition, he was devoted to his home and family. Today, his achievements are recognised and his memory revered rather than reviled.

*Marquês de Pombal square, Vila Real*

## Castro Marim

Castro Marim is set on high ground ahead, only a short drive away through the salt and mud flats of the Reserva Natural do Sapal, see feature page 68. Long a place of strategic importance, as its castle and fort testify, the town makes little concession to the tourist boom along the coast.

Finds from the neolithic period, suggest Castro Marim was fortified and a port even before the Phoenicians set up trading posts. The Romans, who named it Baesuris, and Moors paid particular attention to the defences, the latter raising it to a town of some note. Under the forces of Dom Sancho II, it was recaptured in 1238 and granted its first charter by Dom Afonso III (1277). At this time, the Moors had not been completely driven out of Portugal so Afonso built stronger defences and Castro Marim became an important Christian outpost. This role was further compounded when Dom Dinis persuaded Pope John XXII to found a new, exclusively Portuguese, religious military Order of Christ and use the castle as headquarters. The new Order, which emerged from the disbanded and discredited Knights Templar, was to be an added line of defence against Moorish incursions. The years of the Order's sojourn at Castro Marim between 1319 and 1334 were a period of expansion, especially under the Grand Mastership of Henry the Navigator. With the Moors finally expelled from the Iberian peninsula, the Order of Christ moved its headquarters to Tomar. The town prospered as a port but in the 17th century, after 60 years of Spanish rule, João IV deemed it prudent to restore the castle and build the Fort of São Sebastião on nearby Cabeço Hill. Castro Marim's importance declined rapidly after the 1755 earthquake, which destroyed much of the town. The silting up of the river and the emergence of Vila Real as a more viable port hastened its decline.

There is a sleepy air to Castro Marim, especially since the EN122 was re-routed to by-pass the town. The remains of the **castle** and **fort** dominate two distinct but adjoining hills from where sweeping panoramas clearly show their strategic importance. Inside the castle grounds is the nature reserve office and a small museum. The information provided about the reserve is mainly in Portuguese and there is almost nothing about the castle. Within the inner castle walls are the renovated old square castle with round turrets, a reconstruction of an earlier Moorish fortification, and 14th century **Igreja de Santiago** (church of Saint James). This church served as the Igreja Matrix (parish church) when the village was concentrated within walls which once reached towards the fort and across to Igreja São António nearer the river.

---

## Reserva Natural do Sapal de Castro Marim

Bounded by the Rio Guadiana to the east and the EN125 and EN125-6/EN122 to the south and west, the nature reserve is ideally sited on the main migratory bird route. Once a thriving region of salinas, salt production is now reduced to a small area within the confines of the reserve. The marshes and salinas cover an area of some 2089 hectares which is dissected unevenly by the EN122. Access is easier on the river side of the road but the huge expanse to the west is less exposed to human elements. Paths allow access in and around the salinas for walking and bird-watching.

Huge flocks of flamingos, *Phoenicopterus ruber*, reside alongside a large breeding colony of black-winged stilts, *Himantopus himantopus*, the latter being the emblem of the reserve. Other species include:

avocet (*Recurvirostra avosetta*)
black-tailed godwit (*Limosa limosa*)
Kentish plover (*Charadrius alexandrinus*)
ringed plover (*Charadrius hiaticula*)

sanderling (*Calidris alpina*)
redshank (*Tringa totanus*)
little tern (*Sterna albifrons*)
white stork (*Ciconia ciconia*)

---

## Pastoral route to Alcoutim

A delightful pastoral route to Alcoutim follows the course of the River Guadiana, reached by continuing along the EN122 towards Beja then taking the first right turn, 6km (4 miles) past Azinhal, signposted Alcoutim. **Azinhal** is one of the last locations of the dying art of bobbin lace, *renda de bilros*. The road winds gradually downhill past slumbering white hamlets to reach the river at **Foz do Odeleite**. Yachts bob gently on the water, a reminder that the sea is not too far away, and paper white narcissus, *Narcissus papyraceus*, make a showy mass early in the year. This is a route to savour and take at a leisurely pace passing through backwaters such as **Alamo**, rustic **Guerreiros do Rio** and **Laranjeiras**. First indications that Alcoutim is close come with a clear view of the frontier town of Sanlúcar de Guadiana and its omnipresent Moorish fort across the river in Spain.

## Alcoutim

Alcoutim comes into sight round the next corner, its white houses with their red sloping roofs ranged around the ruins of the castle. Skirt round the edge of town to meet the EN122-1 then continue down to the centre. Fortunately, ancient Alcoutim has retained its identity, with new development kept separate by the tributary Ribeira de Cadavais to the north. The usual tide of Phoenicians, Greeks, Carthaginians, Romans, Visigoths and Moors left their mark as this was a port and defensive position on the Guadiana. Alcoutim was recaptured from the Moors about the same time as Castro Marim (c 1238) and, similarly, its castle underwent extensive alteration. Because of its strategic position it also had links with the Order of Christ downstream at Castro Marim. A brief moment centre stage came to Alcoutim in 1371 when Kings Fernando I of Portugal and Henrique II of Spain met mid-river to sign a peace treaty between the two countries. Subsequently as less traffic began to venture upriver to trade and cross border hostilities subsided, Alcoutim became a quiet retreat. The town's position as a far flung outpost and the locals' need for new excitement manifested itself in the emergence of a new occupation, smuggling. Alcoutim became a centre for an illegal trade in tobacco and snuff which, by the 17th century, appears to have involved most of the town.

A climb up the cobbled streets, probably accompanied by scurrying hens, leads to Alcoutim **castle** whose ramparts provide the best views over the town and across to Sanlúcar de Guadiana which is quite close at this point. Inside, the grounds have been landscaped and a pleasant museum erected over exposed Iron Age, Roman, Arabic and medieval foundations. Fragments of pottery are also displayed along with an exhibition of photographs taken in Alcoutim. Down by the riverside, a ferry crosses the water to Spain overlooked by the Igreja Matrix from its prime position on the river bank. The Igreja de Nossa Senhora da Conceição, built on the site of an earlier 16th century chapel by order of Dom João IV, sits higher up the hillside. A sprinkling of cafés offer light refreshment, with lunch at the riverside restaurant, *O Soeiro*, an option except on Sundays.

## Rural Villages West of Alcoutim

Some of Algarve's more rural villages, where many aspects of an older way of life prevail, can be reached along the EN124 between Alcoutim and Barranco do Velho. The road is very good and fairly straight as far as **Martinlongo** then begins to twist through Cachopo to Barranco do Velho. A revival of rural crafts

*From Alcoutim castle looking towards Sanlúcar de Guadiana in Spain*

is being encouraged, especially in Martinlongo, and a choice of villages along the way might include **Giões**, **Mealha** for old Celtic type round houses now used as storage, **Cachopo** and **Castelão** south from Feiteira. This is where to come to find the real Algarve, but a word of warning, many of the tracks are only fit for four-wheeled drive traffic after the winter rains.

# Practical Information

## Hotels and Restaurants

Quality hotels are thin on the ground from Faro eastwards but below are listed a few of the best ones. Advance booking is advised as most are used by tour operators.

### FARO

**Hotel Eva** (tel. 089 803 354). Four-star hotel centrally situated overlooking the harbour with snack-bar and restaurant.

**Hotel Dom Bernardo**, Rua Gen. Teófilo da Trinidade 20 (tel. 089 806 806). Three-star hotel about 10–15 minute walk from the harbour with garage.

**Hotel Faro** (tel. 089 803 276). Three-star hotel in square overlooking the harbour with restaurant.

**Hotel Ibis**, EN125 Pontes de Marchil (tel. 089 806 771). Three-star hotel on way out to airport and one of the French Ibis chain of hotels. Restaurant and car park.

**Estalagem Aeromar**, Praia de Faro (tel. 089 817 189). 3km from airport and close to beach with snack bar and restaurant.

**Cidade Velha**, behind the Cathedral (tel. 089 271 45). Best cuisine in Faro. Moderate to expensive. Closed Sunday.

**O Gargalo**, Largo do Pé da Cruz 30 (tel. 089 273 05). A Portuguese favourite for fish.

**Green**, Rua Pé da Cruz 9 (tel. 089 213 03). National and international. Moderate.

**Parque**, on road leading to airport (tel. 089 817 150). Has a good reputation amongst the locals.

**Roque**, Praia de Faro (tel. 089 817 868). By lagoon with big terrace and excellent for fish. Moderate. Closed Wednesdays.

**Camané**, Praia de Faro (tel. 089 817 539). Excellent fish cuisine in a little wooden house. Moderate to expensive. Closed Mondays.

### OLHÃO

**Hotel Ria Sol**, Rua Eng. Humberto Delgado 37 (tel. 089 705 267). Two-star and the only hotel in Olhão. Bar but no restaurant.

**Aquário**, Rua Dr João Lucio (tel. 089 706 539). Located near the Igreja Matrix of Rua Vasco da Gama.

**Chez Henri**, The port, Fuzeta (tel. 089 794 725). French/Portuguese cooking and fish.

## TAVIRA

This includes accommodation along the coast close to Tavira. In Tavira centre itself there are only residencials, one listed below, and pensions.

**Almargem, Cabanas** (tel. 081 201 67). Low-rise apartment complex between EN125 and shore.

**Aparthotel Nascente, Cabanas** (tel. 081 205 17). Modern complex of apartments and villas on shore at Cabanas. Pool, tennis, restaurant and bars.

**Hotel Apartamento Eurotel, Quinta das Oliveiras** on EN125 (tel. 081 324 324). Three-star hotel in rural surroundings 2km outside Tavira. Offers all facilities and free bus to sister hotel on beach at Altura.

**Marés, Residential** (tel. 081 325 815). Situated right on the riverside near the market, parking opposite. Private facilities with air-conditioning and satellite TV; it also has a restaurant.

**Pedras da Rainha, Tavira** (tel. 081 201 81). Village complex of apartments and villas at Cabanas.

**Pedras d'el Rei, Santa Luzia, Tavira** (tel. 081 325 352). Village complex of apartments and villas on coast near to Barril.

**Quinta do Caracol, São Pedro** (tel. 081 224 75). 1km from Tavira just off EN125. Part of the Turismo de Habitação chain. Individual apartments in converted 200-year-old farmhouse. Pool, tennis and bar. Luxury. Closed between 31/10–15/12.

**Quinta das Oliveiras**, on EN125 (tel. 081 324 324. Villas and apartments set in 25 acres. Same facilities as Eurotel above which is set in same grounds.

**Tavira Garden Resort, Vale Caranguejo** (tel. 081 324 222). Self-contained apartment complex 700m from Tavira with Restaurant Babilon.

**Á de Abade, Santa Luzia**, Largo da Igreja (tel. 081 381 861). Small cosy restaurant. Open Mon. Wed & Fri for lunch. Dinner every evening from 6.30pm except Sundays.

**O Monte, Quinta Velha, Cabanas** (tel. 081 208 17). On left entering Cabanas. Comprehensive menu. Basket meals. Closed Tuesdays.

**Marisqueira Quatro Aguas, Tavira** (tel. 081 325 329). Algarve cooking. Closed Mondays.

**Patio, Tavira**, Rua António Cabreira (tel. 081 230 08). Over the old bridge on the east side. Traditional Portuguese and French cuisine in old house with roof terrace. Moderate.

## VILA REAL DE SANTO ANTÓNIO (MONTE GORDO)

**Estalagem Oásis, Manta Rota** (tel. 081 951 644). Fronting sand dunes. Half-board.

**Hotel Guadiana, Vila Real** (tel. 081 511 482). Central on riverside. Three-star and refurbished.

**Hotel Alcazar, Monte Gordo**, Rua de Ceuta (tel. 081 512 184). Four-star close to sand dunes.

**Hotel dos Navegadores, Monte Gordo**, Rua Gonçalo Velho (tel. 081 512 490). Three-star about five minutes away from beach.

**Hotel Vasco da Gama, Monte Gordo** (tel. 081 511 321) Four-star on beach.

**Hotel Casablanca, Monte Gordo**, Rua Sete (tel. 081 511 444). Four-star low-rise. No restaurant. Swimming pool, bar and coffee bar.
**Eurotel Altura, Praia da Altura** (tel. 081 956 45). Four-star apartment hotel with restaurant.
**Á Chaminé, Altura**, Sitio da Alagoa (tel. 081 958 581). Locally recommended restaurant.
**O Infante, Altura** (tel. 081 956 817). On EN125 near exit off Via do Infante, IP1. Portuguese and international cuisine.
**Manuel d'Agua, Castro Marim** (tel. 081 531 480). Portuguese restaurant. Closed Mondays.
**Marés, Altura**, Praia Alagoa (tel. 081 956 563). Locally recommended restaurant.
**Pão Quente, São Bartolomeu do Sul** (tel. 081 412 33). Restaurant along EN125-6 Castro Marim road.

## Places of Interest

### FARO
Old town (Vila a Dentro) and Arco da Vila
**Museu São António**, Rua de Berlim, 9am –1pm & 2pm until evening
**Museu Arqueológico** (old town), 9am –12.30pm & 2 –5.30pm closed weekends & holidays
**Museu Etnográfico**, Praça da Liberdade, 9.30am–12.30 pm & 2–5pm closed weekends & holidays
**Museu Maritimo**, harbour, 9.30am–12.30pm & 2–5.30pm Mon–Fri, 9.30am–1pm Sat, closed Sundays & holidays
**Museu Judeus**, at Jewish cemetery on Rua Leão Penedo, 9.30am–12.30pm Mon-Fri only

### OLHÃO
**Museu Municipal**, Largo da Lagoa, Oct–May 2–4pm Mon–Fri, 10am–12 noon & 2–4pm Sat; June–Sept 4–8pm Mon–Fri, 10am–12 noon & 2–8pm Sat, closed Sundays & holidays
**Parque Natural da Ria Formosa**, Quinta de Marim (tel. 089 704 134). Head office and grounds of the reserve. 9pm–12noon & 2–5pm Mon–Fri, closed weekends & holidays. Children under 12 free

### VILA REAL DE SANTO ANTÓNIO
**Reserva Natural do Sapal de Castro Marim** (tel. 081 531 141). Free entrance to castle at Castro Marim where office located.
**Ferries**: Vila Real to Ayamonte in Spain. Daily 8.45am–7.30pm every 40 minutes. Ferries out to sand bars check times locally at Turismo.

## Sports and Leisure

**Animaris Ria Formosa, Faro** (tel. 089 806 840). Lagoon boat safaris for bird-watching, scuba diving, fishing and watersports.

**Aqualine, Altura** (tel. 081 446 88). Junction of EN125 and motorway slip-road. Water theme park.
**Tennis**: Clube de Ténis de V.R.de Santo António (tel. 081 410 14).
**Sailing**: Club Náutico do Guadiana, Rua do Brasil 6, 8900 Vila Real de Santo António (tel. 081 439 03).

## Tourist Offices (Turismo)

### Regional Office of Algarve
Avenida 5 de Outubro, 8000 Faro. Tel. 089 800 400, Fax. 089 800 489.

### Tourism Posts
**Alcoutim**: Praça da Rebública (tel. 081 461 79).
**Castro Marim**: Praça 1° de Maio, 2–4 (tel. 081 531 232).
**Faro**: Rua da Misericórdia, 8–12 (tel. 089 803 604).
**Monte Gordo**: Vila Real St° António) Avª Marginal (tel. 081 444 95).
**Olhão**: Largo da Lagoa (tel. 089 713 936).
**Tavira**: Rua da Galeria (tel. 081 225 11).

# 6. CENTRAL ALGARVE:
# Faro to Albufeira

In contrast to eastern Algarve where broad sweeps of sand edge a littoral zone which itself is barely above sea level, west of Faro the whole character of the coastline changes dramatically. Cliffs rise abruptly from the sea, unequally worn and cut by a restless Atlantic over millennia into intriguing configurations and shapes, all liberally edged with golden sand. The result of this natural artistry is Algarve's biggest asset. Bays, coves and inlets, looked over by a scattering of rock stacks and arches, occur one after another offering beaches of great beauty and character. Unfortunately, the developers have been here in force converting once small fishing villages into gleaming modern resorts which often stand shoulder to shoulder. Manicured golf courses surrounded by luxurious accommodation are squeezed in between the high-rise hotels and the inevitable supermarkets. Amongst all the gleaming white concrete, resorts of character still exist; resorts which have refused to sell out totally to modernity and where fishermen happily share the beach with visitors. Once beyond Albufeira the density of development reduces appreciably and here there are still stretches of largely undeveloped coastline where peaceful coastal walks are possible.

## West of Faro

To explore the coast west of Faro, there is little option but to travel out along the EN125 unless the train is used. For travellers not in a hurry, the train serves this central section of Algarve reasonably well and it offers a delightfully slow way to explore the area. There are plenty of stopping places, but occasionally these are quite distant from the towns they serve, as is the case for Albufeira which is served by Ferreiras station, 6km (3¾ miles) away. For motorists, **São Lourenço**, less than 16km (10 miles) outside Faro, is a worthy stopping place if only to see the outstandingly beautiful *azulejos* in the church, one of the most remarkable in Portugal.

Legend relates how a small medieval hermitage dedicated to São Lourenço on this spot was allowed to fall into disrepair. In 1722, when the village was desperate for water and in the process of sinking a new well, they

# Azulejos

The Portuguese fascination with surface decoration extends to *azulejos*, coloured ceramic tiles, which are inescapable throughout the country. They are not unique to Portugal, it is just that the Portuguese have a passion for them and use them imaginatively in a whole variety of ways from simple patterns to creating large scenes or even documentaries to decorate churches, water fountains, railway stations, palaces, public buildings and house fronts.

This love affair started around the 15th century, inspired by tiles with a geometric pattern imported from Seville. Home production of essentially blue tiles started and the patterns were established in firing by separating the colour with rivulets of linseed oil or by ridges of clay. In the 16th century, the Italian majolica technique was introduced by which the clay tile was covered with a white enamel which could be painted onto directly. This greater freedom allowed the Portuguese to introduce a design element to create patterns and by the 17th century coloured tiles, chiefly dark blue, yellow, green and white were used to make up either geometric, carpet or tapestry designs, often based on a module of four tiles. Exotic designs with animals, fishes and flower motifs made an appearance too, but the polychrome fashion waned with the appearance of Delft blue. Europe had been captivated by the imported blue and white Chinese porcelain and the Dutch responded by developing a delicate blue and white tile which quickly found favour in Portugal.

Towards the end of the 17th century, narrative tiles began to appear telling a story of events in life like harvesting grapes, fishing or hunting and these increased in size and realism to become very popular. Tile painting rapidly became recognised as an art form, both in its creation and use as a complement to architecture to enliven interiors. One of the recognised masters, António de Oliveira Bernardes, together with his son Policarpo, set up a school in Lisbon which rapidly became influential in the development of this art. A number of beautiful works in the first half of the 18th century are often assigned with authority to the Bernardes; the works of António can be seen in the chapel of Nossa Senhora da Cabeça in Évora and those of Policarpo in the church of São Lourenço in Algarve. Quite a number of artists became well known but one outstanding craftsman remains unknown to this day apart from the initials P.M.P. which adorn his works.

Blue and white tiles dominated throughout this period but by the mid 18th century polychromy returned to favour. In 1755 an earthquake shattered much of Lisbon. During the rebuilding phase, when the demand for tiles was high, a large number of factories opened not all maintaining the previous high standards. The use of *azulejos* for the exterior decoration of church façades and house walls was imported in the 19th century when the royal family and other emigrants returned from Brazil where they had moved to escape the French invasion. One of the best places to trace the history and development of *azulejos* is in the Museum of Azulejos in Lisbon.

petitioned the saint with promises to build a new church. Sure enough, the villagers were richly blessed with abundant water and were moved to keep their part of the bargain. As the *azulejo* panel on the outside wall indicates, the church was built in 1730, although the carved and gilded altarpiece by Manuel Martins was not completed until 1735. The church is only small but the interior is almost entirely covered with painted tiles, the walls, vaulted ceiling and cupola depicting the life and martyrdom of São Lourenço. The actions depicted in the various panels are explained in a leaflet (available in English) which can be purchased at the door. The ceiling tiles here, including those in the cupola, were painted by Policarpo de Oliveira Bernardes but there is a view that the panels of the nave were by a painter of his school.

Just down the road from the church is the cultural centre, a German owned commercial art gallery, where visitors are free to wander around to inspect the paintings by local and foreign artists. The centre is also used for concerts and other cultural events.

At one time the EN 125 ploughed through **Almancil** but now there is a bypass so it is necessary to turn off to enter the town. Except as a through route to Quinta do Lago and Vale do Lobo, there seems no reason to visit Almancil, it is away from the coast and generally ignored by tourists, except shoppers from the nearby resorts. It has at least some interesting coffee stops. Coffee and carrot cake at the *Beanfeast* can be followed by a browse in the English bookshop, *Griffin Books*, directly below, or, for an old English tea shop ambience, *The Teapot* offers tea and coffee with home-made cake in the peaceful garden behind.

**Quinta do Lago** and the longer-established **Vale do Lobo** are both exclusive developments offering luxury accommodation. Set amongst 2000 acres of pine forests and lakes on the edge of the Ria Formosa reserve, Quinta do Lago has attracted leading international investors in Bovis Abroad, Trafalgar House, Orient Express and Forte Hotels. The result is a low density development amongst highly manicured, well watered gardens laid out to a master plan by the main developer, Planal S.A. White. Villas and apartments, a mix of private and shared ownership, are scattered in truly enviable positions around the golf courses and on the lake side. Vale do Lobo offers more of the same and both offer recreational facilities second to none. Golf features strongly, Quinta do Lago offers 72 holes on three top class golf courses with a further three nine-hole courses at Vale do Lobo. Apart from golf, sport figures prominently. Roger Taylor runs a tennis centre and Barrington a fitness and leisure club

*Striking azulejo tiles in São Lourenço church*

with tennis, squash and cricket facilities, but there is also a horse riding school and water sports available.

There are two top class hotels in the area, Quinta do Lago hotel is an Orient Express hotel of the highest standard with pools, gymnasium, tennis courts and a snooker room while the Dona Filipa in Vale do Lobo is a little older without health club facilities but guests have access to Club Barrington and to the São Lourenço golf course.

## Golf in Algarve

With such a mild and sunny winter climate, Algarve offers golfers the opportunity to play their sport all year round and a sharp awakening of interest in the game in recent years has led to a dramatic increase in the number of golf courses. Many of the courses enjoy idyllic settings, often along the coast, but more importantly, they are designed by well known names, like the Vale do Lobo course designed by the late Sir Henry Cotton and constructed to championship standards. From east to west, Algarve's 16 golf courses include:

**1. Pinheiros Altos, Quinta do Lago**: set in 250 acres of pinewood, this course, designed by the American architect Ronald Fream, blends two nine-holes of contrasting character. The longer outward nine-holes are played in undulating countryside beneath umbrella pines but the return nine are played through a lakeland beset with water hazards. The total distance of the 18 holes on this par 71 course is 6049m. Apart from clubhouse and restaurant facilities, there is a special golf academy with teaching facilities including a contoured driving range, putting and chipping greens and coaching by professionals.

**2. San Lourenzo, Quinta do Lago**: this 18-hole (6238m) par 72 championship course was designed by the American Joseph Lee in conjunction with William Roquemore. Although this is the newest of Algarve's golf courses, it has been ranked amongst Europe's top 50. It is set amongst lakes and pines bordering the Ria Formosa nature reserve, offering plenty of variety with water hazards around to add some spice. It is reserved primarily for guests of Dona Filipa and Penina hotels but available to others at quiet times.

**3. Quinta do Lago**. Currently, there are four separate nine-hole courses which can be used in combinations to produce golf from 6205 to 6488m in length and all par 72. Three of the courses were designed by William Mitchell and the fourth by Joe Lee. Modifications are in hand to combine these into two 18-hole courses. B & C will be known as Quinta do Lago TPC and A & D will combine into Quinta do Lago Ria Formosa course. Rolling woodland and strategic lakes provide enough challenge to have attracted the Portuguese Open Championships on no fewer than six occasions. Apart from the usual clubhouse facilities, it also boasts one of largest driving ranges in Europe.

**4. Vale do Lobo**. Designed by the late Sir Henry Cotton, there are three nine-hole courses which can be interchanged to provide a variety of challenges. The most famous hole here is the 7th, a long par three, which borders the edge of the cliffs and where a 218m carry is required to stretch over two gaping ravines. The yellow and orange nine-holes are par 36 and the green par 35. In addition there is a 245m driving range with practice bunkers and an 80m contoured putting green.

**5. Vilasol**. This residential holiday resort located 4km north of Vilamoura boasts an 18-hole (6183m) par 72 championship course designed by the English architect Donald Steel. The opening nine wind through fig, pine and cork oak with the natural undulations of the land and water hazards to negotiate before turning towards the club house to face a valley of umbrella pine. It was the venue for the Portuguese Open in 1992, the first year it was open, and again in 1993.

**6. Vilamoura I**. This is the oldest of the three Vilamoura courses, built in 1969 under the guidance of the English architect Frank Pennick, and arguably still the best. A total distance of 6331m takes golfers through 18 holes on this demanding par 73 course which cuts through ranks of pine on a greatly undulating site. The World Ladies Amateur Championship was played here as well as the Portuguese Open and the Algarve Open.

**7. Vilamoura II**. Originally designed by Frank Pennick and laid out as a nine-hole course in 1976, a further nine holes were added under the guidance of the American Robert Trent Jones in 1985. The outward, original, nine holes are played through umbrella pine and the return uses higher more open ground of quite different character. The full 18 holes provide a par 72 course stretching over 6256m. Lessons from the club professional are available and the facilities include a driving range and practice putting green.

**8. Vilamoura III**. The latest of the trio at Vilamoura is a 27-hole parkland course designed by the American architect Joseph Lee. The course is divided into three nine-hole loops all par 36. These include the Marina course (3180m), Pinhal (2935m) and Lago (2953m), each of which has a different character, although all are relatively open and level with strategic sand and water creating the hazards. It is a good course for players with a higher handicap. Facilities include lessons and clinics by the club's professionals, a modern driving range and practice greens.

**9. Pine Cliffs**. Lying between Vilamoura and Albufeira, the Pine Cliffs Golf and Country Club offers an attractive nine-hole course (2324m par 33) laid out by architect Martin Hawtree. Against an Atlantic backdrop, this undulating course is set just behind the jagged red cliffs which line Falésia beach and offers a respectable challenge. Striking at the heart of even the most confident, the 6th hole, the Devil's Parlour, requires a carry of 205m across rugged cliff tops to hit the green. Golf here is available to estate residents and guests at the onsite Sheraton Pine Cliffs Hotel. Racing driver Nigel Mansell, with a villa on the estate, is the club president.

**10. Salgados**. Situated west of Albufeira near Galé beach, this 18-hole (6075m) 72 par course was designed by Portugal's Pedro Vasconcelos with added refinements by the American Robert Muir. It opened in 1994. Low-lying wetlands have been used in the design to create 14 water hazards. Considering that the course uses semi rough for general play and there is a near constant Atlantic sea breeze to consider, it adds up to a fair challenge. Facilities include a driving range and practice green.

**11. Vale de Milho**. Located just 2km east of Carvoeira, this nine-hole par 27 course was designed by the former Ryder cup player Dave Thomas and opened in 1990. Only 970m in length, there is plenty of challenge from this course which flows over sloping land and is beset with water and out-of-bounds hazards. The clubhouse also incorporates squash courts, swimming pool, jacuzzis and gymnasium.

**12. Carvoeiro Club: Quinta do Gramacho**. Located near Carvoeiro, this course, and the one below, was designed by the American Ronald Fream. This nine-hole layout achieves a distinct design achievement with nine fairways but 18 greens and 18 independent tees creating the effect of playing a completely different set of holes on the second circuit. Undulating terrain, natural vegetation, artificial lakes, wall hazards and fast greens make this 18-hole (5919m) par 72 circuit quite demanding.

**13. Carvoeiro Club**. This 18-hole par 71 Vale da Pinta course, which measures 5861m, winds through groves of mature almonds, figs and olives. True to American standards, designer Fream has made sure the deep greens are well protected with even deeper bunkers, 59 in all! It shares the same clubhouse as the Quinta do Gramacho as well as the driving range and the practice bunker and green.

**14. Alto Golf Club**. Situated near Alvor, a short distance from Portimão, this was the last course designed by the late Sir Henry Cotton. Laid out over and around two valleys, this 18-hole (6125m) par 72 course fully meets Henry Cotton's philosophy of being testing for low handicap players while still providing an enjoyable game for the ordinary club player. It is a parkland course with tight fairways, long rough and difficult sloping greens and, if that is not enough, there is the challenge of a long par 5 at the 16th over a testing 604m. Personal lessons by professionals are on offer as well as a golf clinic, driving range and practice bunker.

**15. Penina**. Just 5km west of Portimão, this three course complex is based around the luxury class Hotel Penina. The 18-hole (6439m) par 73 championship course was designed by the late Sir Henry Cotton in 1966 and was the first in Algarve. Essentially flat, the wooded terrain has enough hazards with water, ditches and bunkers to overcome before the elevated greens are reached. Numerous championships have been played here with no less than five Portuguese Open championships.

The other two courses, the Monchique and the Quinta, are both nine-holes. Facilities for the complex include tennis courts, a swimming pool, a driving range and putting greens.

**16. Palmares**. Located just east of Lagos, this is another coastal course alongside the extensive Meia Praia beach and claims to be one of the most scenic in Algarve. Opening in 1975, this 18-hole (5961m) par 71 course was designed by English architect Frank Pennick to include five link holes on the sand dunes close to the beach with the remaining 13 spread over gently rolling hills well sprinkled with almond trees. It has hosted a number of popular amateur events including the TAP open and the annual Almond Blossom Amateur tournament. Facilities include a driving range, putting area, and a pitch area.

**17. Parque da Floresta**. Situated in a peaceful location behind the village of Salema, 16km west of Lagos, this is the most westerly of Algarve's golf courses. Spanish designer Pepe Gancedo has engineered a spectacular 18-hole (5888m) par 72 course winding over some dramatic countryside. To illustrate the diversity of the course, the 6th hole demands a drive over a vineyard, the 9th over a creek to a plateau green, the 15th has a tee shot over a ravine filled with eucalyptus trees and there is a water hazard with an overhanging green at the 11th. In addition to all the usual clubhouse facilities, there is a driving range and a practice putting green.

Quinta do Lago abuts the western edge of the Ria Formosa natural reserve which has now been opened up, with the co-operation of the estate developers, Planal S.A., to allow access for the public to two nature trails, see p 89 for more details. Signs and directions to the reserve are totally lacking but, once through the entrance to the Planal estate, following signs to 'Praia' and the Quinta do Lago hotel over endless roundabouts leads to it. The road eventually terminates in a car parking area.

## Quarteira

The next resort moving westward is Quarteira, the ugly duckling of Algarve unlikely ever to turn into a swan, and one which many people are happy to overlook. A huddle of drab concrete tower blocks, reminiscent of the worst type of building in eastern Europe from the Communist era, creates a first impression which must throw many tourists into a state of shock on arrival. Spirits rise a little when the promenade is reached, although the beach here is interrupted with unsightly breakwaters. Better still is the beach running eastwards out of town which offers a clear run of sand. It is hard to believe that this was once a pretty fishing village but the fisherman are around still, which adds some atmosphere as does the weekly local market, held on a Wednesday. On a positive note, Quarteira is distinctly more Portuguese than most resorts in Algarve and there is some good Portuguese eating around as at *Ze do Norte*, in Quatro Estradas, where speciality dishes from northern Portugal are included in the menu. Similarly, *Duas Sentinelas* on Estrada de Quarteira is another with a strong Portuguese flavour where the locals turn up in force for the *cozido à Portuguesa* and the oven cooked kid. The resort is actually very popular with the Portuguese themselves; many buy apartments here, and it is largely for them that bullfights are arranged in summer.

*The beach at Santa Eulalia*

## Vilamoura

In total contrast, Vilamoura, to the west of Quarteira, is another purpose built resort stylishly laid out around a marina and the largest resort area in Portugal. One difficulty for the visitor is that Vilamoura has no village at its heart and consequently nowhere to visit. A plethora of roads and road signs contrive to confuse which makes it more difficult to leave than enter. The Romans were here first and built Cerro da Vila near to the present marina. There are more than enough vestiges left, including some mosaics, to make it a worthwhile visit. Cerro da Vila was built for business and pleasure which is exactly the theme of the modern Vilamoura. Apart from watching the activity around the marina, which is lively in the summer months, Vilamoura is a place for doing rather than spectating. There are three golf courses (see feature p 78), a casino, facilities for tennis, squash, volleyball, football and snooker at the Rock Garden club or the chance to go out deep sea fishing from the marina. If all that is too much to contemplate then there are very fine beaches either side of the marina for crashing out or taking a dip. The more westerly beach has acres of sand and it is possible to walk out along here as far as Falésia beach with its colourful cliffs. Vilamoura is the heartland of a lot of quality time-share development but there is plenty of accommodation besides including the superbly equipped 365-roomed *Marinotel*.

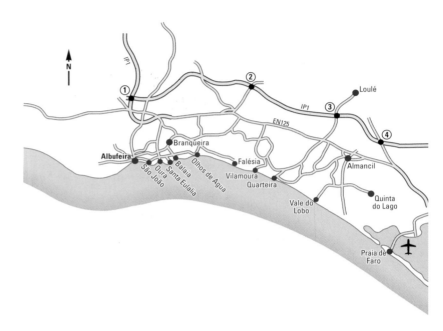

## Resorts and Beaches en route to Albufeira

To make further westerly progress, side roads offer an alternative to the EN125. **Praia da Falésia** marks the start of the spectacular cliffs which are a feature of the coastline all the way to Sagres. The compensation for staggering down the 75 steps to the beach is not just the abundance of shells in the sand here but the sight of the multicoloured cliffs behind. A café at the top of the steps is strategically placed and on hand for refreshments. In contrast, the cliffs relent a little at **Olhos d'Água**, a little further up the coast, and it is possible to drive down to the promenade although traffic is banned in summer. Tucked into a narrow cleft, this small fishing village is full of character and as picturesque as any in Algarve with a bonus that it has been largely overlooked by the larger tour operators. Fishermen share part of the beach which is enclosed by pine topped cliffs given extra interest by the sculptured rock stacks. Apart from the small fish market along the promenade, there are also café restaurants. Much of Olhos d'Água, particularly the shops and accommodation, lies inland and uphill from the front.

Olhos d'Água is on the fringes of the Albufeira conurbation and from here it becomes progressively built up. Even here, as in other parts of Algarve, signs indicating 'Praia' (beach) often occur which have no correspondence to the map. It is not just every cove which has a name, a longer beach too may

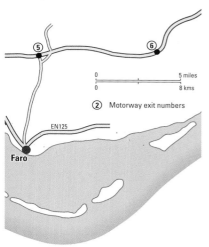

0 ——————— 5 miles
0 ——————— 8 kms

② Motorway exit numbers

EN125

Faro

be sectioned and known by several names. A road connection seems to be the only qualification required to be awarded a distinct epithet. Following signs to uncharted beaches is about the only chance to get off the beaten track in this part of Algarve and it can bring interesting rewards; try the route to **Santa Eulalia**. The small cove which first appears is bigger in reality and an attractive beach opens out on both sides. Nearby **Balaia beach** is dominated by a hotel complex of the same name.

**Praia da Oura** has yielded its identity entirely to the developers. A narrow one-way road, known as the Strip, leads down to the cove which was once Oura. The Strip now is lined with an abundance of bars and cafés with a smattering of gift shops, restaurants and minimarkets. This is the place to be for the young and lively in summer which these days is synonymous with drugs and trouble. Out of season this reputation totally evaporates. Endless white houses and apartments jostle for space on the hillsides down to the cove. The beach, too small to accommo-date all the summer population lying down at the same time and shared with a few fishing boats, is served by a terrace café restaurant.

# Albufeira

Albufeira is an international resort especially popular with the packaged tour operators. The old village at the heart of the town with its winding streets and whitewashed houses is still there but swamped by development on a massive scale. Virtually the whole of the amphitheatrical hills surrounding the old village are full of modern architecture, of whitewashed villas, apartments and hotels. Pubs, fish and chips, *Fred's Bar* and *Kiss* disco are all part of the modern scene like the dual carriageway ring road, the sophisticated glass palace of a town hall, and the huge *Modelo* supermarket and shopping precinct.

The Romans liked it too. They were here, called it Baltum and built a castle. Later the Visigoths came followed by the Moors who renamed it Al-Buhera (Castle on the Sea). Albufeira prospered as a trading port under the Moors for almost five centuries. In the rest of the country throughout this period, the Moors were being resisted and slowly pushed southwards. By

85

*Olhos d'Água beach*

1189 the Christians regained Albufeira but were only able to hold it for two years. Finally, in 1250, it was recaptured by the Knights of St James in the reign of Dom Afonso III. The instant loss of Moroccan trade brought poverty in its wake. By 1527 it had regained some prosperity as a fishing village and a census at that time recorded 320 family houses. Its castle remained an important element in defence, not just against the Moors but also against French and English privateers who harassed the Algarve coast in that period. Dom Sebastião visited the castle in 1573 to inspect the defences just five years before he set sail from Lagos on his ill-fated expedition against the Moors.

The earthquake of 1755 which shattered Lisbon also devastated much of Algarve. Albufeira suffered badly and its castle was almost completely destroyed. There was still more suffering in 1833 when the town was virtually burnt to the ground by Miguelist guerrillas after a siege and battle that was part of the War of the Two Brothers.

Sardine and tuna fishing brought back prosperity to the town in the second half of the 19th century, especially with the opening of canning factories, and steady demographic growth was recorded until 1930. A decline set in from then which was only reversed in the 1960s when efforts were made to promote its splendid beaches, charming village character and wonderful climate to a new growing industry, tourism. It succeeded beyond its wildest dreams and has now grown into a prosperous cosmopolitan resort which attracts visitors all year round. Chameleon-like, its character and appeal changes throughout the season. In winter, it is lent a graceful air by members of the golden age enjoying retirement to the full, but this totally changes when a riotous younger set takes over in summer intent on cramming half a lifetime into two weeks. As a base, it has the advantage of being placed almost centrally on the coast, roughly 85km (53 miles) to the Spanish border in the east and to Sagres in the west.

## The Town

Much of the old, central area has been pedestrianised with walkways attractively paved in *calçada*, small square cut stone. Hewn by hand with a hammer and chisel, blue and pink granites are mainly used but these are supplemented by softer, coloured or white stone for ornamental work. On foot is easily the best way to explore the old centre and a good place to start is in Avenida da Liberdade, near the bus station, where there is plenty of car parking space. This leads down directly into **Largo Eng. Duarte Pacheco**, a large square with a fountain and beds of exotic birds-of-paradise flowers which is the heart of Albufeira. Face-lifted over recent years, cafés and restaurants now line the square with their tables spilling out onto the pavements. It is a great place to sit and watch the world go by and most of it does! Following the short road out of the south-west corner leads into **Rua 5 de Outubro**, the main shop-lined pedestrianised way which leads towards the beach. On the left here lies the tourist office. The road leads through a tunnel cut through the rock beneath the *Sol e Mar Hotel* to the promenade by the main beach. It is an inviting beach with seemingly plenty of space, but there are enough bodies around in high season to cover it wall to wall. Atlantic rollers often crash onto the beach here, as they do throughout much of Algarve, to the delight of the surfers, but such days are not so good for young children, especially since the sea is also tidal.

Returning back through the tunnel, mount the steps by the tourist office to reach the upper road and turn right for a short diversion to the domed church of **São Sebastião**, especially to see the 16th century Manueline doorway and the Renaissance side door. Following the road out here leads, after a good 25 minute walk, to the site of the gypsy market held every first and third Tuesday in the month. Head back now on the upper level passing the steps to enter the region of the **old town** which was once enclosed within the castle. *Azulejo* panels on the wall mark the position of entrances to the old castle, like **Porta da Praça** almost opposite the entrance to Sol e Mar Hotel. It takes only a few moments to wander the cobbled alleys, down Rua Henrique Calado to pass the **Chapel of the Misericórdia** which originates from the 16th century and thought to be built on the site of a mosque. It is no stranger to renovations but at least the Manueline doorway remains. Return back through the next alley on the right, Rua do Cemitério Velho. Plunge into the alleys again, down Travessa da Igreja Velha to pass beneath an arch which was once part of the castle and back along Rua Nova which leads to *Ruinas restaurant*. This restaurant was once part of a castle tower but this is best appreciated by viewing its easterly wall from across **Fishermen's Beach** visited next. Before descending steps, notice the *azulejo* panel marking another castle entrance, Porta de Sant'Ana. Fishermen's Beach where two worlds meet is one of Albufeira's more colourful corners. Here jumpered fishermen mending nets or landing their catch from small fishing boats, share the beach with scantily dressed bathers bent on nothing more than undiluted pleasure and relaxation. Return without climbing steps by following Rua Cândido dos Reis back into Largo Eng. Duarte Pacheco.

East of Albufeira is seemlessly built up. It blends into **Areias de São João** which claims the eastern end of Albufeira's beach as its own and beyond into Oura. Inland from this complex is **Montechoro** which is distinguished only by a large hotel of the same name. Out to the west, it is surprisingly undeveloped and it is possible to find a way onto the rugged cliffs and walk out towards Galé.

## Practical Information

Albufeira has never succeeded in building up a reputation for good eating. Restaurants change hands frequently and chefs move around, but perhaps the most compelling reason is that there are too many customers in summer. Restaurants get crowded out and it is often necessary to wait for a table or to make a booking to be sure to get in. Moving a little out of town offers better prospects, like *Kudos* on the road out to Branqueira where starters include

# Quinta do Lago Nature Trails

Set amongst woodland, salt marsh and dunes, the two nature trails are laid out with information points to increase awareness of the diversity of flora and fauna, particularly avifauna in this area. The **blue Quinta do Lago trail**, a walk in total of 2.5km (1½ miles), heading out in a westerly direction concentrates more on the flora although there are still plenty of birds around. Two information stations illustrate trees and shrubs which can be seen around including the umbrella pine, *Pinus pinea*, the carob tree, *Ceratonia siliqua*, the mastic tree, *Pistacia lentiscus*, and the dwarf fan palm which is a European native palm, *Chamaerops humilis*. Some of the marsh vegetation includes the glassworts, *Anthrocnemum* and *Salicornia* species. Look on top of the dunes for sea holly, *Eryngium maritimum*, and behind the dunes for thrift, *Armeria pungens*. Watch out for kingfishers, *Alcedo atthis*, around the lake at the turning point of the trail.

The **yellow São Lourenço trail**, a little shorter at 2km (1¼ miles), heads out east and concentrates on the bird life. Four information stations detail the wild life and details about the salting tanks built by the Romans to salt fish. Birds which can be seen here include the black-winged stilt, *Himantopus himantopus*, which is mostly a summer visitor but a good population stays all the year round which is also true of the hoopoe, *Upupa epops*. Egrets, *Egretta garzetta* are often around, they can be seen throughout Algarve, but this is also a good area to spot the azure-winged magpie, *Cyanopica cyanus*, which flits about between the umbrella pines and there is a chance here to see the graceful avocet, *Recurvirostra avosetta*. Morning and late afternoon visitors in summer may also encounter a chameleon, *Chamaeleo chamaeleon*, which are not uncommon in the dunes and the pinewoods.

If the beach and a dip calls after strolling around the nature trails, Ilha de Faro with its miles of sand lies just across the footbridge.

brie and mango moneybags. In the same area and providing good food is *The Cockerel*, an English-run restaurant, which goes all traditional on a Sunday but offers a more varied menu in the week. On the road from Montechoro towards Ferreiras, a few hundred metres beyond the Repsol petrol station, is *Fernando's Hide-a-Way*. An unlikely name maybe, but this Portuguese-run restaurant offers some of the best food in the area presided over by Fernando himself, a lively character who has learnt English entirely from tourists. Wild boar, suckling pig and fish *cataplanas* make the menu but his *cabrito* (baby goat) is the best in Algarve.

## *Hotels and Restaurants*

### ALBUFEIRA AREA

This region, which includes Areias S. João, Montechoro, Praia da Oura, Olhos d'Água and Falésia, offers a massive amount of accommodation of all standards. Apartment hotels seem particularly popular and there are a great many. Much of the accommodation is taken up by the international tour operators throughout summer which can present problems for the independent traveller. Advance bookings are strongly recommended from July through to September.

**Hotel Sheraton Pine Cliffs, Apartado 644, Praia da Falésia** (tel. 089 501 999). Relatively new five-star hotel with Moorish architecture. Superb position, lacks nothing in facilities and guests have use of a nine-hole golf course, expensive.

**Hotel Apartments Olhos d'Água, Olhos d'Água** (tel. 089 501 811). Rooms and apartments available, three-star quality but plenty of facilities including restaurant.

**Aparthotel Oura Praia, Oura**, Areias S. João (tel. 089 586 655). A four-star rated establishment, pleasant rooms.

**Hotel Topázio, Areias S. João** (tel. 089 586 205). A three-star hotel, small for these parts with only 46 rooms. Swimming pool, bar and restaurant.

**Hotel Montechoro, Montechoro** (tel. 089 589 423). Recently renovated, this four-star hotel is located at the back of Albufeira and a good distance from the beach. Good facilities without being too expensive.

**Hotel Apartments Cerro da Algoa, Cerro da Algoa, Albufeira** (tel. 089 588 262). This four-star hotel has a mixture of 257 rooms and 53 apartments. Superb indoor swimming pool with jungle theme, large outdoor pool.

**Hotel Sol e Mar, Albufeira**, Rua José Bernandino de Sousa (tel. 089 586 721). Superbly positioned four-star hotel with great sea view and right in the heart of Albufeira.

**Estalagem do Cerro, Cerro da Piedade, Albufeira** (tel. 089 586 192). Four-star with plenty of facilities including restaurant.

**Hotel California, Albufeira**, Rua Cândido dos Reis (tel. 089 586 833). A three-star hotel which could not be more central.

**Kudos Restaurant, Estrada do Branqueira, Albufeira** (tel. 098 515 651). An interesting menu includes mango and ginger duck at reasonable prices.

**Castelo do Bispo, Estrada do Ourada, Albufeira** (tel. 089 586 754). On a cliff top west of Albufeira, menu has an Italian influence but food excellent and price accordingly high.

**Os Arcos, Albufeira**, Rua Alves Correia (tel. 089 513 460). Popular restaurant with roof terrace offers fairly traditional Portuguese fare at inexpensive prices.

**The Cockerel, Branqueira, Albufeira** (tel. 089 542 210). English-run restaurant with interesting menu and reasonable prices.

**Fernando's Hide-a-Way** (tel. 082 541618), on road from Montechoro towards Ferreiras. Excellent Portuguese food from fish and prawn cataplanas to pork in wine sauce, large portions and very reasonably priced.

## ALMANCIL AREA
This includes the up-market areas of Qinta do Lago and Vale de Lobo where accommodation prices are generally on the top side.

**Hotel Quinta do Lago** (tel. 089 396 666). A modern five-star luxury hotel in the Orient Express chain. Health club facilities, indoor and outdoor pools, 72 holes of golf on the doorstep. Restaurant with international and Portuguese cuisine and an Italian restaurant.

**Hotel Dona Filipa,** Quinta do Lago (tel. 089 394 141). A five-star luxury hotel in the Forte chain which has been opened since 1969 and the general decor is beginning to look like it. Clients can use the Club Barrington's facilities and have free reign on the San Lourenzo golf course. It has two restaurants.

**Porta da Quinta, Vale do Lobo,** Estrada Almancil (tel. 089 399 304). Congenial atmosphere with live music and good food at reasonable prices.

**Casa Pituxa, Vale do Lobo,** Almancil Rd (tel. 089 396 238). A popular Portuguese run restaurant where pre-booking is advised, reasonably priced, closed Sundays.

## QUARTEIRA
In contrast to the previous areas listed, Quarteira is decidedly down market but its three-star hotels are much more reasonably priced. All the following offer a pleasant location with good facilities including a swimming pool.

**Hotel Dom José,** Av. Infante Sagres (tel. 089 314 310)

**Hotel Zodiac,** Fonte Santa (tel. 089 389 589)

**Motel Pinhal do Sol,** Sitio do Semino (tel. 089 302 834)

**O Arco Restaurant,** Rua Eng. Duarte Pacheco (tel. 089 314375). An arched dining room with rustic furniture provides a pleasing ambience to enjoy good food. Prices above average but so is the food.

**Duas Sentinelas,** Estrada de Quarteira (tel. 089 389 522). Best to book a table in this popular restaurant. Good food at moderate prices.

**Ze do Norte,** Quatro Estradas (tel. 089 397 321). Menu lists some northern specialities, prices reasonable and the food is good.

## VILAMOURA
**Hotel Atlantis Vilamoura,** Apartado 210 (tel. 089 389 977). A five-star hotel sited close to the marina. At an age when it has lost its sparkle, but with indoor and outdoor pools and three restaurants.

**Marinotel,** (tel. 089 389 988). A large hotel situated alongside the marina. Excellent facilities including a health club, a tennis club and two restaurants.

**Aparthotel Olympus** (tel. 089 302 528). This is a fairly new four-star apartment hotel situated close to the marina which offers tastefully furnished apartments with 2–4 rooms, all with air conditioning. There is a restaurant, swimming pool and tennis court.

**Estalagem da Cigonia**, Centro Hipico de Vilamoura (tel. 089 302 577). A good rural setting and the restaurant is highly regarded for its regional cuisine. In addition there are a good number of apartments available in this area.

## Places of Interest

**Atlantico Aquatic Park**, EN125, Almancil (tel. 089 397 282).
**Cerro da Vila**. Archaeological site close to Marina.

## Sports and Leisure

### Bowls
**Club Praia da Oura** (tel. 089 589 135). Open to residents and non-residents daily from 9.30am.
**Vilamoura Lawn Bowling Green** (tel. 089 321 260). The only championship-sized green in Algarve and open to the public.

### Bridge
**Rock Garden, Vilamoura** (tel. 089 321 170). Session are held every Monday and Thursday, 2pm to 6pm.

### Golf
There are plenty of opportunities for playing golf in this area on high class courses, see the feature on p 78. Prices vary and the cost indicated here by $ is comparative between the courses and intended as a rough guide only. All have buggies for hire. Those open to the public include:

Pinheiros Altos (tel. 089 394 392) 18 holes, $$
Quinta do Lago (tel. 089 394 340) 18 holes, $$$
São Lourenço (tel. 089 396 522) 18 holes, $$$
Vilamoura I (tel. 089 389 908) 18 holes, $$
Vilamoura II (tel. 089 321 562) 18 holes, $$
Vilamoura III (tel. 089 380 724) 18 holes, $
Vila Sol (tel. 089 302 144) 18 holes, $$$
Pinecliffs, Sheraton Hotel (tel. 089 501 999 ext 4076) 9 holes $

**Balaia Golf Driving Range** (tel. 089 501 273), 50 base driving range open to public 9am–12 noon & 1–5pm, free use of clubs. Tickets from Balaia Village reception.
In addition, the **Barrington Golf Academy**, Vale de Lobo (tel. 089 396 622) has practice facilities including an 18 hole putting green, chipping greens with bunkers and full practice facilities.

### Health and Fitness
**Barringtons, Vale de Lobo** (tel. 089 396 622). Includes a health spa and beauty saloon.

## Horse Riding
**Black Horse Riding Stables, Quinta da Sadade**, Vale de Parra (tel. 089 591 829). Experienced guide leads all rides, lessons available.
**Centro Hipico da Vilamoura I**, Vilamoura (tel. 089 302 577).
**Horses Paradise, Almancil** (tel. 089 396 864). Also lessons by qualified instructors.
**Pinetrees Riding Centre, Estrada do Ancão** (tel. 089 394 369). Scenic riding area, lessons by qualified instructors and residential riding holidays also available.

## Tennis
**Balaia Village** (tel. 089 501 273). Four tennis courts open to the public at Hotel Balaia.
**David Lloyd Tennis, Vale de Lobo** (tel. 089 396 991). Coaching at all levels, tournaments, social tennis and a Junior Club Saturdays at 10am.
**Roger Taylor Tennis Centre, Clube Vale do Lobo** (tel. 089 304 145). 12 courts.

# Tourist Offices (Turismo)

## Regional Office of Algarve
Avenida 5 de Outubro, 8000 Faro. Tel. 089 800 400, fax. 089 800 489.

## Tourism Posts
**Albufeira**: Rua 5 de Outubro (tel. 089 512 144).
**Quarteira**: Avª Infante de Sagres (tel. 089 312 217).

# 7. ALGARVE'S WEST COAST: Albufeira to Lagos

Once west of Algarve, holiday developments reduce dramatically and again once beyond Portimão. Through the 1970s and '80s, in the heyday of the tourist boom when developers could not throw buildings up fast enough, a much cursed narrow bridge over the Ria Arade at Portimão proved such a bottleneck to traffic that expansion to the west of the bridge was never seriously attempted. Although dreaded by motorists, the bridge proved a blessing in disguise for preserving part of Algarve from the worst excesses of the developers. With the opening of the new bridge over the river at Portimão in 1992, the traffic now sweeps effortlessly by but with the builders in their wake. However, new and more rigorous building controls administered from Lisbon are now in place which are intended to restrict over-development.

A symphony of eroded sea cliffs, gullies, grottos, stacks, arches and endless beaches continues west of Albufeira throughout the whole of this section reaching a spectacular crescendo at Ponte da Piedade, near Lagos. Extensive watery inlets at both Portimão and Alvor add both variety to the coast and still more opportunities for bird spotters. With a few exceptions the beaches are quieter along this stretch, particularly those where a vehicle is needed, but still as picturesque. Indeed, there are so many fine beaches along Algarve's coastline that the task of ranking them into an order of perfection would defy any committee but the beach at Marinha would be a contender for the short list. Cliff walks following the coastline are possible at a number of sections here but these are not necessarily gentle walks since the terrain dips and rises quite dramatically in places.

## Praia do Castelo and Galé

Heading inland from Albufeira to join the EN125 assures a faster journey west but there is little of interest along this route before Lagoa, except perhaps for Alcantarilha and Porches. Following smaller roads by the coast offers much more of interest while not necessarily excluding the two places mentioned.

Leave Albufeira westerly following signs to Castelo or Vale de Parra to head close to but not exactly along the coast. At a crossroads a couple of miles out of town, follow signs left to **Praia do Castelo** to arrive in a parking area. Steps lead down onto a fine sandy beach scenically enclosed in a rocky coastline and served by a café restaurant. There are smaller sandy coves on either side. Compared to Albufeira and the eastern side of Albufeira, there is very little building here, although small villa type developments are appearing. **Galé**, the next area along the coast, is growing into a resort but primarily with villa developments rather than hotels although these too are appearing. There is no need to stand up on the beach at Galé to get a sun tan, the sand here will take an awful lot of bodies without ever looking full. To the west, the cliffs decline leaving a broad sweep of sand backed by dunes which extend all the way to Armação de Pêra. To the right the cliffs still remain, not so high but fantastically sculptured into a series of sandy coves. A footpath at the rear connects the coves which are graced with rock features.

## Alcantarilha

The coast road, which initially led out of Albufeira, continues to join the Armação de Pêra road. A right turn here allows for a short diversion to Alcantarilha to see the Capela dos Ossos (Chapel of the Bones). Although Alcantarilha lies on the EN125, tourism seems to have passed it by except to look in on the chapel. The **parish church** itself is rather plain but the chancel is Manueline from around the 16th century. Round the corner from the main door is the tiny chapel packed floor to ceiling with grinning skulls and the rest of the remains of former parishioners. This is their fate after being dug from the cemetery. It is customary here, as in other Mediterranean countries like Greece, to exhume the bones from the graveyard after a suitable period — around five years — and store them separately in an ossuary. Such chapels as this are unusual for the bones are normally stored out of sight in small boxes.

## Armação de Pêra

From Alcantarilha the road heads south into Armação de Pêra. Prepare to don rose coloured spectacles on entering the town. A depressing assembly of high rise buildings of no architectural merit crowd untidy streets. One resident commented that if they were all painted pink from top to bottom then visitors would flock in to see them. They are not painted pink so it is either a matter of averting the gaze or keeping the rose coloured specs firmly in place until the attractive promenade and long, long beach is reached. Almost the first greeting on the promenade is the *Hotel Garbe* which has a superb position above the beach but backing directly down onto it. The bar terrace, with a view down over the swimming pool and the beach, is great place for a spot of lunch and open to non-residents.

Armação de Pêra started life as a small fishing community attached to the safer inland village of Pêra. Since *armação* is the name of the device used to trap tuna fish, it suggests that villagers from Pêra were up and down from the coast setting their traps and finally decided to settle. It had some importance since a fort was built here in the 18th century to ward off attacks by pirates. Under the protection offered by the fort, the settlement steadily grew into a town in its own right. Fishing is still an important activity but dreams, hopes and aspirations have turned now to a new paymaster, tourism. Turning a sow's ear into a silk purse is never easy but Pêra has an advantage, it claims, in having the longest beach in Algarve, although others could make the same claim and perhaps with more justification. Nevertheless, its promenade softened with palm trees, outdoor cafés and the beach are worth some time. East along the promenade from Hotel Garbe is a small Turismo and further east the fort. Apart from outer walls, the **fort of Santo António**, built 1760, is hardly recognisable and contains a chapel dedicated to the saint of the same name. **Fishermen's Beach** is reached where the road descends to sea level and here also lies the heart of the old town. Looking east, a vast stretch of sand can be seen stretching endlessly into the distance until it merges at some unknown point with Praia de Galé.

West of Armação de Pêra the cliffs rise again and the road leads past two holiday developments of quality, **Vila Lara** and **Vila Vita Parc**, before reaching Senhora da Rocha. The coastline is back to all its cragginess and here, sitting on a bluff dividing two coves, is the simple white church of **Nossa Senhora da Rocha** (Our Lady of the Rocks) which was built in the 17th century. Visigothic capitals used in its construction suggest a much earlier temple existed on this location. This headland is a favourite spot for weekend fishermen too, who are able to cast their lines down the 30m (100ft) vertical cliffs directly into the sea. From this vantage point it is possible to look down on beaches both sides of the bluff. The larger beach to the west is popular despite the endless steps down which need to be negotiated.

## Festivals

Not a summer weekend passes without a festival taking place somewhere in Portugal. They are deeply bound up with religion and are usually held to celebrate a saint's day (a *festas*) or a religious pilgrimage (a *romario*). In addition there are some popular festivals, music festivals for instance, but even these may have a religious connection.

Every village in the country has at least one celebration to look forward to in the season, while bigger villages and towns may have a number. Months are spent planning the events, and organising committees work hard to raise money to decorate the village and the route of the procession. On the day, the villagers gather for mass then walk in procession carrying images of their patron saint, often to music provided by the local brass band. Do not for one moment think that these are entirely solemn occasions, for once the church procession is over, the folks let their hair down and really go to town, especially in the evening. Often dressed in local costume, the villagers dance and drink the evening away to music blared through speakers from brass bands or from groups of folk singers. Some of the larger events are attended by street vendors and travelling fun fairs creating a lively market atmosphere. Fire crackers add to the noise as celebrations move towards a climax.

Apart from these local celebrations, there are also big events in the calendar, like Easter and May Day, which are celebrated nationally. Some dates to look for include:

**February**
Carnival time at Loulé held the week before Lent.

**March/April**
Easter is celebrated everywhere but some of the biggest processions are held at Faro, Alcantrilha, Algoz and Lagoa.
Loulé celebrates again on the second Sunday after Easter with a Romaria e Festa de Mãe Soberana (Sovereign Mother).

**May**
May Day celebrations, usually in the form of folk festivals, at Albufeira and particularly at Alte.
Festa da Pinha (Festival of the Pine): first three days of May at Estói.
Festa da Espiga (Grain Festival): second week at Salir.
Country fair: Vila Viçosa, last two days.

**June**
Festejos de Santo António: Reguengos.
Feira de São João: one of the biggest festivals for this celebration is at Évora, end of month.

**July**
Feira da Nossa Senhora: Faro, around mid July.
Beer Festival: Silves, third week in July.

**August**
Shellfish Festival: Olhão.
Festa e Feira da Senhora dos Martires (Our Lady of the Martyrs): Castro Marim around the middle of August.

**September**
Algarve Folk Music and Dance Festival: held right across the province, concludes with grand final on Praia da Rocha beach.

**October**
Feira de Santa Iria: Faro.

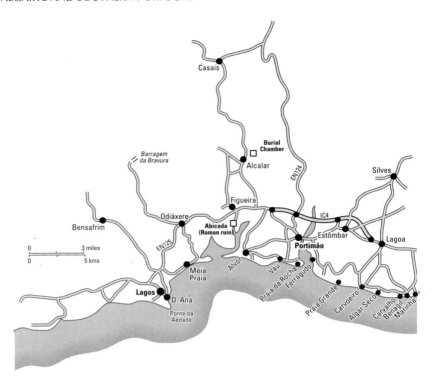

## *Porches*

To avoid a maze of uncharted tracks, the best option to make westerly progress is first to follow the road back to Porches on the EN125. Its history is long, reaching back to Roman times, but the earthquake of 1755 destroyed its castle and main church. Now, Porches is known throughout Algarve for its pottery and this is the place to buy anything from an ornamental Algarvian chimney pot to a two-sectioned dish for olives and their stones. **Porches Pottery** itself is one of the oldest and where the factory artists can be seen at work hand painting plates, pots and dishes. This is also the place where hand painted *azulejo* murals can be bought off the shelf or commissioned to a personal design. A couple of miles back along the EN125, at the artisan's village, an unlikely sounding Yorkshireman with the name of Klaus Schoon has combined his passion for wine with his wife's love of pottery. Here you can sample free, and buy, some of Portugal's finest wines, but it might be safer to wander around the aisles of pottery first.

## Praia de Marinha

Head west again along the EN125 to the next port of call, Praia de Marinha, followed by the small fishing village of Benagil. Just 3km (approx. 2 miles) west of the Porches roundabout, is the road left to Benagil but the turn is not permitted. Use the entrance to the International School a little further on to turn round, as the signs indicate. Turn right now down the narrow lane and where Benagil is signed straight on, fork left and follow signs to Praia da Marinha; park in the area provided. A footpath off west leads down to this spectacular beach which is served by a small café in season. Very popular with residents who know its location and visitors who manage to find it, it does not generally get overcrowded.

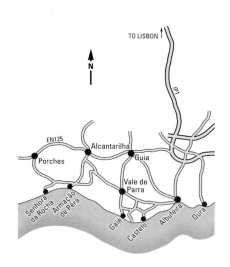

## Benagil and Praia do Carvelho

Return back up the road to follow the Benagil signs. **Benagil** is a small fishing village totally untouched by tourism. There is a pleasant café, at the top of the hill before the road descends to the small bay which harbours the fishing boats, passing a restaurant part way down. The village of Benagil lies on the next hilltop after passing through the bay. **Praia do Carvelho**, another of Algarve's spectacular beaches lies just west of Benagil and is reached by turning left through the village and continuing a short distance on a good track. Access to this completely enclosed beach is down steps through a tunnel cut at the rear. This marks the easterly spread of the extensive resort area surrounding Carvoeira. From Praia do Carvelho it is necessary to return through Benagil and continue on an inland sweep to circumnavigate the Atlantico holiday complex before heading towards Carvoeira. More holiday development follows, including *Hotel Crystal* and, shortly afterwards, *Hotel Almansor*. Before dropping down into Carvoeira, turn left following **Algar Seco** signs. This is another piece of coastline famous for its natural rock sculptures and where steps lead down amongst the pitted and worn cliffs through rock arches to grottos and inlets for those bent on exploration. Without significant sand, the sea is clear here and good for snorkellers.

## Carvoeira

Nestling between steep hills, Carvoeira centre certainly has charm but it is not easy to appreciate why it is virtually swamped out of existence by sugar-white tourist developments which cram the hillsides further than the eye can see, especially when the beach is small and the metered parking area even smaller. Fishing boats share the beach, if they are not being used for taking trips out to the grottos, which is overlooked by a terraced café restaurant specialising in sardine lunches. There is another beach, Paraiso, reached up the road to the west, around the corner and down a long flight of steps. Summer sees them both packed wall to wall with bodies.

## Lagoa

Escaping inland via the one-way road system leads through vineyards to the junction with the EN125 and busy Lagoa which lies just across the main road. It is a provincial town rather than a resort which is good for shopping and has a lively municipal market open each morning selling the local produce which is farmed around the town. Algarve is not noted for producing  wines of merit but Lagoa's red and white wines have achieved at least local recognition and the co-operative is not content to leave it there. It has been granted IPR status (*Indicação de Proveniência Regulamentada*) and hopes eventually for full recognition as a fully demarcated area. Lagoan vines are grown throughout an extensive region stretching almost from Albufeira to Portimão.

## Ferragudo

Staying with the EN125 out of Lagoa leads inland over the new suspension bridge to by-pass Portimão. Before Portimão there is an interesting diversion to Ferragudo on the east side of the Ria Arade which is best reached by following the old road. This is located by turning left at traffic lights on the EN125 shortly out of Lagoa, which leads to Estombar and Portimão, to pass the Slide and Splash water theme park. Signs indicate the route left to Ferragudo just before the old bridge is reached.

Ferragudo, an old fishing village, perches on a hill overlooking the estuary of the Ria Arade and facing Portimão. It offers nothing but atmosphere, a jumble of sloping cobbled streets and narrow alleyways with a hint of Moorish architecture but, with the new bridge at  Portimão relieving access problems, it has recently become fashionable and houses are being renovated and restaurants opened. Access to the beach, Praia Grande, and the picturesque Castelo São João de Arade, is just beyond the village. This castle, now a private residence, together with the Forte of Santa Catarina on the opposite bank guarded the entrance to this important river which was once navigable inland as far as Silves. Windsurfers love the Praia Grande. This fine sweep of sand is well protected from the Atlantic breakers by a mole to the south which has made it one of the finest beaches in Algarve for windsurfing.

Equipment can be hired on the beach where there are also cafés and restaurants. Other small sandy beaches lie within easy reach to the east.

## Portimão

Over the river estuary lies the bustling major port and industrial centre of Portimão. Despite being perhaps the busiest and, until recently, the most congested town in Algarve, it still attracts tourists for shopping and for its waterfront atmosphere. Once the main road traffic had little option but to crawl through the narrow streets clogging up the whole town. Now, the new suspension bridge and a vast new road system keeps unnecessary traffic away from the centre which has changed not just the face of Portimão but visitors' perception of it. If Portimão itself is not directly involved in tourism, next door **Praia da Rocha** certainly is and has expanded so rapidly in recent years that it now merges without distinction into Portimão.

Second only in importance to Olhão as a fishing village, Portimão's estuary harbour has attracted settlement and traders from the earliest times. The Phoenicians, Greeks and Carthaginians were all thought to have had a presence, as did the Romans who are believed to have called it Portus Magnus although considerable uncertainty clouds its early history. Fishing remained its primary industry under centuries of Arab occupation and later, when conquered by the Knights of the Order of Santiago in 1250. In 1452, Portimão was raised to the status of a town, but in the 16th and 17th centuries it was troubled by the activities of pirates which led to the construction of forts on both sides of the estuary. Like much of Algarve, Portimão suffered considerable destruction in the earthquake of 1755. The introduction of a canning factory in the 19th century brought a new prosperity and the town developed into a major fishing port.

Following the nose on a Portimão walkabout is certain to lead up the river to the café area below the old bridge where the air is filled with the aroma of grilled **sardines**. Freshly caught sardines are grilled by the thousand, mostly on outside charcoal grills, for a busy lunch and supper trade and this is the place to eat them. Sardines are extremely popular amongst the locals and they have a place at every barbecue, but traditionally, in restaurants, they are served with boiled potatoes. There is a growing trend in tourist areas to serve them with chips which is alienating the traditionalists amongst the Portuguese and driving them towards a dwindling number of truly Portuguese eating places. From the end of the quay here, beneath the bridge, there is a view over the boatyards and the mud flats to the graceful suspension bridge which has done so much to relieve Portimão from the stranglehold of congestion. At one time there was the thrill of watching the fishing boats unload their catch at the quayside along here but a new port area across the river where the fishing boats now dock has diminished the atmosphere.

If there is time before the call of sardines, perhaps the best place to start a walk around is at the Turismo located at the head of Largo 1 de Dezembro

*Ferragudo castle*

found by heading south from the gardens by the river, Praça Visconde de Bivar, along Rua Judice Biker. **Largo 1 de Dezembro**, named to commemorate the ending of 60 years of Spanish rule, features a small park with benches. The *azulejo* tiled backs to the benches illustrate ten illustrious episodes in Portuguese history. Shoppers will have no hesitation in heading westwards out of the north end of this square to join the pedestrianised **Rua Vasco de Gama** just a couple of blocks further along. This runs northward to join the also pedestrianised **Rua do Comércio** and the two together, with a number of similar but smaller side streets, offer some of the best shopping in town. Designer clothes and shoes, handicrafts, leather goods, pottery and crystal are all on display but the gypsy stalls can offer bargains, especially in table cloths. A new exhibition hall for contemporary art along this route stands to the left, on the site of the old market. Portimão does not have too much to offer in monuments but a diversion at this point, over to the right past the children's play area, leads to the **parish church** which is believed to have originated in the 14th century. Like many other buildings in Algarve, it was destroyed in the earthquake of 1755 but rebuilt and traces of the original still

*Portimão boatyard*

exist which include a portico with four small columns. Three naves inside contain examples of 18th century *azulejo* tiles.

Fully equipped yachts tied alongside the main harbour offer the thrill and excitement of deep sea shark fishing, but there are also more gentle cruises, perhaps in a traditional Portuguese gaff-sailing boat, to explore the grottos or the beaches along the southern coast. Brightly painted, shallow draught boats make inland trips up the river Arade to Silves.

## Algarve's Fishing Industry

The warm Atlantic coastal waters teem with fish and the tradition of sea fishing in Algarve is long, stretching back to Roman times. Tanks used by the Romans in the 2nd century to salt fish can still be seen today on the São Lourenço nature trail on Quinta do Lago reserve and in the grounds of the Ria Formosa Natural Park at Marim. Although at least 200 species of fish are known from this area, two in particular have dominated the industry. One of these is the tuna fish, of which there are actually three different species, and the other is the humble sardine.

Throughout the breeding season, shoals of tuna migrate along the southern shores of Algarve heading for spawning grounds in the Mediterranean and return along much the same route after spawning. The method used to catch them until fairly recently was to set a floating trap, an *armação*, which was introduced and first used by the Moors. This Y-shaped floating structure, angled to catch the main flow, was anchored to the bottom, and a series of nets guided the fish to an inner section where they were effectively trapped ready for slaughter. Fishermen on support vessels were on hand and ready to accomplish the bloody slaughter which was known as the 'bullfight of the sea'. Knowledge that a top-sized tuna fish can be as long as 3m (10ft) and weigh more than 750kg (1650lbs) adds some perspective to the highest recorded catch of 42,000 specimens near Tavira in 1881. With such an abundance of tuna, and sardines, the introduction of canning factories in the 1860s improved export opportunities and brought a new prosperity to many of the fishing villages along the south coast. Tunny-fishing became a Crown monopoly under Afonso III in 1249 and a provincial one in Algarve from 1773. Over fishing eventually led to a rapid decline in tuna numbers and the virtual collapse of the industry throughout the early part of the 20th century which was followed by closure of many canning factories.

Much of Algarve's fishing fleet is nothing more than a vast armada of small boats, usually less than 15m (50ft) long, concentrated at two main ports, Olhão and Portimão, although boats can be seen in virtually every village along the coast. Generally these boats fish within 5km (3 miles) of the coast although larger boats work in deeper waters fishing for sea bream, red mullet and skate. Sardine fishing is big business and Algarve's annual catch, reaching 100,000 tons in a good year, is exceeded in Europe only by Spain. Shoals of small sardines searching for plankton often drift into the warmer coastal waters allowing an army of small boats, usually fishing at night using lights to attract the fish, an opportunity to land economical catches but the more serious sardine fishing is done by trawlers using drift nets. Again, overfishing and declining fish stocks in the 1930s hastened the decline of the sardine canning industry.

Sardines account for just less than half the total present day catch with horse mackerel, scabbard fish, hake, mackerel, whiting, conger eel, skate, sea bream and tuna together about equalling the sardine catch. The rest is made up of a bewildering variety of other species which make the stalls on the fish markets look so interesting. One of these other species is the octopus which is caught in a special earthenware pot known as an *alcatruz*. Up to 72 pots are attached to a line at regular intervals and laid on the sea bottom parallel to the shore with a buoy marker. Sometimes the pots are baited with cockles or muscles but often it is just the inviting safe refuge which attracts the octopus. Pots are checked daily.

Fish farming is now a growth industry, especially within the lagoon area of Ria Formosa reserve, which is particularly important for high value shellfish.

## Praia da Rocha

Praia da Rocha, adjoining Portimão, occupies the coastline to the south. It must have been a pretty resort originally, when confined to the coast, but crystal white high-rise development on a massive scale has expanded the resort area inland to merge with Portimão. Riddled inland with major roads, only the heart of the resort by the coast has anything to offer. Hotels, shops, bars, clubs and even a casino rub elbows in a fairly compact area. A tree decked and flower lined promenade rides above a wide stretch of sandy beach backed by more of Algarve's sculptured cliffs. This leads at its eastern end to the old **Forte of Santa Catarina**, now a terrace café and restaurant offering fine views over the mouth of the estuary to Castelo São João de Arade on the far bank. Restaurants also line the rear of the beach down at sand level, all connected with paved walkways. At the western end of the beach, a tunnel has been cut to allow access to some of the smaller bays beyond.

*Alvor parish church (Igreja Matriz)*

## *Vau·and Alvor*

Building density diminishes moving westward to the next resort, **Vau**. A convoluted coastline between the two hides nothing but small bays and more beach. For those seeking life in the slow lane, Vau fits the bill and offers a more relaxing atmosphere than Praia da Rocha with an equally fine beach overlooked by a café restaurant. White houses and apartments increase again on approaching the picturesque hilltop village of **Alvor**. Overlooking a river of the same name, Alvor is said to have been founded by the great Carthaginian general Hannibal and may have been the original Portus Hannibalis, a name which sometimes gets attached to Portimão. Fortified with a castle under the Moors, it was attacked and captured by Crusaders under D. Sancho I who were on their way to mount an attack on Silves, the Moorish capital at that time. The Arabs quickly reconquered Alvor and held it until 1250, until the Moors were finally expelled from Algarve. Flattened by the earthquake of 1755, the village was rebuilt but Alvor lost its castle.

Now, in a village full of character, jostling houses on sloping narrow streets cluster below the bright yellow and white **parish church**. Rebuilt in the 18th century after the earthquake, the church is distinguished by two very fine Manueline doorways, particularly the main doorway, whilst the three nave interior has columns constructed from the red sandstone of Silves and polychrome *azulejo* tiles decorating the chancel side walls. Streets running west lead down to the harbour side on the river estuary which is also the location of the fish market. Around the village, modern developments, a mixture of high and low rise buildings, are growing steadily as they are by the seashore which lies to the south. Acres of sand stretch both east and west. To the east they are backed by

*Beach at Vau*

more of Algarve's picturesque sculptured cliffs but to the west the cliffs run out and the beach is backed by dunes. There is a broad scattering of cafés along the back of the beach here which, for a change, has easy access.

Keen **bird watchers** may choose to stay at Alvor. Both the Alvor and Odiáxere rivers emerge at this point creating a massive wetland area which teems with birds and is a stopping off place for a wide variety of wading birds during times of migration. Pressure is mounting to prevent development encroaching here and to gain reserve status to protect the wildlife.

## Neolithic site near Alcalar

This huge expanse of water leaves no option but to return inland to rejoin the EN125 to head for Lagos. Before Lagos is reached, there are a couple of sites of historic interest, one a neolithic site and the other a Roman villa, which are quite challenging just to find. Shortly after turning left on the EN125 watch out for and take the road on the right signposted Alcalar 4km. Keep left at a fork just 1.5km (1 mile) later to head into the small village of Alcalar. A fraction beyond the village is a junction signposted left to Artesanato Garrafeira and Fonte de Pedra right. Park here to cover the remaining short distance on foot by heading down the track to the right and looking almost immediately for the passageway on the left marked out with wire fences. This leads uphill to the neolithic barrow which surrounds a megalithic burial chamber from around 2000 BC, now exposed so that the main circular chamber and access tunnel are clear to see.

## *Vila Abicada*

Now for the Roman Vila Abicada. Return by the same route back to the EN125 and turn right towards Lagos. After around 2km (1¼ miles) turn left exactly opposite the road signposted off right to Figueira. The track immediately bears around to the right but turn left almost straight away to continue up a cobbled track alongside Vila Arco Iris. From the main road it is just less than a mile (1.4km) to the site although it might seem longer. Follow the track as it crosses the railway line and keep right past a row of cypress trees, then farm buildings followed by more cypress trees until the track ends in a farmyard. The site of the villa, adjacent to the farm, is fenced and locked but the old lady at the farm has the role of custodian and in the fullness of time should appear with the key. In any event, there is a good view through the open fencing. Foundation walls of the villa remain with some excellent and extensive mosaics mostly of geometric design. The artefacts found here are now contained in the museum at Lagos.

## *Barragem da Bravura*

There is another popular side trip to the reservoir, Barragem da Bravura, to consider before Lagos is reached. It is a 10km (6¼ miles) diversion inland from Odiáxere to this popular picnic site which has a café in season. Set amongst drab, cistus covered hills and filling the confluence of two large valleys, this not especially pretty reservoir provides largely irrigation water for the farmers and especially for the citrus groves. It is good for wild flowers in early spring with *Narcissus bulbocodium* on show as well as a number of orchid species.

The EN125 squeezes through Odiáxere itself, although a well regulated traffic system keeps the traffic flowing through the narrowest sections. Beyond, Lagos is soon reached where a left turn at the initial roundabout leads down the riverside to extensive but invariably busy parking areas.

# Lagos

Picturesque and lively, Lagos has succeeded where much of Algarve has failed, in creating a resort of charm, elegance and character in the midst of a busy working town. There is much to explore, a castle guarding the estuary, old town walls, a riverside promenade, gardens, pedestrianised streets and squares colourfully decked with pavement cafés, restaurants and shops, not to mention its museum, churches and monuments.

Occupying an important estuary location, Lagos has seen the footprints of the Phoenicians, Greeks, Carthaginians and the Romans, who called it Lacóbriga. When the Arabs took over in the 8th century, they renamed it Zawaya, surrounded it with walls and used it as a trading base to conduct business with North Africa. Their defences were insufficient to stop the town eventually being recovered by the newly emerging Portuguese nation in 1249 under Dom Afonso III. The story of Lagos does not end there for a key role in the history of the country still lay in store. Recognising its potential as a naval base, Dom Dinis was along in the 14th century to strengthen the castle and raise its walls. Portugal did not have a navy at that time so Dom Dinis invited a Genoese to found one. Under João I Portugal was still having troubles with Castile but after that was resolved in 1411, he adopted an aggressive policy towards Morocco. In 1415, a fleet of mighty Portuguese warships was assembled at Lagos from where it sailed to capture Ceuta. João I had married Philippa of Lancaster, daughter of John of Gaunt, Duke of Lancaster, in 1387 and their son Henry, after the capture of Ceuta, went to Lagos and gathered about him a team of pilots, cartographers and navigators in a venture which launched Portugal into a golden era of exploration and built them a great maritime empire. Henry himself won a place in history as Henry the Navigator (see feature p 121). Gil Eanes, a local man born in Lagos, proved to be one of Henry's most distinguished captains. By 1434, Madeira and the Azores as well as North Africa had been charted and the edge of the world moved as far as the stormy promontory of Cape Bojador on the west coast of Africa. Until then, nobody had ever sailed beyond it but Gil Eanes broke the barrier, sailed around and found more coast and safer waters beyond opening up a further chapter of exploration.

Young Dom Sebastião liked Lagos and, in 1576, made it the capital of Algarve which it remained for exactly two centuries. Full of crusading zeal, Dom Sebastião came to Lagos in 1578 with a force of men to lead an expedition which ended in disaster at Alcacer-Quiber in Morocco. His army of 18,000 men was destroyed and as many as 8000, including Sebastião and many young nobles, were slaughtered.

Lagos suffered as badly as anywhere else in Algarve from the earthquake of 1755. It was flattened and little remains now of its earlier architecture except some parts of the town walls. Although rebuilt, it was never able to recapture its former glory and settled to a life based around the fishing industry. By the end of the 19th century, it had recovered some prosperity and was productive enough to require 40 canning factories but overfishing brought inevitable decline. Its history is by no means finished for Lagos has now turned to tourism and looks set to enjoy another success.

## The Town

Although Lagos offers plenty of opportunity for exploration, interest centres mainly on the part of town nearest the river and the following route encompasses much of it. Starting in the main square, **Praça Gil Eanes**, named after Lagos' famous explorer, the first point of interest is the unmissable statue of the young pink-faced Dom Sebastião cast in his stone suit of armour. The statue has not received too much good comment and one view is that young Sebastião looks more like a 'biker'. Love it or hate it, at least it is more memorable than some other statues around Algarve. Taking the centre road out of the square, Rua Afonso d'Almeida, leads into the main pedestrianised **Rua 25 de Abril** filled with pavement cafés. A brief diversion to the right into Rua Lima Leitão leads to Turismo where a street plan can be picked up. Antique shops and *artesanato* shops which line Rua 25 Abril press for attention but it is equally important to save time for the museum which is one of the most interesting in Algarve. Continue ahead and slightly right into Rua da Silva Lopes which terminates opposite **Igreja de Santo António** which also contains the museum.

Completed originally in the early 18th century, the church was restored after the earthquake to retain its fine Baroque carving. Inside is free of furniture except for a few seats, but the upper walls are covered in exuberantly carved and gilded woodwork full of fat-faced cherubs. The eight blue and white *azulejos* panels depicting scenes from the life of Santo António which line the lower walls are the work of Joachim Rastilho, a local man from Loulé, and these were added in the restoration work after the earthquake. Even the ceiling is elaborately painted while the paintings on the walls are framed by carvings. If the tombstone on the floor carved with the name of Hugo Beaty comes as a surprise, then it helps to know that the church was connected with the army regiment that used to be quartered in the town and Hugo Beaty, an Irishman, was a commander.

A side door in the church leads into the **museum** for which there is a small charge. Much of the story of Algarve, ancient and modern, is told through relics, artefacts and models in a small but well organised museum which is diminished for most visitors because the information is presented only in Portuguese. Mosaics, frescoes, Corinthian capitals and pottery from the Roman period include some remains from nearby Vila Abicada while earlier, prehistoric remains from Caldas de Monchique and Bronze Age relics from Vila do Bispo are also displayed. In the folklore gallery, models are used extensively to depict life and lifestyles in the more recent past and there are fine examples of local crafts including lacework, embroidery, basket weaving and carving. There are bits and bobs of everything from animals preserved in bottles to sardine nets and lobster pots including many artefacts from former African colonies.

Turn towards the riverside on leaving the museum to enter Praça da Republica. For the former slave market, **Mercado dos Esravos**, turn northwards to head for the small gallery at a confluence of two roads. When the caravels sailed boldly out of Lagos in search of discoveries and wealth, they returned not just with gold, cinnamon and spices but with a human cargo, slaves. The market here, now a small gallery, has the dubious distinction of being the first place in Europe, in 1441, to sell slaves. This trade in African slaves proved very profitable, helping to pay for Henry's voyages of discovery in the first instance but continuing on for centuries afterwards. On the west side of this square is a statue of Henry the Navigator himself.

Castellated town walls dominate the statue of Gil Eanes, the famous explorer, as well as the scenery while walking southwards by the riverside towards the **Fort Ponta da Brandeira** at the estuary of the Ribeira de

Bensafrim. Originally 17th century, this compact fort has been renovated and a small museum incorporated dedicated to Henry the Navigator and the age of discoveries. There is a charge to gain entry to the fort which includes the museum but, if time is pressing, this is the one to miss. The museum is nothing more than blown up posters with information only in Portuguese and the rest of the fort is taken up with a snack bar/restaurant. There are some small beaches and grottos on the seaward side of the fort but the best beach is **Meia Praia** across the river. Some 4km of sand stretch out invitingly but it takes transport to get there which may be a boat trip in season.

Most of the hotels and accommodation have been squeezed out of Lagos itself and lie largely to the south enjoying the best of both worlds. They are easily within walking distance of Lagos and on the doorstep of some spectacular but small beaches such as **Dona Ana**. Reached by descending steps between a couple of restaurants, the sandy cove embraced by colourful rocks is as picturesque as it is intimate and a coastal footpath heading towards Lagos discovers more similar coves all accessed down steps.

Algarve's most sculptured and most famous stretch of coastline lies just to the south at **Ponta da Piedade**. Stations of the cross line the route down to the lighthouse on the headland where there is plenty of room for parking. Here the headland has been cut and shaped by the power of the elements over centuries leaving an assembly of offshore stacks, arches and grottos which change shape with every angle. There is a narrow footbridge to take the intrepid out a little further for even better views but vertigo sufferers would be wiser not to attempt it. Steps lead down between the rocks to a small jetty where fishermen spend summer days taking visitors out on trips to see the grottos.

# Practical Information

## Hotels and Restaurants

See the introduction for further details of houses in the TURIHAB (TH) and Turismo Rural (TR) schemes.

### ARMAÇÃO DE PÊRA
**Casa Bela Moura**, Alporchinos (tel. 082 313 422). Recently constructed house, eight rooms all with private facilities. Close to Senhora da Rocha. Meals available, facilities include swimming pool.
**Hotel Garbe** (tel. 082 312 194). Superbly situated comfortable middle-sized four-star hotel. Many rooms renovated in 1995, heated outdoor swimming pool.
**Vilalara** (tel. 082 314 910). One of the earlier hotels but good position by the ocean. Apartments and suites available. Offers good facilities with six tennis courts and a Thalasso centre with sea water pools and mud baths but no indoor pool. Gourmet restaurant.
**Vila Vita Parc** (tel. 082 313 068) A complete five-star touristic development

with rooms, suites and villas in extensive gardens. Five restaurants, five swimming pools, two beaches and tennis courts.
**Restaurant Clipper**, Av. Beira Mar (tel. 082 312 327). Portuguese run restaurant providing good food at moderate prices.
**Gatsby**, Rua Dr Manuel d'Arriada 109 (tel. 082 313 535). His cataplana or piri-piri shrimps are usually accompanied by Fado or live music and the price is still moderate.
**Restaurant Quinta da Saudade**, Vale de Parra (tel. 089 591 761). A comfortable English-run restaurant offers home made cuisine and, in addition, a full vegetarian menu.
**Ze Leiteiro**, off Rua de Praia. Cheap and cheerful, enough meat or fish for most appetites at a fixed price. Very popular.

## CARVOEIRA AND SURROUNDS
**Motel Alagoas, Lagoa** (tel. 082 52 268). Situated directly on the EN125, this three-star motel offers 41 apartments, a swimming pool and private parking.
**Hotel Almansor, Praia Vale Covo** (tel. 082 358 026). A large, modern hotel close to small beach. Well equipped with two tennis courts, two restaurants an outdoor pool and a health centre.
**Hotel Apartments Crystal, Vale Centeanes** (tel. 082 358 860). This four-star establishment offers 100 rooms and suites with two restaurants, two swimming pools and a health club.
**Hotel Dom Sancho, Praia do Carvoeira** (tel. 082 357 301). This 51-roomed four star hotel could not be closer to the beach. Restaurant and two swimming pools.
**Teodoro's Restaurant, Praia do Carvoeira** (tel. 082 357 394). Overlooking the beach, Teodóro's is particularly good for fish and not too expensive.
**O. Lotus, Lagoa**, Rua Marquês de Pombal, 11 (tel. 082 52 098). An interesting menu including typical Portuguese dishes, good food at moderate prices.

## LAGOS including Dona Ana and Meia Praia
**Hotel Golfino, Praia Dona Ana** (tel. 082 769 900). Large, well situated four-star hotel close to beach. Plenty of facilities including indoor and outdoor pools and restaurant.
**Hotel de Lagos**, Rua Nova da Aldeia (tel. 082 769 967). Located not altogether conveniently in the heart of Lagos, this 300-room four-star establishment has tennis courts, a heated outdoor pool and health centre with Turkish bath.
**Hotel Meia Praia, Meia Praia** (tel. 082 762 001). Good three-star hotel with swimming pool, tennis and children's play area.
**Restaurant Alpendre**, 17 Rua Antonio Barbosa Viana, Lagos (tel. 082 762 705). International restaurant with high class food, on the expensive side but good value.
**O Jardim, Meia Praia** (tel. 082 62 259). Opens only in season. Garden restaurant with fairly traditional menu including pizzas, moderately priced.
**O Lamberto**, Rua 25 de Abril 21, Lagos (tel. 082 763 746). Family run restaurant with good food biased towards fish and reasonably priced.

**O Trovador**, Lagos (tel. 082 763 152). Close to Hotel Lagos, this is a cosy restaurant with international cuisine of a high standard, moderate prices.
**Ze do Porco**, Lagos. Close to the fish market and mainly fish on the menu, the food is good and the prices very reasonable.

### PORTIMÃO including Praia da Rocha and Alvor
This is another area which is hugely supplied with accommodation but mostly directed at the packaged tourist and taken up by the big tour operators. Out of season there should be no problem finding accommodation on arrival but it is very different in high season.
**Casa Trés Palmeiras, Vau**, Apartado 84 (TR) (tel. 082 401 275). Clifftop situation, superb house with five rooms, all with private facilities, and swimming pool.
**Hotel Jupiter, Praia da Rocha**, Av. Tomás Cabreira (tel. 082 415 041). This four-star hotel with 180 rooms is well equipped with both indoor and outdoor pools, restaurant, grill and private parking.
**Hotel Algarve, Praia da Rocha** (tel. 082 415 001). This pre-70s five-star hotel has a fantastic site on the beach with an attractive outdoor pool and tennis courts.
**Hotel da Rocha, Praia da Rocha**, Av. Tomás Cabreira (tel. 082 24 081). A more modest three-star establishment with 77 rooms but reasonable.
**Hotel Apartments Oriental, Praia da Rocha**, Av. Tomás Cabreira (tel. 082 413 000). Apartment accommodation with four-star facilities including swimming pool, gardens, parking but no restaurant.
**Hotel Penina, Portimão** (tel. 082 415 415). More than a hotel, it is a five-star resort with olympic size swimming pool, tennis, three golf courses, horse riding centre and five restaurants.
**Hotel Alvor Praia, Alvor** (tel. 082 458 900). Large five-star hotel superbly situated with own beach and good outside pool.
**Hotel Delfim, Alvor** (tel. 082 458 901). This 312 roomed three-star hotel offers an outdoor pool with other sporting facilities including tennis.
**Hotel Apartments Encosta do Vau**, Encosta do Vau (tel. 082 415 592). 74 apartments in this four-star hotel with an outdoor pool and gardens.
**Vila Rosa de Lima, Estrada da Torre** (TR) (tel. 082 411 097). Quiet inland location, just north of the EN125 between Portimão and Lagos. Restored Algarvian house offering high standard of accommodation. Just four rooms, all with facilities, and swimming pool.
**O Bicho, Largo Gil Eanes 12, Portimão** (tel. 082 22 977). Essentially a fish restaurant and the place to try *bacalhau com natas* or seafood rice at moderate prices.
**Falésia, Praia da Rocha**, Av. Tomás Cabreira (tel. 082 23 524). This is the place to try fish kebab and *cataplana* at moderate prices.
**Capacho, Alvor**, Rua Poeta António Aleixo (tel. 082 458 126). International cuisine with Portuguese bias, game in season; good value for money.

*Praia de Rocha*

## Places of Interest

**Lagos Museum**, entrance through church of Santo Antonio or separate entrance next door. Open 9.30 am–12.30 pm and 2.00 pm–5.00 pm; closed Mondays and Holidays.
**Slide and Splash**, Vale de Deus, Lagoa (082 341 685). Aquatic park.
**The Big One**, EN125, Areias Alcantrilha (082 322 827). Aquatic park.
**Zoomarine**, EN125, Guia. Entertainment park with rides, swimming pool and sea lion and dolphin shows.
**Vila Abicada**. Remains of an old Roman villa in isolated location (see details on p 108). Farmer has the key for access.

## Sports and Leisure

### Golf

There is a selection of high class golf courses in the area open to the public which are described in the feature on p 78. Prices vary and the cost indicated here by $ is comparative only between the courses. All have buggies for hire unless otherwise stated.

Alto Golf, Praia do Vau (tel. 082 416 913) 18 holes, no buggies, $$
Gramacho, between Lagoa and Carvoeira (tel. 082 52 670), 18 holes on 9 fairways, $$
Palmares, Meia Praia (tel. 082 762 953) 18 holes, $
Parque da Floresta, Budens (tel. 082 65 333) 18 holes, $
Penina (tel. 082 415 415 ) 18 holes, $$$

Vale de Minho, Carvoeira (tel. 082 358 502) 9 holes, no buggies, $
Vale da Pinta, between Lagoa and Carvoeira (tel. 082 52 670) 18 holes, $$

**Pitch and Putt**
**Alvor Golf**, Sitio da Dourada (tel. 082 459 781), nine-holes on par three course, $.

**Horse Riding**
**Black Horse Riding Stables**, Quinta da Saudade, Vale de Parra (tel. 089 591 829). Selection of interesting rides including moonlight beach rides for experienced riders.
**Vale de Ferro Riding**, Mexilhoeira Grande (tel. 082 96 444). Over 30 different treks in the scenic foothills of Monchique also lessons by qualified instructor.

**Microlights**
**Algarve Microlight Centre**, Lagos (tel. 082 62 906). Experienced pilots on hand for microlight rides. Open Monday to Saturday 9am to 12pm.
**Ten Pin Bowling**, Av. Tomás Cabreira, Praia da Rocha (tel. 082 83 818). Four lanes of American-style bowling. Open 2pm to 2am.
**Torralta Bowling**, Alvor (tel. 082 459 211). Four lanes also snooker and pool tables.

**Tennis**
**Hotel Penina** (tel. 082 415 415).
**Clube Carvoeira** (tel. 082 357 847).

## Tourist Offices (Turismo)

**Regional Office of Algarve**
Avenida 5 de Outubro,  8000 Faro. Tel. 089 800 400, fax 089 800 489.

**Tourism Posts**
**Armação de Pêra** (8365) Avenida Marginal (tel. 082 312 145).
**Carvoeira** (8400 Lagoa) Largo da Praia do Carvoeira (tel. 082 357 728).
**Lagos** (8600) Largo Marquês de Pombal (tel. 082 763 031).
**Portimão** (8500) Largo 1° de Dezembro (tel. 082 236 95).
**Praia da Rocha** (8500 Portimão) Rua Tomás Cabreira (tel. 082 222 90).

# 8. THE BARLAVENTO

The southern coastal areas from Lagos to Sagres then north as far as Aljezur are amongst the least developed and wildest in Algarve. Not for nothing are these extremities known as the Barlavento (windward) which manifests itself around the Sagres peninsula where there are few windless days, verified by the sight of wind-cut trees, low shrubs and little cultivation. Gone are the intricately sculptured convolutions of the cliffs around Ponta da Piedade. The cliffs become more rugged until at Sagres they tower defiantly, impervious to the relentless pounding of the ocean. Pockets of sandy beach gain a foothold to the south whilst huge stretches of fine sand face an unremitting sea to the west. Burgau and Salema still manage to retain much of their fishing village character despite some development. This area was once regarded as a far-flung outpost but easier access makes it more vulnerable to outside interference. Development controls have been tightened and the coast from Salema as far north as Sines declared a protected zone, so there is hope yet.

## Luz

A new road from Lagos (EN125) has imposed its imprint over the old ambling route to Sagres, so the left turn to Luz arrives sooner than expected. The country ambience immediately makes itself felt and, early in the year, huge swathes of Bermuda buttercups, *Oxalis pes-caprae*, carpet the fields in a brilliant yellow glow. Increasing housing density announces arrival at Luz, where the narrow road ahead squeezing between the houses suddenly opens out into the square. A one-way system operates down left between the church and Fortaleza restaurant, situated in what was a 16th-century fort, to the shore and along the narrow promenade to the car park.

Luz was a centuries old fishing village before tourism arrived but has become part and parcel of the surrounding crush of villas and apartments. All the development is small scale rather than huge, the lines of the white buildings softened with tumbles of purple bougainvillaea. *Hotel Belavista da Luz* has recently made an appearance as the only hotel in Luz. Beautifully appointed, it offers luxury at a very affordable price and all its bedrooms, two especially designed for disabled guests, overlook the sea and heated outdoor pool. Cafés and souvenirs share the compact area behind the ample sized sandy beach. The lure of the obelisk on the cliff top is an irresistible challenge. Those undeterred by the steep climb are rewarded with views of blindingly

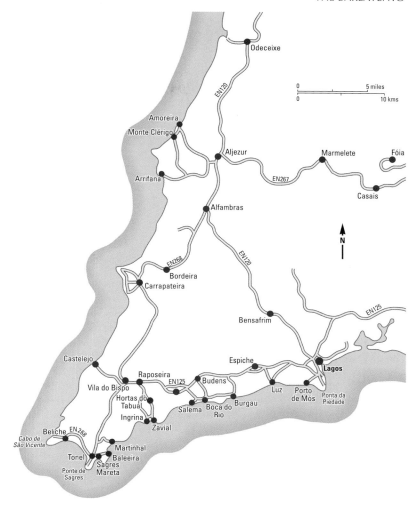

white Luz and west along the coast. A springtime bonus are the flowers, including orchids such as *Ophrys bombyliflora* (bumblebee orchid) and *O. vernixia* (mirror orchid), which grow on the hillside.

## Burgau

Burgau is reached by returning to the EN125 and continuing westwards. Creeping development greets arrivals but this has not as yet become overly intrusive. Driving down into Burgau can be a problem at the best of times as

*Luz*

space is very limited, better to turn right at the junction by the bus shelter above the village and park. The old village houses form a cramped cluster on the steep slope down to the harbour where café/bars and restaurants oversee the activities of local fishermen. Fortunately, tourist amenities are kept small scale due to lack of space and Burgau still manages to retain something of its original character.

Continuing along the narrow top road parallel with the coast leads to Boca do Rio, becoming a track nearer the shore. This undeveloped pocket was once an area of salt pans and marshy ground but a sandy strip edging the shore is the draw now. Paper white narcissus, *Narcissus papyraceus*, add splashes of white in winter whilst the yellow hoop petticoat daffodil, *Narcissus bulbocodium*, hides on the headland beneath the ruined castle. A large fenced area surrounds the site of a Roman settlement awaiting excavation, some remains of which edge the beach.

## Salema

A track leads to Salema, just over the next headland, but there is access to the EN125 at Budens which itself is thought to be of Roman origin. Salema's heart is still its fishing quarter and narrow street of fishermen's houses rising up the cliff side, but development has burgeoned on the approach from the EN125 and on the hill to the west. That apart, the beach is fairly extensive and Salema remains relatively uncommercialised.

Back on the EN125, pass through Figueira and, in around 2km (1¼ miles), look on the right for one of the oldest churches in Algarve, the **chapel of Nossa Senhora de Guadalupe**. Thought to have been built in the 13th century by the Knights Templar, the church was most probably used for worship by Henry the Navigator who lodged for a time in the nearby village of Raposeira. A road off right heads from Raposeira to the beaches of **Ingrina** and **Zavial** 4km (2½ miles) distant. Follow signs to Ingrina and Hortas do Tabual keeping left at a fork in 1km (approx. ½ mile) to reach Zavial beach.

## Vila do Bispo

Vila do Bispo stands at the junction of the EN125 with the EN268 where north leads to Aljezur and south to Sagres. Known as Santa Maria do Cabo before 1515, the town was donated by Dom Manuel I to the bishop of Algarve and renamed Aldeia do Bispo, later becoming Vila do Bispo (Bishop's Town). Agriculture is the dominant industry here, so the town exudes a sleepy rural atmosphere. It contains little in the way of sights but for the Igreja Matrix and a couple of windmills, one of which is a restaurant.

## South to Sagres

The flattened landscape becomes ever more inhospitable as the route presses southwards, now on the EN268, through increasingly cowed vegetation with hardly a tree in sight. It is hard to believe the wealth of flora which finds a roothold here beneath the stunted shrubs which provide protection from the fierce wind and the voracious appetite of sheep and goats. The whole area is a botanist's delight in spring and similarly for bird-watchers during the migrations of spring and autumn. A left turn leads through the Quinta do Marinho development to **Praia do Martinhal**. The beach of fine sand backed by dunes stretches from low cliffs, where there was once a Roman settlement, to Sagres fishing harbour at **Baleeira**. Signs of habitation increase as Sagres is neared but the brooding presence of the fortaleza (fortress), squatting on the horizon directly ahead, captures all attention, the 6km (3¾ miles) dramatic sweep of coastline on the right towards the Cabo de São Vicente spur momentarily ignored.

## Sagres

In all probability, Sagres **fortress** served as Henry the Navigator's head-quarters (see feature page 121) and site of his School of Navigation. Activity seems to have continued here after Henry's death until Sir Francis Drake laid waste to the fortresses of Baleeira, Beliche, Sagres and Castle of São Vicente in 1587, when Portugal was under Spanish rule. This seemingly mindless act was as likely nothing to do with piracy, but more a means of securing safe passage round the cape to the Mediterranean for Spain's enemies. Unfortunately, Henry's archives and library, which would have contained precise details of his enterprises, and his Vila do Infante were destroyed in the attack. For 44 years the fortresses lay in ruins until Dom Filipe ordered their reconstruction in 1632. With the restoration of the Portuguese monarchy (in 1640), Dom João IV continued rebuilding them, ensuring the use of the most up-to-date specifications. Destroyed yet again, this time by a natural catastrophe in 1755, the fortresses lay waste for a further 40 years. Their rebuilding in 1793, on the orders of Dona Maria I, was without purpose and short lived. Beliche and Sagres were abandoned to the elements whilst São Vicente continued life as a lighthouse. The rise of tourism has awakened interest in these remote sites and they are now enjoying a new lease of life.

The present impressive frontage of the Sagres fortress was reconstructed after the 1755 earthquake on the orders of Dona Maria I, in 1793. This effectively seals off the rocky plateau of the steep cliffs at the tip of the spur, now frequented by anglers perilously fishing off rocky ledges. Woollen jumpers are a speciality of the vendors plying their wares on the car park outside the fort, no doubt hoping for a gusty day and good sales. If it is quiet, drive through the fortified gateway and park. Immediately inside is the neglected 'Rosa dos Ventos', a large wind compass laid out on the ground. Discovered in 1928, a question mark hangs over its actual age but many believe it to be contemporary with Henry the Navigator. The small white domed **Igreja da Santa Maria** was probably around during the time of Henry since it appears on charts of the fortress used by Sir Francis Drake, the originals of which are in the British Museum. Other buildings of value and character have been destroyed or disfigured, including one thought to have been part of Henry's school. The lavatorial style of the new museum lacks both taste and vision, being completely devoid of empathy with its surroundings. This is but one of a growing number of museums in Algarve, exhibitions really, which have nothing to show and with explanations usually only in Portuguese. Entertainment comes in the form of a bracing walk to watch the anglers who populate the rocky fringes of the bare plateau high above the turbulent waters.

Once remote and isolated, Sagres is rapidly becoming surrounded by the trappings of tourism but there is little evidence of its long history. Since time immemorial, it provided shelter to ships afraid to round the cape when strong north or west winds were blowing. By the time Henry arrived on the scene though, Sagres lay in ruins, its population forced to abandon the village after constant attacks by North African pirates. One of his first tasks was to repopulate the village and provide fortifications and protection to defend the coastline of his domain. Sagres continued to flourish after Henry's death and, under Dom Manuel I, was created a parish in 1519. Today, accommodation includes a *pousada* and the luxury *Hotel Apartamento O Navegante*. Plus points are the good beaches of **Tonel** and **Mareta**, but beware of strong currents. There is also good food available. Stop for a coffee in the square before continuing on.

The 6km (3¾ miles) ribbon of the EN268 to Cabo de São Vicente speeds on through wind battered terrain. A blip amongst the wilderness of the cape is the small **Fortaleza de Beliche** perched on the cliff edge, just before reaching the lighthouse. Its chapel, dedicated to Santa Catarina, was commissioned by Henry the Navigator shortly before his death. Built to keep watch over the Beliche inlet, between it and Sagres where ships once sought refuge from strong northerly winds, it fell foul of Drake's orgy of destruction in the area. Later reconstructed, the fort now serves as a small hotel with a restaurant of some repute and from here a steep path leads down the cliff to Beliche beach.

## Infante Dom Henrique — Henry the Navigator 1394–1460

Foundations of the British connection with Portugal were cemented in 1385 when, with the aid of English archers, João I defeated the Castilians at the battle of Aljubarotta. In gratitude for English assistance in securing Portugal's independence, the Treaty of Windsor was signed in 1386 as a declaration of lasting peace between the two countries. More than anything, it served as formal confirmation of an earlier Anglo-Portuguese Alliance in 1373. As a further seal of good intent, John of Gaunt, Duke of Lancaster, a signatory to the Treaty, gave his daughter Philippa of Lancaster in marriage to João I. They were married in Porto cathedral on 14 February 1387 and their third son Henry, later known as Henry the Navigator, was born in 1394.

A serious son of an equally studious and serious mother, Henry's curiosity regarding seafaring matters was most likely developed whilst as a child growing up close to the Douro riverside in Porto. What motivated Henry is a matter of conjecture but expeditions were still very much bound up with the Crusades. Interest in voyages of discovery was fuelled by talk of the legendary Christian kingdom of Prester John, and its untold riches, said to lie somewhere in Africa. Conquering Moorish lands in North Africa was a prerequisite to gaining access into the hinterland of that continent; the seeds had been sown to think of wider possibilities.

With a fleet of 200 ships, the building of which Henry himself supervised, he set sail from Porto with his father and brother on a Crusade against Ceuta in North Africa where they won a resounding victory. A lasting impression on Henry was not so much the victory itself but the oriental riches they looted. What of these lands from where such a wealth of gold, silver, silks and spices originated? Henry returned to Portugal a thoughtful man but his energies were still channelled into taming the north coast of Africa. Only later, on hearing tales from other sailors, was Henry drawn into the search further afield although he himself remained a landlubber after his foray to North Africa.

To pursue his quest, Henry approached his brother the regent, Dom Pedro, and asked for a grant of land at Cabo de São Vicente. In October 1443 he was granted his request under terms which included Sagres, documented thus — `and that he be given by us the said Cape and one League of Limit around it', a grant confirmed by his nephew Dom Afonso V. Taking himself off down to the untamed wilds of Sagres in Algarve, Henry established an observatory and school of navigation, where he devoted time, effort and money into improving navigational aids and boat design. Using revenue from his position as Duke of Viseu, Governor of the Algarve and also Governor of the Order of Christ, he gathered together experts in astronomy and astrology, cartography and geography as well as knowledgeable mariners. His shipyard at Lagos built the boats, from where they set sail, the red Cross of Christ emblem of the Order of Christ prominently displayed on their white sails. Trading gradually took over precedence from crusading as Henry developed a tidy business from financing and equipping excursions down the west coast of Africa.

A huge leap forward came in the form of a new boat, the caravel, which Henry and his team designed and perfected. The caravel's light weight gave it manoeuvrability and speed and its shallow draught the ability to sail close inshore. Another advantage was the need for a smaller crew and thus more storage space for goods.

Under Henry's patronage Gil Eanes, of Lagos, finally passed Cape Bojador on Africa's west coast in 1434, a barrier beyond which 15 earlier expeditions had been too afraid to penetrate. Explorers were encouraged to set up trading posts at each new landing place, where they erected stone pillars (*padrões*) topped by crosses and engraved with the Portuguese coat of arms. They also brought back samples of plant life, fruit and nuts. It was to be a further decade before Gil Eanes returned with the first human cargo of African slaves, which prompted an escalation of trade along the west coast of Africa.

An austere man who shunned worldly pleasures in favour of a monkish existence, Henry remains something of an enigma. His striving after wealth was inconsistent with a frugal personal image — wealth to fuel his life's interest at Sagres seems more probable than personal gain. By the time he died at Sagres in 1460, his expeditions had reached as far as Sierra Leone.

*Beliche Fort*

## The Peninsula

Little imagination is required to appreciate the myth and mystery which has been woven into the fabric of this wild outcrop of land ever since man first ventured here. According to ancient writers, there was a temple on the promontory to the Phoenician god Melqart `king of the city' who was head of the pantheon of gods of Tyre. Melqart was equated with the Greek god Herakles but the temple was supposedly dedicated to Kronos under Greek influence. There is no tangible evidence of the temple but to the Romans the peninsula was their legendary `Promontorium Sacrum' (Sacred Cape). Their belief that it was the end of the earth was probably compounded by larger than life sunsets, experienced when the atmospherics are right, as well as fear of what lay beyond the confines of the Mediterranean and Europe. The most westerly point of the promontory got its present name from a shrine dedicated to São Vicente (St Vincent). Legend relates how, after his martyrdom at Valencia in Spain, the body of São Vicente arrived at the promontory in a boat guided by ravens who stayed to guard the shrine erected over his remains. A more acceptable story is that his body was brought here by citizens of Valencia, escaping persecution by the Caliph of Córdova. They built a stone chapel on the site which was later enlarged by the Visigoths. In 1173, ravens apparently accompanied the ship which transferred São Vicente's relics to Lisbon for safekeeping, which are now in Lisbon cathedral, and the raven figures in the arms of Lisbon and of Vila do Bispo, the local *concelho* (council) of Cabo de São Vicente.

Although the exact location of Henry the Navigator's home is speculative, what evidence there is supports its siting at **Cabo de São Vicente**. A Franciscan convent was founded here by the Bishop of Algarve, Dom Fernando Coutinho, at the time Sagres was elevated to parish status in 1519, but it suffered under Drake's attack of 1587. The castle was later restored by order of Dona Maria I and occupied the tip of the cape where the lighthouse was constructed in 1846. One of the most powerful lighthouses in Europe, it was electrified in 1906 and has a penetrating beam which, if it was not for the curvature of the earth, is reckoned would be seen by shipping some 90km (56 miles) distant. The lighthouse grounds are open for visitors to wander around and, if a keeper is about, climb the 73 steps to the top of the tower to view the 3000 watt lamps. Even without entrance to the lighthouse tower, the sight of creaming foam and curling swell surging 70m (230ft) below is mesmeric. Perhaps an even more amazing sight, especially at weekends, is the mass of extra long fishing rods and their owners all jockeying for a death defying perch on the cliff edge.

## To Aljezur

Just before reaching Vila do Bispo, on the return up the beautiful and remote west coast, a small road off left indicates **Praia do Castelejo**. This is the first of a series of dramatic sandy beaches washed by Atlantic rollers and backed by dunes or cliffs. It is great place to enjoy the natural delights of wide open spaces away from the congested south coast. Peel off left to skirt Vila do Bispo, keeping on the EN268 in the direction of Aljezur. Umbrella pines and eucalyptus line the road through low scrub-covered hills punctuated with occasional clusters of glaringly white hamlets. At **Carrapateira**, a hamlet only slightly touched by tourism, tracks fan off left to the beaches of **Amado**, just after the Escola Primario (primary school) and through the village to the magnificent **Bordeira** beach. Follow the track to rise onto the cliffs from where the thundering surf and superb dune backed beach can be best appreciated. Once past Carrapateira, the countryside mellows and more trees appear in the landscape. The junction with the EN120 is reached at Alfambras where a left turn heads directly to Aljezur. A right turn here connects with Lagos on the coast. On the outskirts of Aljezur, a left turn towards Arrifana on the coast soon divides. Go left for the beach and small fishing harbour of **Arrifana**, where there are facilities and the remains of a 17th-century fortress, but go right to reach the quiet beaches of **Amoreira** and **Monte Clérigo**.

## *Aljezur*

Set strategically inland from the coast, Aljezur is watched over by its ruined castle, the old town clinging snugly to the steep hillside below. Its name stems from the time of the Arab occupation but there was likely habitation on the site before that time. The area has been inhabited since prehistoric times as tombs at the slate mines of Corte Cabreira and at Vidigal copper mines verify. At one time, the Ria de Aljezur was navigable to the town but silted up by the 14th century. Arab rule was ended in 1246, when the distinguished commander Dom Paio Peres Correira captured the castle. As master of the important Order of Santiago he was responsible for much of the reconquest of Algarve. The town was granted a charter in 1280 by Dom Dinis but, tucked away in the hills, Aljezur became effectively a backwater. By the 18th century, mosquitoes breeding on the sluggish river below the town caused frequent malaria epidemics. To circumvent the problem the Bishop of Faro, Dom Francisco Gomes, suggested resiting the town further away from the river. An added impetus for such a move  was probably the 1755 earthquake which badly damaged the town and castle. A new church was built, around which modern Aljezur clusters, but the bishop's plan only partially succeeded as many of the townspeople refused to move.

An agricultural area, Aljezur has the reputation for growing the best sweet potatoes in Portugal which is reflected in the local gastronomy. To drive up to the **castle**, keep ahead through the steep narrow streets to the top, or walk by first following the main road right to cross the river and parking on the left by Turismo. The walk up to the castle through old Aljezur takes in the recon-structed 16th-century pillory, Igreja Misericórdia and the Igreja Matrix. Once up at the castle, its strategic position becomes more obvious as a gap through the band of rolling hills between Aljezur and the sea reveals itself.

*Carrapoteira*

Choices now consist of returning south to Lagos, following the EN120 all the way via the typical Algarvian village of **Bensafrim**, or heading inland to the right of new Aljezur on the EN267 to Monchique. The 15km stretch of road from Aljezur to Marmelete has been completed for a number of years but has not yet found its way on to many maps. This route rises to follow along a ridge of hills and makes a superb alternative run back to the coast. Northwards continues up the EN120 to Odeceixe on the Algarve Alentejo border and another quiet beach.

# Practical Information

## *Hotels and Restaurants*

### ALJEZUR
**Hotel Vale da Telha** (tel. 082 981 80). Facilities include a pool, tennis, shooting and horse riding. No restaurant.

### LUZ
Apart from hotel below, accommodation in villas and apartments.
**Hotel Belavista da Luz** (tel. 082 788 655 and fax 788 656). Four-star luxury at a reasonable price. Restaurant with excellent menu open lunch and dinner to non-residents. Heated outdoor pool, gymnasium, tennis and health club.
**Residencial Vilamar**, Estrada do Burgau 10 (tel. 082 789 541). Three-star open 1/5–31/10. Restaurant/bar.

**SAGRES**
**Pousada do Infante** (tel. 082 642 22). Pool and restaurant.
**Fortaleza do Beliche** (tel. 082 641 24). An annexe of Pousada do Infante.
Only four rooms with good restaurant.
**Hotel Apartamento O Navigante** (tel. 082 643 54). Three-star but many facilities including a pool, squash and bar/café/restaurant.

**SALEMA**
**Estalagem Infante do Mar** (tel. 082 651 37). Restaurant and pool.
**Hotel Salema** (tel. 082 653 28). Three-star with a bar.
**Casa Grande, Burgau** (tel. 082 694 16). Restaurant in an old winery in 1900s Portuguese Mansion. Home cooking including vegetarian.
**The Fortaleza Restaurant, Luz** (tel. 082 789 926). Good Portuguese cuisine with English and French highlights, lunch and dinner.
**Restaurant Golf St. António, Parque da Floresta Golf & Country Club, Budens** (tel. 082 653 33). Comprehensive menu.
**Rios Negros, Vale de Boi** (tel. 082 653 30). Traditional Portuguese cooking.
**A Tasca, Sagres** (tel. 082 641 77). A popular fish restaurant.
**Telheiro do Infante, Praia da Mareta, Sagres** (tel. 082 641 79). Wonderful views of cape. Fish with shellfish a speciality from owner's own nursery. Closed Tuesdays.
**O Tiago, Budens** (tel. 082 650 81). Café/restaurant. Tempting no-frills menu in homely surrounds.
**Tinkerbell's, Raposeira** (tel. 082 664 40). On EN125 3km after Figueira on right. Old Portuguese cooking.

## Sports and Leisure

**Hotel Belavista da Luz** (tel. 082 788 655). Health Club, tennis and gym.
**Burgau Sports Centre** (tel. 082 693 50). Wide range of facilities.

### Fishing
**Rios Negros Restaurant, Vale de Boi** (tel. 082 653 30 after 6.30pm Tues–Sat).
Small groups taken out by owner.

### Golf
**Parque da Floresta Golf and Country Club**, Budens (tel. 082 653 33/4). 18 holes, buggies for hire.

### Horse Riding
**Atalaia Equestrian Academy**, Quinta do Monte Bravo, Lagos (tel. 082 761 921). 5 minutes along EN125 towards Sagres.
**QPA Riding Centre**, Fronteira, Bensafrim (tel. 082 672 63 & 675 07).

### Wild Life Tours
**West Algarve Equestrian Centre**, Burgau (tel. 082 691 52). Full and half-day field trips, Algarve & Alentejo Plains with John and Madge Measures.

## *Tourist Offices (Turismo)*

**Regional Office of Algarve**, Avenida 5 de Outubro,  8000 Faro. Tel. 089 800 400, fax. 089 800 489.

**Tourism Posts**
Aljezur (8670), Largo do Mercado (tel. 082 982 29).

# 9. TOWNS AND VILLAGES OF THE BARROCAL

Stretching across much of central Algarve is a region of limestone known as the Barrocal. It provides some of the best farming land in the region which over time has attracted scores of farming settlements now grown into villages and some into important agricultural towns. Although the Barrocal is vague and without clear boundaries, especially to the south, looking at the concentration of inland villages on a map gives a fair indication of the area. The northern boundary is edged sharply by an abrupt change to stony, infertile soils with the consequence that, apart from Monchique, there are no major towns or villages lying north of the Barrocal.

A crude guide to the southern limits is the EN125, the road which divides Algarve as surely as a boundary divides two countries. Concentrated to the south are all the resorts and associated developments which absorb the vast bulk of visitors whilst, to the north, there is space and countryside where almonds blossom, the farmers farm and the villagers watch the world go by. These villages of the Barrocal are the custodians of Algarve's culture and, apart from Silves and Monchique, are little visited by tourists. They have no great monuments of interest and lack sophistication but they have a country way of life which has changed little over decades. Farming subsidies are forcing the pace of change and traditional farming tools and methods, like the horse drawn plough, are giving way to mechanisation, but the old face of Algarve is still around in the smaller villages. Although farming is extensive, not all the landscape is shaped by the farmers and there are untamed areas of scrubland *matos*, where wild flowers abound in spring. There are limestone ridges too near Pena and Alte which defy the farmer and offer good walking opportunities.

The route described omits Silves and Monchique which are the subject of Chapter 10 but concentrates on central Algarve and includes the major towns and a selection of the more attractive or interesting smaller villages. This tour may require more than one day but nowhere is too far away in Algarve so it is easy to break off and return to complete the tour another day.

*Basket maker, Fonte de Benémola*

## Estói

Estói, just north of Faro, is the starting point and easily reached from east or west by using the IP1. Not all days are the same in Estói, the second Sunday of the month is special, it is market day. Estói hosts the biggest and best market in Algarve. It is more than a market, it is a country fair and a day out for the local families who may arrive in a pony and trap or one of the traditional high-wheeled carts.

Proud of its market, Estói seems blissfully unaware of the other treasures within its boundaries. One of these is a remarkable derelict baroque **palace** which was once the home of the Carvalhal family. Built in the 18th century with later additions, it is a fantasy creation of various architectural styles where baroque, neo-classic and rococo styles blend harmoniously. Only the grounds are available for inspection since the house is in a state of decay and closed to the public, although plans are afoot for the restoration of its 28 rooms. The iron gates just north of Estói centre mark the entrance to the estate and, if the personal gate is open, there is no charge to wander in the grounds. A palm shaded avenue leads past stables, now a study centre, towards the terrace in front of the house to enjoy a first taste of the exuberant artwork around the gardens. A voluptuous marble lady drapes herself around a poly-chrome *azulejo* fountain, a theme mirrored on the other side of an assemb-lage of yet more marble ladies. Sweeping balustrades lead down either side to a lower part of the garden and a chapel guarded by an iron grill to protect a statue of the three graces, a replica of Canova's work, which may yet prove to be the work of the same sculptor. Venus and Diana also share the chapel.

*Estói Palace*

The theme of nubile nymphs is maintained in the blue and white *azulejo* panels which decorate the area but busts of prominent people, including the poet Milton, are scattered about keeping a sober eye on events. Climbing the steps from the terrace to the upper level is the nearest approach to the palace itself but the iron railed gate allows a clear view.

Heading west out of the centre leads to Estói's other treasure, the ruins of a 2nd–6th century Roman villa, **Milreu**. Free access is allowed to the protected site during opening hours and an information sheet, available in English at a small charge, shows the ground plan of this peristyle Roman villa and offers some detailed explanation. The striking building with the circular apse on the south of the site was originally a water sanctuary, a nympheum, of the late Roman period before it was converted by the Visigoths into a church complete with baptismal font. No self-respecting Roman villa was complete without its own baths and the baths area here occupied a suite of rooms including a furnace room to heat the water and changing rooms. The smaller basin entered by steps and decorated with a fish mosaic is thought to be for the ladies. There are other mosaics around although some are covered with sand for protection. Finds from the site have been distributed around various museums including those at Faro and Lagos.

## Moncarapacho

Leave Estói heading eastwards first on the Olhão road but taking the left turn to Moncarapacho. Not too much happens in Moncarapacho but the main square offers some parking if the Renaissance doors of the parish church beg

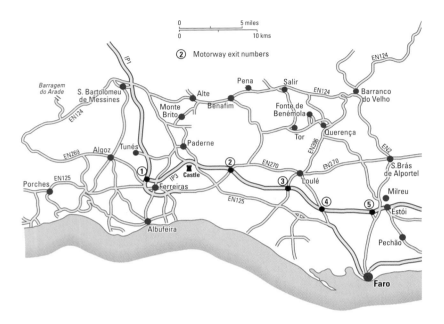

inspection. There is a small museum here of sacred art with a touch of archaeological interest which is the passion of the local priest. Its opening days are limited to Monday, Wednesday and Friday from 11am to 3pm. The focal point of interest in this area is not so much the town but the nearby mountain, **Cerro de São Miguel**, which has the distinction of being the highest point around. Leave Moncarapacho on the Santa Catarina road and look shortly for a left turn which leads through almond and olive groves initially in a winding ascent to the scrub covered summit. It is ruined as a beauty spot by the over-rich garnishing of unsightly aerials but the views from this elevation (410m/1345ft) are extensive, particularly down towards the coast.

## São Brás

The onward route to the next destination, São Brás, leads through Santa Catarina which is the home of the Colina da Rosa Country Club for tennis, squash, swimming and snooker. São Brás, or to use its full name, São Brás de Alportel, is very much a rural town which busies itself with agricultural activities but it is worth a stop to visit its **ethnographical museum** at 61 Rua Dr José Dias Sancho. Housed in an old mansion, the museum has corridors and alcoves filled with farming equipment, kitchen utensils and traditional costumes. If it is time for coffee and cakes, try the almond cakes, a local

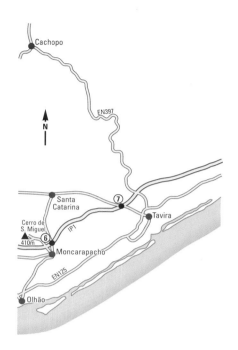

speciality, at *Chaplins café* on Avenida da Liberdade. Continuing westwards, ribbon development along the road hides the almond groves from view which are at their very best when in blossom in February.

## Loulé

Loulé, the next stop en route, is the largest inland town in Algarve and a centre famous for its handicrafts. Occupied by both the Romans and the Moors, Loulé's castle is believed to be of Moorish origin although it was rebuilt in the 13th century. Only a few remnants of the walls and castle remain although they now provide an august home for the Turismo office found on Rua Paio Perez Correira. Next to Turismo is a new museum, the latest in a line of small museums which seem to be sprouting up throughout Algarve, and this one sets out to display a traditional kitchen filled with pots and pans. In the same street as Turismo is the small church of **Nossa Senhora da Conceição** with a simple exterior which belies a very elaborate interior. A brown door opens into a tiny chapel filled with blue and white *azulejo* tiles depicting biblical scenes which contrast sharply with the heavily carved and gilded altarpiece. From here a wander around some of the narrow cobbled streets of the old centre to the south reveals dimly lit workshops where artisans are busy creating articles in copper, leather, cane and an assortment of other materials all of which are offered for sale. The town's tradition for handicrafts is as old as the castle itself.

Saturday morning finds Loulé in a bit of a fever, with the local traders setting up the weekly market around the Moorish municipal **market** building off Largo Gago Coutinho and filling the streets with anything from pumpkins to young chicks. Early morning is when the locals do their shopping before the loaded coaches arrive to spill out tourists by the hundreds. The goods are cheap enough on the market but for quality head down the main **Praça da Republica** to window shop in the boutiques. If Loulé is all a bit overpowering then relax beneath the palms in the **Jardim dos Amuados** next to Largo da Matriz, south of Praça da Republica, and wonder how it came by the name 'Sulky People's Garden'.

Festival time leading up to Lent is taken more seriously by the people of Loulé than perhaps anywhere else in Algarve and for five days they really let their hair down. Street parades, floats, fancy dress, masks and dancing are all part of the celebrations which draw in visitors from throughout Algarve. It is also a time for pranks and these jolly folk delight in hitting each other with plastic hammers; flour bombs and sometimes paint are thrown at indiscriminate targets, usually failing to discriminate between one pretty girl and the next!

## Country Fairs and Markets

Almost every town in Algarve has a municipal market which is open weekday mornings and where locally grown produce is on sale. Many towns also have a market where traders move in to set up stalls for the day and where a much wider range of goods is on sale. Those close to centres of tourism have been hijacked to a large extent by traders who are interested in selling goods to tourists. Away in the smaller towns, the market is an occasion of great excitement for the locals, not just as a social event, but for the opportunity to buy clothes, household goods and perhaps a hen or two which is denied to them for the rest of the month.

Some of the bigger markets traditionally include animals such as horses, cows and goats and these, particularly Estói, have developed into country fairs full of the smells of cooking bacon, the tinkling of beer glasses and the sound of cow bells. Bargains are struck, deals are made in the temporary bars and eating places, while the women finger dress materials, ponder over the dishes of olives or buy up the week's fruit and vegetables. It is a bustling atmosphere alive with interest and where the die hard habits and customs of country folk can be observed which might sometimes surprise and sometimes even shock.

Conveniently, the markets follow a regular timetable and some of the important ones are listed below.

**Weekly**: Saturday: Loulé, São Bras de Alportal. Wednesday: Quarteira

**Fortnightly**: Albufeira, 1st and 3rd Tuesdays in the month. Armação de Pêra 1st and 3rd Thursday

**Monthly**:

1st Sunday: Almansil, Moncarapacho
1st Monday: Portimão
1st Friday: Sagres
1st Saturday: Lagos, Paderne
2nd Sunday: Estói, Lagoa
2nd Monday; Algoz
2nd Friday: Monchique
3rd Monday: Silves
3rd Thursday: Alte
4th Monday: Messines
4th Saturday: Tunes

*The Querença sausage festival*

## Querença

Leave Loulé on the Querença road (N396) to plunge back into the country-side. The road by-passes Querença so two left turns are necessary to enter the village. In contrast to Loulé, Querença is made for relaxing and the village square has that inviting ambience where the only natural thing to do is join the locals at one of the café tables to watch the world go by. Should sustenance be needed, the *Restaurant Bar de Querença,* with its upstairs dining room, has a reputation for good food which draws an evening clientele from miles around. The village can lay claim to one of the most unlikely festivals in Algarve, a sausage festival which is held at the end of January. It starts, as all good festivals do, in church and here a procession emerges from the portals of the 16th century parish church in the square to parade a statue of São Luís to the music of Loulé's silver band. The sausages do not really get hot until the evening when serious enjoyment starts.

Near to Querença, at **Fonte de Benémola**, is a popular circular walk which is a fraction over 3.5km (2 miles) and is comfortably completed in the hour. Details are given in the feature box p 136.

## Salir

From Querença return to the N396 and continue northwards to pick up the N124 and follow signs to Salir. An undulating but good road leads through a varied landscape with views towards the northern serras. Leave the road to motor into Salir but expect to park below the main village. The town square, looked on by the church, occupies a prime position right on the summit and is the natural gathering place for the townsfolk, especially with a café on hand. Spectacular views over the northern countryside usually tip the scales in favour of lingering for refreshments, especially if children are in the party, for behind the church is a small park with seating and a play area. Salir was once a Moorish stronghold complete with a castle but this has long since fallen into ruin although some parts of the walls still remain and can be found to the west of the square. Of particular interest is the building material favoured particularly by the Moors known as *taipa* which is made up from clay, sand, straw and water and used to build the castle walls, although it is sometimes seen in walls forming field boundaries.

## Fonte de Benémola Walk

This is a short, circular walk just a fraction over 3.5km (2 miles) long taking around about an hour if not too many distractions are encountered on the way. As a source of spring water the *fonte* is very popular with the locals who are usually there patiently filling a selection of plastic bottles. It is not unusual to find the village ladies washing out sausage skins in the river, especially if the sausage festival is looming! To find the start, head up the N396 from Loulé to pass Querença by turning left following signs to Torr and picking up signs to Fonte de Benémola. Park by the deserted house at the start of the track on the right.

Follow the track upstream along the side of a shallow valley between scrubland on one side and cultivation on the other. In spring time there is a good selection of wild flowers along the way, including flowers like the cheerful yellow *Anemone palmata* and orchids like the sombre bee orchid, *Ophrys fusca*.

A wooden bridge in the area of the *fonte* provides a crossing place for the return leg on the other side of the river. Part way down the track on this side, a basket maker has a rustic workshop and he is often there hand-making delightful baskets in all shapes and sizes. Check the prices, he offers the best bargains in Algarve. Turn left on meeting the road to cross the bridge over the river, watch out for kingfishers, and return shortly to the car.

## *Alte*

Beyond Salir, the road continues to pass the small village of Pena lying at the foot of a dominant limestone ridge which offers opportunities for both walkers and climbers. Watery Alte, the most visited of all the villages in the Barrocal, is the next stopping place. This pretty village is famous for the quality of its spring waters which have drawn the Portuguese here over centuries, long before its discovery by tourists. Leave the car in the area of the fountains on the eastern edge of town as Alte's narrow cobbled streets are best explored on foot. Starting with the fountain area, the first encountered, **Fonte das Bicas**, is backed by an attractive blue and white *azulejo* panel showing a monk and a girl at the well. Beyond, the road follows along the river to the **Fonte Grande** which has a number of springs and where a mill has been converted into a restaurant. The whole area is a popular picnic spot with rustic bridges, leafy willows, walled seats and picnic tables. Heading westwards, cobbled streets lead between trim flower decked, whitewashed houses into the village and to the parish church with its 16th-century Manueline portal. Cafés, as well as handicraft shops, take advantage of the passing tourist trade.

---

## Farming in Algarve

Although farming in Algarve has been a principal occupation down the centuries, the land is worked only in small plots and by a vast number of families working for themselves who generally have no need to employ labour. At harvest times when there may be extra work, members of the extended family lend a hand or the village community helps out. The use of machinery is increasing but only in a small way since its application is limited by the small size of the farms.

Traditional farming has made good use of drought resistant fruit trees and relied on cereal and vegetable crops grown beneath. Such fruit trees include almond, fig, olive, carob and vines which are widespread throughout Algarve although there is generally a greater concentration of them in the *sotovento*, the leeward eastern side. Fruit farming, once a success story, is no longer producing the valuable exports it once did. Visitors in January and February are delighted by the sight of many thousands of almonds trees in bloom, perhaps not thousands but millions for in the 1960s there were reckoned to be over four million. Not all the trees flower at exactly the same time since there are two basic types, those with hard shells and those with soft shells, and there are a range of varieties grown. The nuts are harvested around the end of August when they are knocked down from the trees with sticks. A further drying period is required to help with the removal of the outer husk which, by August, has usually split with the heat of the sun. The nuts are extracted from the shells by machine. Almonds (*amêndoas*) became a significant export industry for Algarve around the turn of the 20th century but in latter years the trade has dwindled to virtually nothing in the face of more intensive cultivation methods employed in other countries, especially California, and from the lack of new plantings to replace old trees.

It is a similar story with figs (*ficos*). Figs have played a significant role in feeding Mediterranean people for thousands of years, providing fresh fruit in the summer and dried fruit for the rest of the year. A number of different varieties is grown in Algarve of which some mature in May–June whilst others are harvested in August–September. Figs for drying are laid out on cane mats in the sun and turned daily until the process is complete by which time green figs have turned brown and the blue ones almost black. There was a time when Portuguese figs were considered the finest available but Turkey has gradually taken over Algarve's traditional markets in Europe and America and by the mid 1970s Algarve's export trade had dwindled to insignificant.

The story is similar for olives (*azeitonas*) too, with declining production, particularly in the last 25 years, but perhaps for a different combination of reasons. Government price controls failed to reward the growers sufficiently, increasing land use for tourism, especially in the coastal areas has been responsible for the decline in the number of olive trees, as with other fruit trees, and problems with pests and diseases have seriously reduced the quality.

Citrus fruit, on the other hand, is a growth industry. It is crop which requires irrigation but has been grown in the province for centuries, mostly around Silves. Now, with the completion of large reservoirs in the early 1970s and the technology and power to sink deeper bore-holes, a considerable expansion has taken place and citrus fruits are widely grown throughout much of the region with new plantations appearing annually. They will grow anywhere which is frost free and preferably free of strong winds which excludes the most westerly of the province. Algarve is a great place to be in April when the heady scent from the waxy white blossom fills the air. Oranges are the most important of the citrus crops and a great number of varieties are grown to spread the supply throughout the season. Varieties such as 'Newhall' are amongst the earliest which fruit from October through to January when the main crop variety 'Baia' is ready which keeps supplies going until the lates take over to ensure a flow of oranges through until June. Mandarins and clementines are also widely grown as are lemons but grapefruit production is insignificant.

Farming with animals too is important in the province and few farms are without livestock. Goats in larger flocks often tend to be farmed in open scrubland which provides suitable grazing and are mostly seen inland around Monchique, Loulé and Castro Marim. Their milk is used for cheese-making and their meat is appreciated throughout Portugal. Sheep are just about as widely kept but with most farms owning just a small number. The same pattern of animal husbandry is also observed with cows and pigs which are also popular.

*Milreu*

## To Paderne

Side roads provide an interesting route onwards through pleasant countryside and small villages to Paderne. Maps generally fail to show the way with clarity but the following details should help. Start by heading back eastwards from Alte but take the first narrow but surfaced road on the right which heads for Monte Brito. This route leads first through a shallow valley to a fork reached about 1.6km (1 mile) later where it is necessary to stay right. Care is needed when Monte Brito is reached for the road turns sharp left on a blind corner and care is needed again at the next junction where the road joining from the right has priority although the road markings are fairly obscure. Keep straight on here but turn right at the next junction and left again shortly to head into Paderne. On entering Paderne, turn right with the traffic flow and right again on joining the main Boliqueime–Purgatorio road. For the castle, turn left just past the cemetery and either park in the *fonte* area, reached shortly, and proceed on foot to enjoy a 30 minute walk, or drive the rough but stable tracks all the way to the castle.

Paderne **castle** now stands in ruins but it occupies a romantic position on a hill surrounded on three sides by the Ribeira Quarteira. It was built in the time of the Moors but captured during 1249 when Algarve was finally regained by the Portuguese in the reign of Afonso III. Now only the outer walls remain to hint of its past glory but a chapel inside dedicated to Our Lady of Ascension suggests that the castle was restored and remained in use for some centuries after its capture. Traces of a plaster frieze inside the chapel are thought to be from the 16th century. The chapel side of the castle looks down over a medieval arched bridge built on Roman foundations arising from

139

the time when the river was once navigable. By this bridge are the remains of an old water mill as there are by the river on the other side of the castle.

The N270 from Paderne leads south back towards the IP1 and Albufeira, a convenient distribution point for all parts of Algarve, and to the conclusion of this tour.

# Practical Information

## *Hotels and Restaurants*

See the introduction for further details about houses in the Turismo Rural (TR) and Agroturismo (AT) schemes.

### ALTE
**Alte Hotel**, Montinho, Alte (tel. 089 68 523). A modern low-rise three-star hotel in country location. Offers a high standard of accommodation, 24 rooms and two suites all with private facilities. Swimming pool, tennis courts, gardens and a shuttle bus to the beach.
**Casa de Alte**, Largo de Igreja (TR) (tel. 089 684 826). Centrally situated, this five-roomed house is part of the Turismo Rural scheme but has limited facilities.

### ESTÓI
**O Branquinho**, Estói. Small restaurant, typically Portuguese and inexpensive.
**Restaurant O Familiar**, Coiro da Burra, Estói (tel. 089 91 440). Strong on grills but also regional dishes, moderately priced. Folk singers on Sundays. **Monte do Casal**, Cerro do Lobo (tel. 089 91 503). Situated between Estói and Moncarapacho, this international restaurant has been converted from an old coach house and is highly rated throughout Algarve. It has a great many palette ticklers including mousseline of crayfish wrapped in smoked salmon, but take a loaded credit card.

### LOULÉ
**Loulé Jardim Hotel**, Praça Manuel de Arriaga (tel. 089 413 095). Quality accommodation in modern three-star hotel situated close to the heart of town. Swimming pool.
**Restaurant Avenida Velha**, 40 Av. Jose Costa Mealha, Loulé (tel. 089 416 735). Excellent food from a Portuguese menu at moderate prices.
**Casa dos Arcos**, 23–25 Rua Sá de Miranda, Loulé (tel. 089 416 713). Good for both seafood and meat dishes and at reasonable prices.
**Bica Velha**, 17–19 Rua Martim Moniz, Loulé (tel. 089 633 376). A restaurant of good reputation, fine food but expensive.
**Aux Bons Enfantes**, 116 Rua Eng. Duarte Pacheco, Loulé (tel. 098 620 096). A French restaurant which serves excellent food but on the expensive side.

## MONCARAPACHO

**A Caravela**, Rua D. Maria Purificação Palermo. Located a short distance out of Moncarapacho on the Tavira road, this restaurant is run by a Portuguese couple who have lived in the USA and know how to blend Portuguese food to European tastes. Good food at moderate prices.

## QUERENÇA

**Quinta da Várzea** (AT) (tel. 089 414 443). Located on country estate just north of Querença, this Quinta offers nine rooms with lounge, dining room and swimming pool. There is also the opportunity for guests to participate in some of the estate activities, like cheese-making.

**Restaurant de Querença.** Upstairs dining room serves specialities including wild boar and venison, moderately priced.

**Quinta de Olival**, Querença (tel. 089 62 969). Good local specialities but a little on the expensive side.

## SANTA BÁRBARA DE NEXE

**Hotel Apartments La Reserve** (tel. 089 904 749). Small, quality four-star hotel in a huge estate with good facilities including restaurant, swimming pool and tennis courts; expensive.

## SÃO BRÁS DE ALPORTAL

**Pousada de São Brás** (tel. 089 842 305). Located just above the town with 23 rooms, swimming pool and tennis court. Newly renovated in 1995.

# Places of Interest

**Estói Palace.** Open 9–12 noon and 2–5pm, closed Sundays and holidays.
**Milreu Roman Ruins.** Open 10–12 noon and 2–5pm, closed Mondays.
**Loulé museum**, Rua D. Paio Peres Correira. Open 9am–12.30pm and 2–5.30pm, closed Saturday and Sunday.
**Moncarapacho museum.** Open Monday, Wednesday and Friday 11am–3pm.

# Sports and Leisure

**Colina da Rosa Country Club**, Santa Catarina (tel. 081 971 469). Offers tennis, squash, swimming, snooker and bridge.

# Tourist Offices (Turismo)

**Regional Office of Algarve**, Avenida 5 de Outubro, 8000 Faro. Tel. 089 800 400, fax. 089 800 489.

**Tourism Posts**
Loulé (8100) Edifêcio do Castelo (tel. 089 639 00).
São Brás de Alportel (8150) Rua Dr Evaristo Gago, 1 (tel. 089 842 211).

# 10. SILVES AND SERRA DE MONCHIQUE

## Silves

Silves, Algarve's only truly historic town, and the heights of Monchique exert sufficient attraction to draw tourists away from the beaches and the poolside and they are close enough to be included together in a day's tour. Unfortunately, the coach tour operators take the same view so these places suffer an ebb and flow of visitors but early or late in the day finds them a little quieter.

The best way to approach Silves by road to see the clustered white houses on the hilltop huddled within the old town walls under the powerful dominance of the red sandstone castle, is from the east, from Algoz. Just on the descent towards Silves there is a large pull-off on the right in just about the optimum position for absorbing this daunting view, at least daunting to any would-be invader. Approaching from the south, from Lagoa, also gives a good view on the immediate approach but it is worth the short diversion up the Algoz road to enjoy the best overview. Just after crossing the bridge to enter Silves there is a large parking area, although it is not always easy to find a place, and there is a second area for parking on the riverside just to the west, along the Monchique road.

Silves has been around for a long time, its origins clouded in misty uncertainty, but various finds from the neolithic period and the Bronze Age suggest settlement well before the Romans and probably as early as 900 BC in Phoenician times. A navigable river inland to a secure position with an easily defended hill was attraction enough for the early settlers but it was likely that there were also metal ores around and the mine opened on the top of the hill — now known as the Dog's Cistern — in the castle, can be traced back to the late neolithic period. Coins found in Silves bearing the word Cylpes are of pre-Roman origin, from 206–40 BC, and are thought to have been minted in Silves by a Celtic-Cylpense tribe. By the time the Romans arrived, it is probable that some fortification around the hilltop already existed which they adopted and strengthened to make Silves into an important centre.

*Silves from the south*

Under the Arabs, Chelb (Silves) developed into an important maritime trading centre with ships busily loading cargoes of oranges, lemons, figs, fish, timber and cork at the river quayside. For a time it became capital of Algarve, with sumptuous buildings as well as a fine castle, although the Arab period was not one of great unity. Silves first came to greatness under Prince Bakr ben Yahka who came from Santa Maria (later Faro) to set up a Council of State with a large armed force. Later Banu Muzain, head of an independent dynasty, became the ruler but, in 1053, Silves was conquered by another faction led by Al Mutamid, King of Seville. It was held for only a short time before Banu Muzain moved to recover it, only to lose it again after a long siege in 1063. When Al Mutamid died, his son, also Al Mutamid, took charge and installed locally born Ibn Amar, a governor who also later distinguished himself as a great Islamic poet. Most of the inhabitants of Silves were originally from Yemen and spoke pure Arabic. They revelled in this opulent city of fine houses and bazaars which attracted men of culture, including writers and poets. Often against their will, the people of Silves were drawn into petty squabbles which arose and intensified in the final period of Arab domination. Turbulence followed when the Almoravids from North Africa captured much of Andalucia and Silves to bring an end to the period of autonomous administrative districts which had given Silves so much freedom. A further unsettled period followed with frequently changing leaders but eventually the Almohads, fierce enemies of the Almoravids, took the town of Silves.

By the time the Almohads had finished strengthening the towers and walls of the castle they were yielding to the forces of Don Sancho I supported by some notable Crusaders including King Richard the Lion-Heart and King

143

Philip II of France. It was no easy victory for the Muslims fought with great tenacity and were beaten eventually on 3 September 1189 by thirst. Dom Sancho then took the title of King of Portugal and Silves. However, the Almohads came back with a vengeance and, on 20 June 1191, they recaptured the town. War torn and damaged, Silves was never again to enjoy its former power and prosperity. Enormous efforts were made by the Almohads to restore Silves but it placed a heavy burden of taxation on the people. By 1230, the Almohads themselves had given way to a new Arab faction ruled by Ibn Afan who united Algarve with southern Spain. This proved insignificant since, in 1242, Silves finally and irrevocably fell to the Portuguese as did Faro and Algarve as a whole in 1249.

Disentangling Algarve from the grip of Spain caused some initial problems. Infante Don Alfonso of Castile, who in 1252 became King Alfonso X, claimed that the lands had been given to him by Ibn Mahfot. An intervention in 1253 by Pope Innocent IV brought peace and a family alliance with the marriage of Dom Afonso III to Dona Beatrice, daughter of Alfonso X. Under this agreement, Portugal gained clear sovereignty of Algarve although Alfonso X retained the usufruct, the right to use and gain profit from it. This arrangement, fraught with irritations, lasted only until 1264 when a new settlement was reached by which Alfonso X relinquished usufruct.

Although Silves was rebuilt and its fortifications restored, it never regained its former glory. In time, the River Arade silted up, restricting shipping to smaller vessels which transferred maritime trade away from Silves to Portimão at the mouth of the river. A series of earthquakes, six in the 14th century, more in the 16th century and two particularly severe ones in 1722 and 1755 reduced Silves almost to rubble, to nothing more than a village of some 200 inhabitants. The castle walls, a vibrant reminder of an illustrious past, remained impregnable throughout.

## The Town

A good place to start a tour is down by the waterfront. Arching the river here is a graceful **medieval bridge** by the riverside quay. It is believed to have been built over a similar Roman structure. It no longer looks over a raging river or ships arriving from foreign destinations but over a sleepy tidal river bringing the occasional pleasure cruise from Portimão. Opposite the quay is the **market hall** which teems with locals buying oranges and cabbage or whatever is in season. This market, one of the best municipal markets in the province, reflects the fact that Silves is now a busy agricultural town and the centre of the citrus industry. Steep cobbled streets lie ahead from here to explore the rest of the town. Set off up Rua Francisco Pablos by the market to join Rua 25 Abril where a right turn leads past Turismo into the main square, **Praça do Municipio**. Here, on the Italian-like piazza, is where the locals, and the tourists, gather at shaded tables to drink coffee and watch the world go by.

On the far side of the square, the inviting gateway in the stone tower, Torreão das Portas da Cidade, which was part of the old city walls leads into Rua de Se. It is another uphill climb along a narrow street bounded by balconied white houses to reach the cathedral. Catching the eye first is the raised Manueline doorway to the Misericórdia church opposite the cathedral, purposely raised to accept coffins directly from the back of a cart. The **cathedral** itself was built on the site of a Moorish mosque and building was probably started by Alfonso X, King of Castile, in the period when Castile laid claim to Algarve following the expulsion of the Moors, although it was possibly finished under Afonso III. Earthquakes and neglect left their mark and this Gothic style cathedral required several restorations. The last major restoration, after the earthquake of 1755, effectively ruined the architectural unity and elegance of the building. Silves remained a bishopric only until 1579 after which time the see was transferred to Faro.

On entering the cathedral, beware of unofficial guides who expect payment. Inside, the beautiful Gothic chancel contrasts markedly with the gauche baroque rebuilding of the nave completed after the 1755 earthquake. Dom João II was buried here after his death in Alvor in 1495 but four years later his body was transferred to Batalha although a stone remains. There are various tombs belonging to bishops but there are two friends of Henry the Navigator buried here in a side chapel to the right of the main entrance. Baroque carved and gilded woodwork is seen in the side altars and the apse contains some curious gargoyles.

Continuing uphill from the cathedral leads to the red sandstone **castle**. Waiting to greet visitors is Dom Sancho I clasping an unsheathed sword as he must have appeared when he took Silves from the Moors in 1189. The steps beyond lead up to the southern rampart and from here it is possible to walk around the full perimeter of the walls passing the various turrets and towers while enjoying spectacular views over the surrounding countryside. On the north side lies the true keep, a tower named after Aben Afan, which faces north from where most attacks on the castle were mounted. Within the interior of the castle lies the **Cisterna da Moura Encantada**, Cistern of the Enchanted Moorish Girl, which is of uncertain origin. Part of the vaulted ceiling can be seen above ground but below is a huge hall, 18m (55ft) long and 14.5m (47ft) wide, with a ceiling made up of three vaults supported by pillars, and it is still used for water storage. Apart from some excavations which seem constantly ongoing, the other point of interest is the **Cisterna dos Cães** (Dog's Cistern) over on the west side of the interior. Protected by a grill, this shaft is a former mine exploited by both the Romans and the Moors although there is a popular belief that it led to a subterranean passageway giving access to the river.

Leaving the castle by the same gate, the only one now in use, turn left down steps to the terrace of *Café Inglês* beneath the castle walls. Whilst the terrace itself has a pleasing ambience, the roof garden enjoys an excellent perspective of both the castle walls and the cathedral. It offers home made food, including English cakes, whilst a speciality worth trying is the chocolate desert, St Emillion, which blends brandy and almonds to great effect.

*Silves, Praça do Municipio*

Three series of fortifications defended Silves under the Moors, the castle, the Almedina walls and the outer Arrabalde walls. Parts of the Almedina walls are still intact — best appreciated from the viewpoints to the south of town — but a good section of wall with towers can be seen west of the town hall. Nothing now remains of the Arrabalde walls.

Torreão das Portas da Cidade, by Praça do Municipio, once held a small **museum** but this has transferred to a fine modern building especially constructed around an old Moorish **well** on Rua das Portas, reached from the main square by heading east through the tower gateway and turning right. There are some archaeological artefacts displayed with information only in Portuguese but the main feature is the old well. One final monument but barely worth a special detour, is the **Cruz de Portugal**. This elaborate Gothic cross lies east of the main town on the road of the same name and is protected by a canopy. Its history is unclear but it is thought to have been brought from the north of the country. The base carries a date of 1025 which suggests that it was erected on an Arab plinth.

Orange groves dominate the scenery on leaving Silves towards Monchique. Traditionally, Silves has always been at the heart of the citrus fruit industry but with increasing facilities for irrigation (see feature p 150) oranges are now widespread throughout the province.

## Caldas de Monchique

Deeply incised valleys and tree cloaked hills dominate the landscape as the road twists its way up towards Monchique. Forget Monchique for a moment,

*Even road names appear in azulejo*

the centuries old atmospheric spa town of Caldas de Monchique beckons first. It lies in a green and wooded valley just below a crook in the main road, although little of it is visible from the road. The Romans were here, enjoying the pleasantly warm spa waters (32°C) and curing their rheumatism and respiratory problems and it has been famous for that ever since. Dom João II came here in 1495 to bathe in the waters hoping it would cure his dropsy but died shortly afterwards in Alvor. The spa is still running but under state control and the clinic for the treatment of patients opens from mid-June through until autumn. There are springs besides and locals queue most days with a battery of plastic bottles to fill them patiently from the slow but constant dribble of water whilst the more productive springs are monopolised by the water bottling plant. While the waters are an attraction for some, thousands more visit simply to enjoy the ambience. A smattering of Edwardian style buildings beneath leafy slopes, a peaceful shady square to drink coffee, bars and hand-icraft shops fit harmoniously in this cosy spa town. To sample the verdancy of the wooded valley, head to the south of the village until the incongruous bottling plant is reached, which takes all of five minutes, and descend the cobbled steps to the left to join the riverside. A path follows along the river in this narrow, leafy valley to various picnic places, but it is a linear walk so the return is by the same route. If stimulating refreshment is in order, try the local firewater called *medronho* which is made from the fruit of the strawberry tree (see box p 149).

The journey from Caldas to Monchique is quite short but it brings into focus the importance of the lovely blue seyenite granite which is quarried exten-sively around here and is even exported to Japan. One important feature of

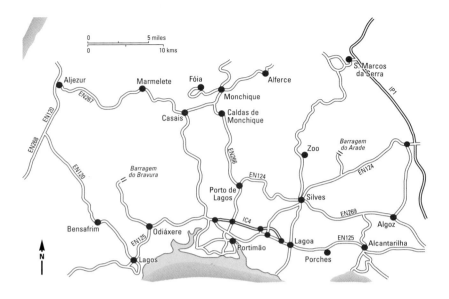

this granite is that it responds well to the hammer and chisel and can be cleanly cut and worked to shape.

## *Monchique*

Monchique itself is something of a curiosity and many visitors wonder why it figures so strongly on the tourist trail. The big attraction is the nearby mountain peak of Fóia and Monchique happens to be the village at the foot of the mountain which interests visitors simply because of its high location. Realising that its popularity is not likely to disappear overnight, Monchique is coming to terms with its flood of tourists and has introduced a one-way system to ease traffic flow and has made some car parking space, mostly through the village just along on the Fóia road.

The main town square, **Largo 5 de Outubro**, complete with bus station and fire brigade is a dull affair despite the water feature recently constructed but it is worth a brief stop to wander the narrow cobbled streets radiating out from the square, searching for handicraft shops selling wicker baskets, wooden items and pottery, and small cafés. A brief 15 minute walk up to the ruined 17th century Franciscan convent of **Nossa Senhora do Desterro** is rewarded by splendid views even though the convent ruins have little to offer. Set off from Largo 5 de Outubro up the narrow, cobbled Rua do Porto Fundo, turn left up the first narrow alley and keep climbing until the impressive, washing festooned

# Medronho

The strawberry tree, *Arbutus unedo*, is particularly common around Serra de Monchique but its enticing strawberry-like fruit is not really too enjoyable as the name *unedo* suggests, you eat only one! However, the locals have found a use for it which keeps them happy all winter, they make an *aguardente* called *medronho*.

Ripe fruit harvested between September and November is placed in a wooden barrel, just covered in water and allowed to ferment. A covering of mud protects the alcohol formed from further conversion to vinegar and a tube is inserted to assist the escaping gasses. All this bubbles away until the fermentation is complete, usually by January, by which time the copper stills are being dusted down. Distillation requires carefully controlled conditions but the farmers of Monchique, using very basic equipment, have turned this into an art form. The mass is transferred to the copper kettle (*alanbic*) — an average one will hold 100kg — which is heated steadily over a wood fire and requires hand stirring occasionally to prevent burning. When the time is right, a serpentine tube is fitted over the top of the kettle which passes also through a tank of cold water. The distillate containing the alcohol condenses in the tube and drips out of the bottom end into a container. Very carefully controlled heating to maintain a slow but steady distillation is essential for a good product. Pure spirits can never be achieved by simple distillation even with the most sophisticated equipment but the farmers do well to get the alcohol strength up to around 43 per cent, similar to gin or whisky.

Although licences to distil have been granted in the past, especially for a travelling *alanbic* (someone who moves around from farm to farm), licenses to sell are tightly controlled. Export is positively banned, largely because a poorly made product may well contain wood spirits, methanol, which is very poisonous and can cause blindness. A commercially made product is available but locals reckon that it is a poor shadow of the real hard stuff. Enjoy your nip!

façade of the ruined Colegio de Santa Catarina is reached and turn left. Bear right at the first opportunity and keep climbing now following signs to the old convent. For Manueline portals, Monchique's **Igreja Matriz** is hard to beat with its cabled columns and nautical knots whilst inside the church are three naves supported by pillars and a wooden roof. Fine *azulejo* polychrome tiles line the lower side walls. If it is not open, and more and more churches are being kept locked these days, ask locally to find the key-holder.

## The Art of Irrigation

With their skill at water management in arid areas, the Moors are popularly believed to have introduced the technique of irrigation into Algarve to extend the natural winter growth period into the summer months. However, the credit really goes to the Romans who built small, shallow reservoirs and dug artesian wells, known as *noras*, for that same purpose. Techniques advanced under the Moors who proved to be masters in this field and they devised the first automated system using oxen power. By a simple cog wheel system, the energy supplied by an ox circling while attached to a horizontal shaft was used to turn a vertical wheel above the well which lowered empty buckets and raised full ones. As the full buckets tipped over the top of the wheel, the water was collected in a channel and delivered to a storage tank. When needed, it was conducted through channels and distributed through furrows cut between the crops.

Many *noras* of this type can still be seen throughout Algarve, although oxen and donkeys were replaced by diesel power many years ago, but hardly any are in use today. One reason is the increasing demand for water which is effectively lowering the water table. Wells are dug down to around 10–15m (30–45ft) but boreholes are now drilled down to 80m (260ft) to secure an adequate supply of water while in some parts it is necessary to drill as deep as 200m (650ft). The energy required to raise water from such depths makes the water expensive. Following on the start made by the Romans, reservoirs (*barragems*) are being increasingly used to harness natural supplies. Mostly these are built in the areas of highest rainfall, in the serras of north Algarve which also offer suitable topography. Several have already been built including Barragem da Bravura to serve the land between Lagos and Portimão and Barragem do Arade to serve the needs of Silves. Many more are planned or under construction including some in the eastern part of the province.

## Fóia

The route up to the summit of Fóia leaves from the main square and snakes its way up the wooded mountainside to the cool heights. It is a good road, well surfaced, and passes a number of well placed restaurants on the way up which offer the opportunity of dining with truly sweeping views. Just before the summit is a *miradouro* on the left but this is more convenient to use on the way down to avoid the difficulty of crossing the traffic flow close to a bend. Summits reaching 902m (2960ft) should be beautiful by right but this one has long since been spoilt by a dense forest of telecommunication masts and aerials. Almost hidden in their midst is a purpose built handicraft centre which is best described as functional, but it is the place to buy a thick jumper should the winds be on the keen side as they often are at this altitude. If you cannot see the top of Fóia before starting out on the day's trip, save it for another day. There is nothing to see if the top is shrouded in mist but on a clear day the views are superb taking in much of the coastline right out to Sagres and Cape St Vincent. A few minutes' walk along the track which leads off the summit towards the east reveals unspoilt countryside with steep terracing and a more natural face of the mountain.

# Practical Information

## *Hotels and Restaurants*

### CALDAS DE MONCHIQUE
**Albergaria do Lageado** (tel. 082 92 616). This three-star *albergaria* (open 1/5 to 31/10) has good facilities including swimming pool, restaurant, gardens and parking.

### MONCHIQUE
**Estalagem Abrigo da Montanha**, Corte Pereiro (off the Fóia road) (tel. 082 92 131). Small, six-roomed inn with restaurant.
**Estalagem Santo António da Fóia**, Alto da Fóia (tel. 082 921 587). An eight-roomed inn perched at some elevation, restaurant and bar.
**Pensão Mons-Cicus**, Estrada de Fóia (tel. 082 92 650). Small three-star establishment with restaurant and gardens.
**Restaurant Quinta do Infante**, Monchique (tel. 082 92 143). Rustically set under chestnut trees between Monchique and Fóia, it is a great place to try the cinnamon flavoured lamb and at a very reasonable price.

### SILVES
**Albergaria Solar da Moura**, Horta do Pochino Santo (tel. 082 443 106). Well situated just outside Silves on the Algoz road, 22 rooms. Good restaurant open to non-residents.
**Quinta da Figueirinha** (tel. 082 442 671). Quietly situated just 3.2km (2 miles) east of Silves on the Messines road, the house is part of the agrotourism scheme and offers three self-contained apartments on a farming estate. No additional facilities.
**Restaurant O Alambique**, Poço Barreto (tel. 082 449 283). Good Portuguese food at very reasonable prices, popular with the ex-pats. Closed Tuesday.
**Retiro da Ponte Romana**, Silves (tel. 082 443 275). Small but popular restaurant on the south side of the river Arade. Rustically furnished with farm tools and old carriage wheels, very reasonable.

## Places of Interest

**Silves Museum**. Open daily 10am–5pm every day except national holidays.
**Silves Zoo**. This lies outside the town to the north. Take the road by the side of the cemetery on the east side of town and the zoo is reached after about 8km (5 miles). It is only small but has fox, wild boar, monkeys, genet, deer, peacocks and a variety of other birds, picnic tables. No charge for entry.

## Tourist Office (Turismo)

**Regional Office of Algarve**, Avenida 5 de Outubro,  8000 Faro. Tel. 089 800 400, fax. 089 800 489.

**Tourism Posts**
**Silves** (8300), Rua 25 de Abril tel. 082 442 255.

# 11. BAIXO ALENTEJO

Cast aside with a name meaning the land beyond the Tejo, Alentejo once considered itself nothing more than an unimportant, sun-baked plain which separated Algarve from Lisbon and the rest of Portugal. Even the inhabitants were regarded as dull witted and the butt of jokes throughout the country. But suddenly, after centuries of neglect, Alentejo is a rough diamond ready to polish and its culture, history and landscapes are bringing a new sparkle to the province. The Alentejans can hardly believe it.

Baixo (lower) Alentejo, with no hotels and very little in the way of accommodation, is particularly unexplored, yet it remains the guardian of an old and unchanging culture in its small towns and villages. It has no hard and fast boundaries, there is no sign to advise when Baixo Alentejo becomes Alto Alentejo but this chapter reaches north as far as Beja, just over two hours away by car from central Algarve. Historical interest centres largely on two towns, agricultural Beja of Roman origins and walled Mértola which lives in the shadows of a long, deep history where Romans, Visigoths and Moors have all left clear footprints. Over in the west of Alentejo, in the middle of nowhere, is an ill defined archaeological trail, rather like a treasure hunt, which provides a fun day and turns up an unexpected castle. Also in the west is the Atlantic coast, incessantly pounded by white surf, but with the charming resort of Vila Nova de Milfontes in the protection of the river mouth and threading all these together are small villages lost in a time of their own and a vast, vast landscape lost under an achingly blue sky.

In contrast to Baixo Alentejo, Algarve has masses of accommodation and in that respect makes a convenient base for exploration. This is the strategy adopted here and tours are described from a base somewhere in the Albufeira region of Algarve from where it is easy to reach the Lisbon road (IP1).

## En route to Mértola

Historic Mértola, enclosed by walls, dominated by its castle and connected to the sea by the once navigable Guadiana river is not just one of the jewels of Alentejo but one of the undiscovered treasures of Portugal. The town and its museums are worthy of a full day but in addition there are a number of excursions close to Mértola to be considered including the old, deserted copper mines at São Domingo, the downstream port of Pomarão from where

*Alentejo scenery*

the ore was shipped away and Pulo do Lobo (the Wolf's Leap), a watery beauty spot along the river (see p 161 for more information on these places).

From central Algarve, the easiest route into Alentejo is provided by the IP1, the Lisbon road and then cutting across country to reach Mértola. To complete the circle, the line of the Guadiana can be followed southwards to reach Castro Marim. Mértola is no great distance from eastern Algarve, about one hour by car, so from a base in that part of the province, it is more convenient to use the Guadiana river route for both legs of the journey.

Do not be misled into believing that the northbound IP1 is a road of motorway standard, although motorway regulations apply with regard to no stopping. It may start off as a dual carriageway road but it soon reduces to an ordinary road on to which houses front here and there and side roads and tracks join directly. Curled and twisted cork oaks picked out by the angular rays of the sun spread their weird shapes on the hillside to dominate the immediate scenery once beyond S. Bartolomeu de Messines. Cork oaks make an important contribution to farm economy in Algarve but Alentejo is a far bigger producer of cork, see the feature on p 155.

Distance can be saved by cutting off the IP1 and taking a route through Almodôvar. The road is well surfaced, although maps still indicate to the contrary, and the route is scenically interesting. Look for this minor right turn off from the IP1, which is signposted Almodôvar, at the top of the hill just 1.6km (1mile) after passing Santana de Serra and turn right again at the next junction. Rolling wheat fields, cork oaks, flat-topped holm oaks, black pigs, storks and always a blue, blue sky provide starkly contrasting scenery so typical of Alentejo. Stay around to the right at the village of Gomes Aires to

# The Story of Cork

The cork oak, *Quercus suber*, grows in coastal regions around the western half of the Mediterranean including the North African coast. It is dominant in Portugal and especially so in Alentejo which is home to around one third of the world's oak trees. Annual cork production from Alentejo alone is sufficient to meet about half of the world's requirements and is a major export earner for the country. Algarve's cork production is by no means insignificant and most of its plantations lie in the north and west of the country.

Growing cork is not for the impatient. On the poor, acid soils of Portugal, it takes around 25 years for a tree to reach the stage where cork can be taken but the slower the growth, the better the quality of the cork. The pigs do not mind how long the oaks take to grow providing that the acorns keep falling. Acorns, black pigs and Alentejo are inseparable and it is not just the cork oak which feeds the pigs but another extensively grown oak, *Quercus ilex*, which produces much loved sweet acorns. Both these oak trees are pruned to create a flat, spreading crown which provides plenty of shade for animals from the burning heat of the summer sun.

Cutting the cork is done in the height of summer when the gnarled, dull grey outer bark is easier to strip. Sharp axes are used to make first a horizontal incision around the circumference then vertical slits to enable the bark to be peeled off, first from the trunk then from the lower part of the branches. Provided that the outer cork layer only is taken and the inner cambium is left intact, the tree suffers no permanent damage and sets about the task of replacing its outer cork layer which takes around 9 or 10 years. Freshly stripped boles take on a wonderful wine red hue which makes the cork oak easy to identify even by the layperson although the colour fades over the years as the cork grows again. A single number painted on a tree identifies the year in which the cork was taken, and where two such numbers are found on different parts of the tree it indicates separate cropping by the farmer to regulate cash flow.

A single cutting can yield anything from 23–45kg (50–100lbs), and after removal from the tree, the curved sheets are sorted, stacked and left in the sun to dry for several months until the fatty substances which fill the millions of air cells have all been dried off. After boiling in water, the then flexible sheets are flattened and again dried in the sun. Not all cork is of the same quality, virgin cork from the first cutting, for example, is not as good so all the cork needs to be graded for various applications. Low grade material and cork waste are used for making composite cork board or for wall insulation, while better quality cork goes to make bottle stoppers for the wine industry, filters for cigarettes, sound insulation in studios, shuttlecocks and a whole host of other applications.

head towards Almodôvar. Just 3km (approx. 2 miles) beyond Gomes Aires there is another short diversion into **Santa Clara a Nova** to visit the **Museu de Etnográfico** and to a ruined castle just beyond. Although the distance is short, the interest here could easily absorb an hour or more and, instead of interrupting the journey to Mértola now, another option is to include it in the nearby archaeological circuit described later. Look for the museum on the right just on entering the village and should it be locked just attract the attention of a local who will fetch the carpenter, also the local mayor and key holder. Housed in the museum is an incredible collection of wooden farm tools including an 1870 threshing machine which would have been drawn by two horses, a Roman balance and jars, pots and pans of all descriptions. Reconstructed within the museum is an 18/19th century Alentejana house with typical furnishing including a family bed which hardly looks big enough for one person, let alone two. Concealed under the pillow is a pistol and under the bed a flowery chamber pot. The museum is overflowing with exhibits and a much needed extension will soon be brought into use which will also house archaeological finds from the nearby Muslim castle, **Mesas de Castelinho**, the next port of call. To find the castle, continue through the village past the front of the church and keep ahead where the hard surface ends and the road continues as track. The castle lies just 2km (1¼ miles) from this point and is reached by following the sign left to Monte do Castelinho. Superbly positioned, the excavated remains show clearly the layout and the walls have been uniformly restored to a height of around 1m (3ft). The only way back from here is to return to the Almodôvar road.

## Almodôvar

Steeped in agriculture, Almodôvar is unexpectedly large but fortunately signs are well placed to direct Mértola traffic through the tortuous streets, around the main square and cleanly out of town. There is an interesting museum here. Just less than 10km (6¼ miles) beyond is the possibility of a short side trip to see a restored and working windmill at **São Miguel de Pinheiro**. Old ovens are being faithfully restored nearby and bread baked from the flour produced by the mill sold from a shop on site. Should lunch be calling, or just a coffee stop, then the café/restaurant *Maria e Antonio* in the village here serves excellent food at very reasonable prices.

Eucalyptus shaded roads penetrate more of Alentejo's rolling, tree dotted plains giving no hint of Mértola until after leading down into a fold when the dramatic walls of the old town spring into vision with startling unexpectedness. There is an excellent viewpoint just before the final descent which is best seen in the evening with the sun behind. For the best view in the morning light, drive straight through the town, cross the new bridge over the river and turn immediately right.

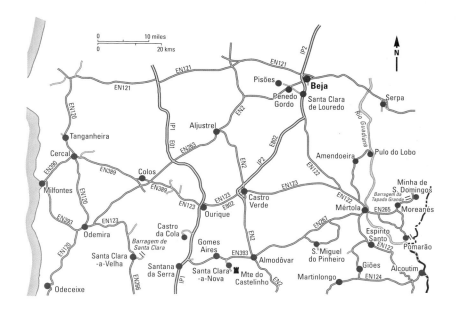

# Mértola

Crowned by a castle and encapsulated by impregnable town walls, Mértola's narrow cobbled streets echo with the sounds of history. For five centuries under the Romans, Myrtilis held a key position as a port situated on the then navigable Guadiana river which was convenient for the export of mineral ores mined at nearby São Domingos. Agriculture also played a role in the prosperity of the town as well as serving as a port to Pax Julia (Beja), all of which attracted people of wealth and power to settle here. Visigoth occupation saw little change and the occupants of the town established themselves as a Christian community. Trade continued unaffected under Islamic domination which was to see Martula twice capital of a kingdom in the 11th and 12th centuries whose territories included Beja. Wall construction and repairs were carried out by the Moors in the 12th century, including rebuilding the mosque. Christian reconquest in 1238 by the Knights of Santiago effectively brought an end to Mértola's long period of prosperity with the transfer of commercial routes to the estuaries at Setúbal and Lisbon. A brief economic revival occurred in the 15th and 16th centuries when Mértola became an important port for supplying cereals to territories in North Africa, but with the river slowly silting up its days as a port were limited. The final blow to prosperity in the region came with the closing of the mines at

*View of Mértola from the east*

São Domingos on 22 April 1968. Reduced to insignificance, Mértola is now making a new bid for prosperity in tourism by preserving its historic past and making it work for a new future.

## The Town

The best place to start is Turismo, in Largo Vasco da Gama, especially for those planning to visit the town's museums. Mértola does not always have enough visitors to warrant having the museums open every day but Turismo will arrange to have them opened up for interested visitors on request. Heading south from Turismo into the old part of town towards the castle leads past the small **Museum of Islamic Art**, although there are plans afoot to move this to a new location. On view here is the finest exhibition of Islamic pottery to be found anywhere in the country. Very early examples of polychrome glazing are seen in some exhibits where each polychrome patch is outlined with a dark band of manganese oxide. Climbing towards the castle, the route leads past the dazzling white **Igreja Matriz** which was once a Moorish *mesquita* (mosque), probably from the 12th century. Today, the square shape of the building and the horseshoe-shaped doors at the rear are the only clues left to read although the mihrab (the prayer niche facing east) is still there, in front of which is placed the main altar. Inside, the attractive rib vaulted roof, supported by columns incorporating some Roman capitals, was constructed in the 16th century, following damage in 1532 by an earthquake which had also destroyed the minaret. Outside, the cone-shaped pinnacles on the roof give some Moorish character to the building.

*Old Roman port, Mértola*

Crowning the hill is the **castle** incorporating much Roman stone and looking quite unscathed by past battles. After being captured in 1238 by the Knights of Santiago, restoration and enlargement work was undertaken and it was around this time, 1292, that the keep was first built. Dom Dinis was along in this same period to rebuild and improve the town walls. By the 1950s the castle was virtually in ruins but now it has been extensively restored.

The view from the top of the keep, open weekday mornings and afternoons, gives a good overview of the town and surrounding countryside and is well worth the effort of climbing the steps. A few Visigothic remains are also on display in the keep. A barrel-vaulted water cistern in the middle of the garrison courtyard, reached by steps, is still in good condition. Below and to the north of the castle is an area of excavation started in 1978 which has produced both Moorish and Roman artefacts. Originally it was a Roman forum and the real treasure is the cryptoporticus discovered here which was acting as the north wall to level the site. It took painstaking excavation over a period of five years to empty the 30m (98ft) cryptoporticus chamber and it produced many fine artefacts in the process, now housed in museums, both locally and in Lisbon. The walls remain in remarkably fine condition, unaffected by the chamber's conversion to a cistern in Moorish times. Overlaying the forum are Moorish houses which have been cleared to reveal kitchens, patios and alcoves. Much of the Roman underlayer has not yet been fully excavated, but it is postulated that the forum site was bounded by a temple and a basilica. For tours around the excavations, including the cryptoporticus, enquire at the tourist office.

Wandering down from the castle towards the riverside and the 18th century clock tower, Torre do Relógio, complete with stork's nest, is the easiest way to find the **Roman museum** which was born from a real twist of fate. The museum is located beneath the *câmera* (town hall), just a few yards to the south of the clock tower in Largo Luís de Camões. After the *câmera* building had been destroyed by fire, clearance of the site for rebuilding revealed the foundations of a former Roman villa. Excavation of the remains went ahead which reduced the level sufficiently to rebuild the *câmera* building on its original level and yet leave space enough beneath to convert the Roman ruins into a rather elegant museum. At the entrance is a headless, toga clad statue from the 1st century AD which was actually found in the town in the 16th century. Illuminated display cases show bits of pottery, coins and weapons while architectural fragments are scattered around including photographs of some pieces now housed in the National Archaeological Museum in Lisbon. Outside, in the same square, is the tribunal building where a mark on the wall records the height of one of the worst floods ever recorded. In periods of heavy rain, the river level can rise abruptly but, on the 6 and 7 December 1876, after copious and incessant rain, the river rose in a huge deluge to flood the town. In the aftermath of the flood, vestiges of some ruins were exposed, including some copper scales of Roman origin, found in an area known as Olive Oil Gulley, which resulted in the government of the day ordering excavations to explore the ancient remains of Mértola.

Walking south from the square while keeping the river in view gives a sight of the **Torre de Rio**, the River Tower, built by the Romans to defend the port and provide access to the water. Its arched structure protected the tower from river floods while still retaining a passageway through the pillars to reach the riverside. The arches are believed to have supported a pier, walled for protection, where soldiers could guard and defend. Just a little further upstream is the modern quayside which is used now only by fishing boats, but river trips bring tourists up from Vila Real in season.

Off Largo de Vasco da Gama, beneath the market hall, lies a small craft workshop where local women spend their days weaving blankets and other woollen goods using traditional methods. Continuing north from Turismo, but keeping ahead when the main road swings right, leads to another of Mértola's remarkable museums, **Museum Basilica Paleocrista.** This basilica was a sacred burial place used first by the early Christians and later by the Moors and the graves lie in two distinct orientations, one followed by the early Christians and a second, this time an easterly orientation, followed by the Muslims. Many of the open graves are there to be seen and around the sides are some of the finds which include grave stele inscribed in Latin and even some in Greek. When demand is sufficient, guided tours of this museum are laid on at 11am and 3pm, but if you are interested in these it is best to enquire at Turismo. Even if the museum is not open, the windows are large enough to allow good views inside.

With so few tourists around, every restaurant in these parts serves traditional food of Alentejo which relies heavily on pork. *Restaurant Avenida,* on the roundabout, is locally popular and has a good, reasonably priced menu which includes wild boar. Another interesting restaurant, *Alentejo*, lies at Moreanes on the road to São Domingos. The meals here are typical Alentejana and served by waiters in traditional costume.

## São Domingos

The journey to São Domingos starts out east over the new bridge and concludes when the lake by the roadside is reached some 18km (11¼ mile) later, although the old **mining village** is just a little further on. It is likely that there was mining activity here in pre-Roman days but the copper ore mingled with gold, silver, iron and tin certainly attracted intense mining under the Romans. Galleries from that period are still visible at the old mine and part of the wooden wheel used by the Romans to remove water from the workings is displayed in a museum in Paris. It continued to be worked under the Muslims, bringing prosperity to Mértola and the region. Activity at the mine picked up again around the middle of the 19th century when it eventually fell into the hands of an English company, Mason and Barry. By 1874, ore production was in full swing and a mineral railway, the first railway in Portugal, connected the mine to the riverside port of Pomarão from where the ore was transported by barge. Mature eucalyptus trees stand all around this region, originally planted as fuel to fire the steam engines. Production reached a peak in 1912 but it was not all from deep shafts, flooding problems had forced a move to open cast mining. As many as 6000 people lived in the town when the mine was in full production but the living conditions of the miners were basic. The rows of single storey windowless houses can still be seen today although many have now been improved. Meanwhile, the English lived in gracious villas. In 1929, at the request of the miners, the editor of *O Século* newspaper was asked to draw up a report on the living conditions but it was suppressed for 45 years. Of the miners houses, he said, 'They only had doors and if they did not look entirely the same as the stables of noblemen of old, it was only because they were even more poor and humble. Each door corresponds to a room, each room to a family.'

The mine closed down in 1968 causing widespread hardship amongst the workers and eventually reducing São Domingos to a population of only 800. Today it is like wandering around a ghost town. Many of the small houses are still there as are the old mine workings, a multicoloured open cast pit and the old hopper feed for the railway.

On the return to Mértola, a diversion to see Pomarão adds a further 28km (17½ miles). The route is signposted and it follows close to the line of the old railway in parts. **Pomarão** sits on the riverside overlooking the redundant docks, quietly reminiscing over the good old days.

To the north of Mértola, on the Guadiana river, lies a waterfall and beauty spot known as **Pulo do Lobo**, the Wolf's Leap. It is a round trip of around 50km (31 miles) out of Mértola and reached by first heading out on the Beja road then following signs to Amendoeira da Serra. The road from there leads

*São Domingos mines*

directly to the riverside. Prepare for the thundering noise where the water, encased by rocks, cascades through 15m (50ft) to arrive with its energy spent in the calm lake below.

## *To Beja*

Beja is easily reached from Mértola and almost as easily from central Algarve. Using the IP1 as far as Ourique then cutting off around Castro Verde following the upgraded road, now the IP2, gives a fast journey. Just before Beja is reached, a side trip leads to Roman ruins at **Pisões**. Turn left from the main road following signs to Penedo Gordo and turn right on reaching the village. Look shortly for a track on the left signposted Ruinas Pisões and motor down this unsurfaced road, keeping left at the fork, for around 4km (2½ miles), until the ruins are spotted. Although fenced, and possibly unguarded, entrance is still possible into these extensive ruins. Although poorly kept and presented, excavations have revealed a villa from the 1st–4th century liberally decorated with floor mosaics with a baths area and pool. Many of the finds are on show at the museum in Beja.

# Beja

Like many of the old towns in this region, Beja evolved well before the car and subsequently has barely been able to accommodate it. Park at the earliest opportunity and be prepared to explore on foot. Dominated by its castle, prosperous and busy Beja blends the old and the new. Narrow cobbled

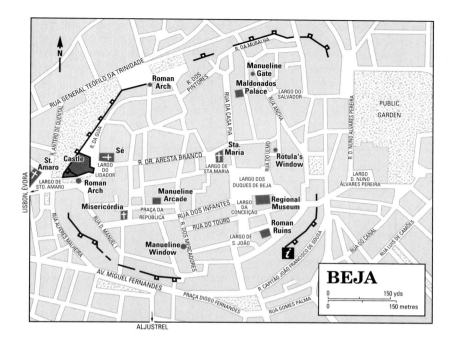

streets wander aimlessly in parts, whilst in the centre a spacious pedestrian-ised shoppingway oozes sophistication. Known as a town from around the 1st century AD, the Romans later called it Pax Julia after peace was made here between Julius Caesar and the Lusitani tribe. They made it the seat of one of three major jurisdictions of Lusitania. Its strategic position at a road inter-section and important farming activity ensured its growth and fortification under the Romans. In the 7th and 8th centuries Beja became an Episcopal see under the Visigoths; and because of its fine architecture and other treasures from that period it is often assumed to have been the Visigoth's capital. Many of these remains can be seen in the museum housed in Igreja Santo Amaro. Under Islamic domination, Beja evolved into a brilliant cultural centre attracting intellectual and artistic Moors to settle here. Battles with the Christians diminished the town which was eventually captured by Afonso Henriques in 1159 but it was not held for long and the town constantly changed hands until it was finally recovered by the Christians under Dom Afonso III in 1249.

## The Town

The **castle** was repaired and rebuilt under the Moors from 1173 to 1178 but, after so many attacks, in the 13th century Dom Afonso III found it necessary to order further renovations as did Dom Dinis. Today the castle, dominated by its keep, stands as a fine example of military architecture. Strongly built with a sturdy elegance and graced by three Gothic windows, the tower has balconies for vertical defence from which boiling oil could be poured through holes in the floor on aggressors. A small military museum is held within the keep and those with the energy can climb the steps inside the 40m (131ft) high tower for a big view which encompasses virtually the whole of the town and the 1173 sq km of territory which makes up Beja. Of the rest of the castle, the thick walls invite a tour for a view of more immediate surrounds.

## Architecture in Portugal

Influenced perhaps by their early history or simply reflecting the nature of the people, Portuguese buildings often have the solidity of Roman construction. Stable rectangular forms have their clean lines emphasised by a neat facing of white plaster which leaves the bare stone of the aperture frames and structural members free. Portuguese architects have always favoured horizontal structures so that most buildings are of no great height and have not shown any inclination towards curves and domes. Even in the Romanesque churches of the north, the curved apse is often ignored in favour of a square wall. The oval plan favoured by church architects of Germany, Austria and Italy in the 17th and 18th centuries was almost completely ignored although Nasoni built the 18th century Clérigos church in Porto to this design. Domes, too, are rare in Portugal and barrel vaulted roofs are by no means common.

In total contrast to this simplicity of line and style, the Portuguese found great delight and demonstrated extraordinary creative talent at surface decoration. This is evident in the decorative sculptures on the Romanesque churches where doorways are often decorated with carvings. The Manueline, Baroque and Rococo periods provided opportunities for expanding this art which was fully embraced by the sculptors, stonemasons and wood carvers of the time.

This same genius for surface decoration spread inside the church, especially to the retable behind the altar which evolved into a highly carved and usually gilded piece of woodwork often embellished with cherubs and vine leaves. Uniquely Portuguese, this style developed until sometimes the whole church interior was entirely covered in carved and gilded wood.

Gothic architecture, which brings together a number of elements like the pointed arch, the principle of the flying buttress as half arches or half tunnel vaults, and generally more slender elements, was introduced to Portugal by the Cistercians and the most outstanding early example is the abbey of St Maria Alcobaça (1178–1252). Gothic architecture only really found support towards the end of the 16th century and reached full expression in the Monastery of Batalha.

The Manueline style, which developed out of late Gothic, sprang from the great riches pouring into the country and it represents Portugal's unique contribution to the world's architecture. Its peak coincided roughly with the reign of Dom Manuel (1495–1521) after whom the style was named but not until much later. Apart from lavish surface decoration, the style also involved some transformation of structural members with a particular passion for twisted columns and ribs. There was no great uniformity within the style and it sometimes borrowed ideas, like sea motifs and other effects like Mudéjar which evolved in Spain from Christian architects absorbing Muslim influences. Most of the finest examples of Manueline occur south of Coimbra with Jerónimos monastery at Belém and especially the Convent of Christ at Tomar famous for its carved stone frames of twisted tree trunks, coral, knots and ropes.

Preoccupied with the Manueline style, the influence of the Italian Renaissance was late in reaching Portugal; it creeps in around 1530 at the earliest. French architects working in Portugal were the first practitioners in this return to the harmony, stability and poise of the Greco-Roman style which extended to statues, portals, retables, tombs and whole chapels. Amongst the most elegant and harmonious of the early works is the chapel of São Pedro in the old cathedral at Coimbra (1537). From the middle of the 16th century, Portuguese architecture responded to changes arising in Italy which evolved the Mannerist style. This involved a shift away from the basic classical proportions to characteristic distortion and exaggeration to present an ideal of beauty opposed to a representation.

Baroque architecture developed in the 17th century and was initially resisted in Portugal. This style is characterised by exuberant decoration, expansive curvaceous form, a delight in large scale and sweeping vistas, with a preference for depth over plane as seen, for example, in the Baroque staircase at Bom Jesus near Braga. It was gold and diamonds from Brazil and the munificence of João V (1706–50) which attracted foreign craftsmen to Portugal and stimulated architectural advances. Complex surface ornamentation was not neglected and the Portuguese took to wood carving with particular enthusiasm and retables emerged with twisted chestnut columns decorated with theatrically gilded grape vines and birds.

The first truly Baroque church is Santa Engrácia in Lisbon which was not actually completed until 1966, whilst the most extravagant project launched by João V was the huge complex of Mafra Palace, near Sintra. A movement away from the dark and ponderous Baroque to the lightness and colour of Rococo represented the dying phase of this style of architecture which faded around the middle of the 18th century.

Near to the castle, in **Largo de Santo Amaro**, stands a **church** of the same name which has been converted into a **museum** housing the remains of the Visigothic era and is one of the most important in the country. The Visigoths inherited much of the Roman style of architecture but added their own refinements to the surface decoration on the columns and capitals and many fine examples are on display in the museum. There is also some fine architecture (see feature p 164) to see in Beja and extraordinary Manueline windows seem to turn up when least expected, like the one on Rua dos Mercadores. A window of a different kind, Rotula's window off Rua do Ulmo covered by a wooden lattice, is remarkably like windows seen in Turkey where women can look out in peace without falling under the gaze of men.

In Largo da Conceicão, in the centre of the old town, lies the convent of **Nossa Senhora da Conceicão** which now houses the **regional museum**. Full of Gothic arches, it was built in 1459 by the 1st Duke of Beja as a convent under the Franciscan Order and converted into the regional museum only in 1927. Inside, on the right, are the portraits of the founders, D. Fernando and his wife D. Brites, who were the parents of Dom Manuel I, and on the left, a small Gothic tomb contains the bones of the first Abbess, D. Uganda. Inside the church are several altars but the most eye catching is the magnificent inlaid marble altar dedicated to John the Baptist whilst gleaming from the chancel is an exuberantly carved and gilded retable which was completed in the 17th and 18th centuries. Adjacent to the church, the four galleries of the cloister with their adjoining chapels form part of the museum and is where early examples of polychrome *azulejo* are to be seen.

# West Coast of Baix Alentejo

## *Vila Nova de Milfontes*

The west coast of Baixo Alentejo is well blessed with beaches but generally well battered by Atlantic breakers and it has only one resort of note, Vila Nova de Milfontes, which lies sheltered in the mouth of the Ria Mira. It can be reached comfortably on a scenic circular tour out of central or western Algarve involving around 260km (162 miles) of travelling. From central Algarve the quickest route is via the IP1 as far as Ourique then heading off west through Colos and Cercal. Tucked neatly into the river mouth, compact Vila Nova de Milfontes has all the airs and graces of a small fishing village finding a new lease of life as a desirable resort. The small 16th-century fort guarding the river entrance is now a private residence but it lends some extra character to the nearby sandy beach. Even though the sea is calmer in the river mouth, swimmers face a risk from the strong currents. There is a second beach facing the Atlantic and yet more sand across the river. Life centres around the fishing jetty where the best restaurant, *A Fateixa*, is to be found and where the Portuguese themselves come to eat. Accommodation is limited which may be why it has retained an unspoilt air although it may feel different when weekenders from Lisbon pour in. There are two options for returning to

*Daily gathering of local sages in Mértola*

Algarve by a different route. First head south to Odemira then either take the slow but scenic route on an ever twisting road through the mountains via Santa Clara-a-Velha to Monchique or by the less tortuous road which follows the line of the coast to Aljezur then to Lagos.

## Archaeological Circuit

An archaeological circuit has been laid out just north of Algarve's border roughly in the vicinity of the Barragem de Santa Clara. Little information is available about the historic remains to be seen but signposts are liberally sprinkled around to direct between the sites. Even so, finding some of them is a distinct challenge rather like a treasure hunt. Most of the 14 sites are old water mills, wells, *necrópoles* and similar, but the prime target is Castro de Cola which is not at all difficult to find and that alone makes the day worth while. The accompanying map supposedly indicates the location of the historic remains but it requires an adventurous spirit to find them all! To find the start, set off northwards on the IP1 and continue to reach Santana de Serra. Stay on the IP1 but look for the minor left turn 10.5km (6½ miles) later which is signposted Castro de Cola. **Anta 2 de Fernão Vaz**, a megalithic monument from the 3rd millennium BC, is signposted on the left a short distance down the road. From now on it is a case of driving on and picking up the various signposts but staying ahead on this road leads to the extensive remains of **Castro de Cola**. Castro de Cola started as an Iron Age settlement then was taken over by the Romans. All that can be seen now are the excavated foundations of many buildings enclosed within the substantial

167

Archaeological circuit

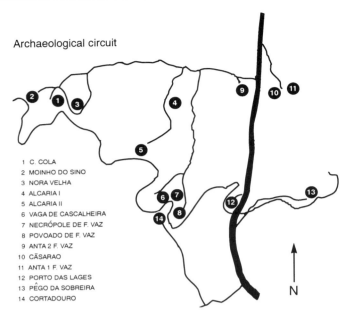

1 C. COLA
2 MOINHO DO SINO
3 NORA VELHA
4 ALCARIA I
5 ALCARIA II
6 VAGA DE CASCALHEIRA
7 NECRÓPOLE DE F. VAZ
8 POVOADO DE F. VAZ
9 ANTA 2 F. VAZ
10 CÃSARAO
11 ANTA 1 F. VAZ
12 PORTO DAS LAGES
13 PÊGO DA SOBREIRA
14 CORTADOURO

N

remains of the outer walls. The nearby restaurant, *O Chaparrinho*, serves excellent food but, be warned, it is very expensive.

# Practical Information

## *Accommodation and Restaurants*

### BARRAGEM DE SANTA CLARA
**Pousada de Santa Clara** (tel. 083 98 250). Perched on the lakeside a bit out in the wilds, good location for fishing and sailing. Six rooms, restaurant and small swimming pool.

### BEJA
**Residential Cristina**, 71 Rua de Mértola (tel. 084 323 056). A four-star *residencial* regarded as the best in town, rooms with private facilities but fairly basic. Centrally situated.

**Residential Santa Barbara**, 56 Rua de Mértola (tel. 084 322 028). Four-star *residencial*, rooms with private facilities but otherwise basic.

**Residential Bejense**, 57, Rua Capitão João Francisco de Sousa (tel. 084 25 001). A four-star *residencial*, all 24 rooms with private facilities.

**Restaurant Central**, Praça da República, 25 (tel. 084 22 189). Centrally situated, good traditional food and inexpensive.

**Restaurant A Esquina**, Rua Infante D. Henrique, 26 (tel. 084 389 238). A fairly large and popular restaurant, prices are reasonable.

## MÉRTOLA

**Casa das Janelas Verdes**, Rua do Dr Manuel Francisco, 40 (tel. 086 62 145). Traditional house in old part of town, member of the Turismo Rural scheme. Three rooms with private facilities.

**Restaurant Avenida**, Rua Dr Afonso Costa (tel. 086 62 458). Well respected restaurant, menu includes wild boar and seafood rice, pricewise very reasonable.

**Restaurant Alentejo**, Moreanes (tel. 086 65 133). Pork and wild boar specialities.

## VILA NOVA DE MILFONTES

**Apartmentos Turisticos Quinta das Varandas**, Quinta das Verandas (tel. 083 96 155). 12 apartments on touristic development.

**Aldeamento Turistico Duna Parque**, Eira da Pedra (tel. 083 96 451). A tourist complex with 27 apartments and 14 villas, swimming pool and tennis courts.

**Pensão do Cais**, Rua dos Carris, 9 (tel. 083 96 268). Modest pension with 20 rooms, all with private facilities.

**Restaurant A Fateixa** (tel. 083 96 415). Mainly fish but good and cheap.

## *Places of Interest*

### BEJA

**Castle**. Open 9.45am–1pm and 2–5.15pm, free entrance to the grounds but a small charge for the keep.

### PISÕES

Remains of Roman villa.

**Visigothic Museum** (in Igreja Santo Amaro). Open 9.45am–1pm and 2–5.15pm, closed Mondays and holidays.

**Regional Museum**, (in the convent of Nossa Senhora da Conceicão). Open 9.45am–1pm and 2–5.15pm, closed Mondays and holidays.

### MÉRTOLA

The low level of visitors at the moment does not justify regular opening times but, if closed, viewing can be arranged through the local Turismo.

Roman Museum, below town hall.

Castle and Keep, also museum.

Museum Paleocristão.

Islamic Museum.

### SANTA CLARA A NOVA

Ethnographical Museum. Opens on request at the moment.

## *Tourist Offices*

### Beja

Rua Capitão João Francisco de Sousa.

### Mértola

Rua da República (tel. 086 62 573).

# 12. ALTO ALENTEJO

First impressions of Alto Alentejo might easily be of a peaceful, empty land-scape of gently rolling corn fields dotted with flat topped oak trees stretching endlessly mile after mile and broken only by farmsteads here and there. Arising out of nowhere are the towns which formed the front line of the country's defence against the old enemy, Spain. Alto Alentejo bristles with them, with walled villages and castles where the echoes of history rumble around the old streets and shadowy figures flit along the castle ramparts — usually visitors these days. The past beckons everywhere in Estremoz, Vila Viçosa, Monsaraz and Murão, but nowhere more strongly than in Évora, and these towns are as rich in culture as any in the country. To discover Alentejo takes time and is a little like opening a well-wrapped parcel: take away the medieval layer to reveal an Islamic wrapping, remove that to see the Visigoth layer and undo that to find an inspired Roman civilisation which left an indelible mark.

Alto Alentejo offers more in accommodation than Baixo Alentejo but it still fails to meet the demand in summer which makes touring without advance bookings risky in high season. There is another very good reason for avoiding high summer, it gets very hot just as it gets cold in winter. Évora, roughly 150km (94 miles) from Lisbon, makes an ideal base for touring the region and most places of interest lie within an easy day's driving. Estremoz would not be as convenient geographically but does have the very tempting 30 roomed *Pousada da Rainha Santa Isabel* located in a 13th century castle with antique furnishings of the period.

## Évora

Historic Évora, which attracts more visitors than anywhere else in Alentejo, is a place of culture listed now by UNESCO as a World Heritage site. It has taken a long time and farmers in the megalithic period would not have appreciated that they laid the foundation stones, still around as menhirs and dolmens. The Celts were here, the Carthaginians passed through, but the first to leave a real mark were the Romans. Lusitani tribes put up fierce resistance, especially further north, but by 60 BC Julius Caesar had set up colonies in the area at Pax Julia (Beja), Myrtilis (Mértola) and Ebora (Évora). Southern Portugal

*Apostles guarding the entrance to Évora Cathedral*

was culturally advanced before Julius Caesar's men arrived and it is likely that the Greeks and Phoenicians had already introduced some crops, including olives, but the Romans are generally credited with bringing vines, wheat and olives with them. Many of these crops were farmed around Évora on *latifúndios*, massive agricultural estates which employed many labourers with no stake in the land. That system introduced by the Romans is more or less still in place today and Alentejo is the only province in Portugal which has large farms under single ownership. The Visigoths followed the Romans early in the 5th century but their footprints have faded, unlike in nearby Beja. Islamic forces took over in 714 and Évora continued to flourish largely under the Ibn Wazir family. Gerald the Fearless (Geraldo Sem-Pavor), an outlaw knight, staged a surprise attack in 1165 to take the town from the Moors. At night time, he drove spears into the outside wall to make a ladder over which he was able to climb to open the doors to the waiting Portuguese. In so doing he regained the favour of the king, Dom Afonso Henrique. Évora remained a cultural centre favoured by the first two dynasties of Portuguese kings and occasionally it was to here that the *Cortes* was summoned. It attracted scholars and artists from far and wide and a Jesuit college was founded in 1559 by Cardinal Dom Henrique, who later became king. During this period it grew to become the most important city in the country after Lisbon. Spanish rule in Portugal at the end of the 16th century marked the start of a long, gradual decline for Évora and here, in 1637, occurred the first serious resistance to Spanish domination. In 1759, the Marquês de Pombal closed the Jesuit college and in 1808, during the Peninsular War, the town fell to the French forces of General Loison and was brutally sacked. The legacy of this rich and varied history is a collection of fine monuments which is returning some prosperity to the town through tourism.

## The Town

Full of Moorish alleys, fine 16th-century granite and whitewashed buildings, wrought iron balconies and arcaded walkways, the old walled town of Évora sits on a low rise and is still home to thousands even though the town has long since expanded beyond its medieval boundaries. The town plan could have been inspired by a spider's web with all roads leading to the centre, and it is around the centre that most of the interesting monuments are to be found. Évora is one of those places which runs away with time but set aside at least a full day and expect to explore on foot.

**Praça do Giraldo** is the hub of the city, if not quite the centre, and a good place to start a tour if only to pick up a street map at Turismo. A huge 16th century fountain dominates one end of this spacious square, more or less in front of the Renaissance style Igreja São Antão built in 1557, whilst the northeast side is pleasingly arcaded. Parasol shaded tables from nearby cafés are set out in the centre in summer adding to the atmosphere. Rising out of the arcaded side of the square is **Rua de 5 Outubro** which leads up towards the summit of the hill, to the cathedral and the Roman temple. A clutch of tourist souvenir shops line the route selling anything from wall plaques to pottery, carpets and items in cork, although eye-catching for its difference is the Egyptian shop. Turn right at the top of the street for the granite **cathedral** with its ill-matched square twin towers.

This grand Romanesque-Gothic structure, one of the finest cathedrals in southern Portugal, was built on the site of an earlier mosque in 1186 and dedicated to St Mary in 1204. The façade fascinates for, matching Gothic widows each side of the door apart, the two Romanesque towers share no other architectural features. The buttressed bell tower has a clock face and is capped by a cone surrounded by a series of turrets similar to those seen on the converted mosque at Mértola, while the other tower has six irregularly placed facing windows and is topped by a single large cone covered in blue tiles. Each of the towers is as sturdy as a castle keep which reflects the role of the church in protecting the people in the troubled times of the early Middle Ages. Between the towers, the deeply recessed porch protects the carved figures of the twelve apostles which were carved by a local sculptor in the first half of the 14th century. The interior is distinctly more Gothic, with three soaring naves and a vaulted roof from which hang mighty chandeliers supported by rosary-like chains. Both the choir and the high altar were remodelled by the German J. F. Ludovice, the architect of Mafra, in the early part of the 18th century. Polychrome marble features strongly in the chancel and especially noticeable are the beautiful columns. A small charge is levied to enter both the cloisters and the Museum of Sacred Art located in the bell tower. The museum is abundantly and richly furnished with religious artefacts, ecclesiastical vestments and jewel encrusted gold and silver chalices and crucifixes from the treasury. Altogether a sobering display of wealth which raises more questions than answers.

The nearby archbishop's palace now holds the excellent **Museu Municipal**. Ornate doorways and windows from the original royal palace of Dom Manuel and the royal church of St Francis have been cleverly incorporated into the structure and form part of the exhibits. The central courtyard has a display of stonework from the Roman and medieval periods whilst the ground floor Renaissance room has work by the French sculptor Nicolau Chanterine with some especially delicate marble pillars from the Paraiso monastery and the tomb of Alvaroda Costa. Chantarine worked in Évora for a period in the 1530s. Upstairs, the collection of 15th and 16th century paintings by Flemish and Portuguese artists easily outshines the period furniture.

Beyond the museum lies the country's best preserved Roman monument, the **Temple of Diana**. It was built in the 2nd or 3rd century AD and, while its actual dedication is not known, it is popularly assigned to Diana. Most of the podium remains but only the north end of the colonnade which once surrounded the temple still stands. Corinthian capitals carved from Estremoz marble grace granite columns which have 12 rather than the more usual 24 flutes and all are in a remarkable state of preservation. The temple was apparently used as a slaughter house until late in the 19th century which

*Temple of Diana, Évora*

may have helped with its preservation in preventing the stone being removed for other building projects. Adjacent to the temple lies the rather grand *Pousada dos Lóios* occupying the 15th century Monastery dos Lóios which is believed to have been built by the nobleman Roderigo Afonso de Melo on the foundations of Évora castle destroyed in 1385. In restoration, the chapter hall was converted into a restaurant opening on to the cloisters and many of the most elegant features of the former building, like a splendid Manueline arch, have been carefully retained. Visitors enquiring at reception are usually permitted to look around between meal times. Next to the pousada is the associated **Igreja São João Evangelistria** which houses tombs of the family. Although a small charge is made for entry, it offers an opportunity to see

18th century *azulejo* tiles painted by the master himself, António de Oliveira Bernardes, illustrating the life of St Laurence Justinian, patriarch of Venice. Squeezed between the church and the old Palace of the Melos (also known as the Cadavals) is the Jardim do Paço with its café/restaurant.

Walking past the old palace and turning right into Rua de Menino Jesus gives a view of the robust medieval **walls** and tower now built into the old palace. Parts of the wall that run through the small garden known as Largo das Colegias are considered to be original 1st century Roman although reinforced by the Visigoths some centuries later. Above the wall here can be seen the palace of the Dukes of Bastos where the kings lived when resident in Évora. Across the main road at the bottom is the modern **university** occupying a group of buildings which were built originally for the Jesuit college in 1559 and regarded as one of the oldest universities in the world. It was closed down in 1759 when the Marquês de Pombal revenged himself by expelling the Jesuits from the country after they blamed him for the great earthquake of 1755 which effectively destroyed Lisbon and devastated large areas of the south. The university was re-established by parliamentary decree only in 1979. Turn left round the corner of the buildings to find the entrance to the **Cloister of Studies** which is well worth a moment or two. It is enclosed by a two tier arcade supported by marble columns and within the arcades are the classrooms which are identified by a tile on the outer wall indicating the subject taught.

From the university take the Rua do Conde da Serra da Rurega to pass around the hilltop back in the general direction of Praça do Giraldo. To the right, at the end of this road, are the sturdy twin towers of Portas de Moura, a former gateway to the medieval town. To the left is the rectangular **Largo das Portas de Moura** with an attractive spherical fountain in white marble built in 1559, and also to the south is the private 16th-century Casa Cordovil eye-catching for its graceful horseshoe shaped Moorish arches on slender columns. Still continuing towards Praça do Giraldo, along Rua da Misericórdia, look for a left turn into Rua da República to find **Igreja de São Francisco**. So many royal weddings took place here in the Middle Ages that it became dubbed the Royal Church of St Francis. Its architectural style is drawn on elements from the late Gothic and early Manueline with more than a touch of the Moorish, like the roof cones which here have the Manueline twist. It was built between 1460 and 1510, with a fine Manueline doorway which embraces the symbols of Dom João II, a pelican, and of Dom Manuel I, an armilliary globe. The main attraction for visitors here is the macabre 17th century Capela dos Ossos, the Chapel of the Bones, the walls of which are entirely covered with the bones and skulls of Franciscan monks exhumed from a nearby cemetery. A Latin inscription over the door warns 'The bones here are waiting for yours'.

Évora seems to overflow with fine buildings from the 15th to 17th centuries, and if cultural overload has not yet taken its toll, the 16th century **Palacio de Dom Manuel** in the park to the south is close by and worth a few moments. Originally a Franciscan monastery, it became the residence of

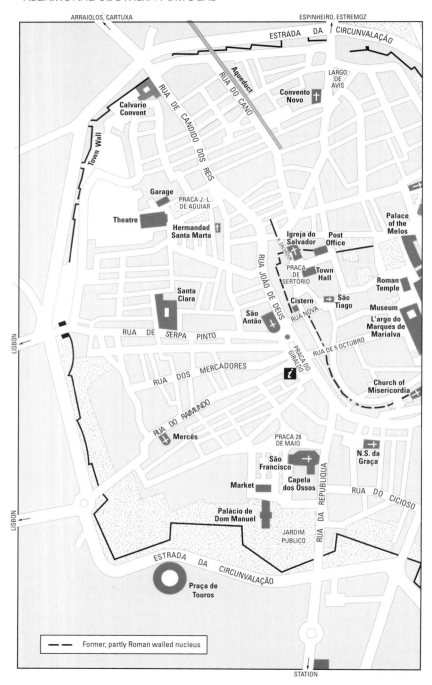

ARRAIOLOS, CARTUXA

ESPINHEIRO, ESTREMOZ

ESTRADA DA CIRCUNVALAÇÃO

Aqueduct

RUA DO CANO

LARGO DE AVIS

RUA DE CANDIDO DOS REIS

Convento Novo

Calvario Convent

Town Wall

Garage

PRACA J.-L. DE AGUIAR

Theatre

Palace of the Melos

Hermandad Santa Marta

Igreja do Salvador

Post Office

R. SALVADOR

RUA JOAO DE DEUS

PRACA DE SERTÓRIO

Town Hall

Roman Temple

Santa Clara

Cistern

São Tiago

Museum

São Antão

L'argo do Marques de Marialva

RUA DE SERPA PINTO

RUA NOVA

RUA DE 5 OCTUBRO

LISBON

RUA DOS MERCADORES

PRACA DO GIRALDO

i

Church of Misericordia

RUA DO RAIMUNDO

Mercês

PRACA 28 DE MAIO

N.S. da Graça

LISBON

São Francisco

RUA DO CICIOSO

Market

Capela dos Ossos

RUA DA REPUBLIQUA

Palácio de Dom Manuel

JARDIM PUBLICO

ESTRADA DA CIRCUNVALAÇÃO

Praça de Touros

— — — Former, partly Roman walled nucleus

STATION

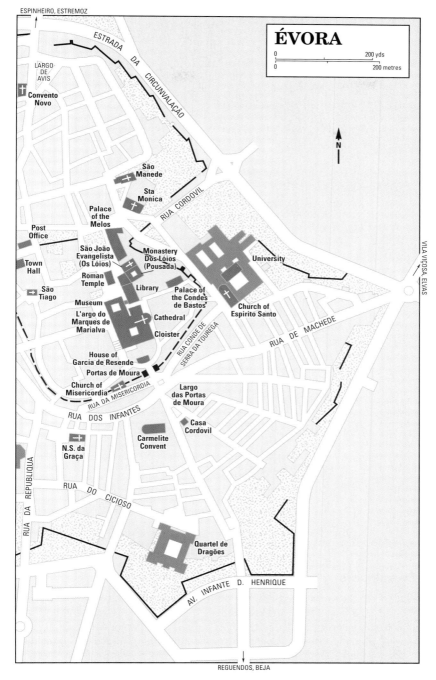

ÉVORA

0 _____ 200 yds
0 _____ 200 metres

ESPINHEIRO, ESTREMOZ

ESTRADA DA CIRCUNVALAÇÃO

LARGO DE AVIS

Convento Novo

São Manede

Sta Monica

RUA CORDOVIL

Palace of the Melos

Post Office

São João Evangelista (Os Lóios)

Monastery Dos Lóios (Pousada)

University

Town Hall

Roman Temple

Library

São Tiago

Museum

Palace of the Condes de Bastos

Church of Espirito Santo

L'argo do Marques de Marialva

Cathedral

Cloister

RUA CONDE DE SERRA DA TOUREGA

RUA DE MACHEDE

House of Garcia de Resende

Portas de Moura

Church of Misericordia

RUA DA MISERICORDIA

Largo das Portas de Moura

RUA DOS INFANTES

Casa Cordovil

N.S. da Graça

Carmelite Convent

RUA DA REPUBLICA

RUA DO CICIOSO

Quartel de Dragões

AV. INFANTE D. HENRIQUE

VILA VIÇOSA, ELVAS

REGUENDOS, BEJA

kings, used by Manuel I, João III and Sebastião as well as the Castilian kings who changed much of the structure of the original building. Now just one restored wing remains since the rest of the original palace was completely destroyed by fire in 1916. Like many of Évora's buildings, it combines Moorish, Manueline and Renaissance influences.

Surrounding Évora are a number of small fortified towns full of medieval character. All are within easy reach and, with a little planning, a number of these towns can be incorporated into a day's tour unless the scattering of megalithic monuments around the area have high priority in which case allow more time. There are some 25 recognised **megalithic sites** of dolmens, cromlechs, necropolis and menhirs, many of which have been declared National Monuments, and all are included in an excellent guide which details their location, published by the Câmera Municipal de Évora and available in English through Turismo. There are other sites besides and one or two of these are included or indicated in the tours described here. The first tour heads out on the eastern side of Évora taking in Évora Monte, Estremoz, Vila Viçosa, Alandroal, Reguengos de Monsaraz, Monsaraz and Mourão before returning to base. It is a tour rich in scenery, sites and history but if time runs out, distances are not so great and it is easy enough to return to Évora and pick up the tour again the next day.

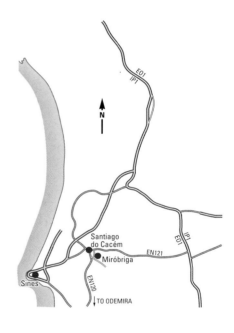

## *Évoramonte*

The EN18 out to Estremoz, signed off the ring road which basically circles the old medieval walls, quickly plunges into the cork covered rolling hills which characterise the scenery in this corner of Alentejo. Medieval Évora-monte, dominated by its **castle,** lies up on the left, a short drive from the modern village. This easily defended steep hill which rises to 474m (1555ft)

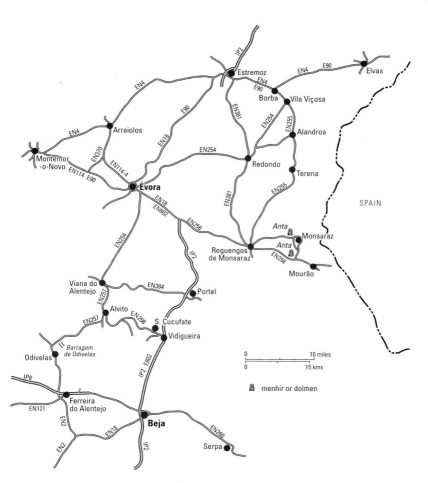

menhir or dolmen

has witnessed settlements from very early times and had a castle in Moorish times which was restored by Afonso III. With this part of the country in a state of near permanent warfare at that time, Dom Dinis continued with restoration and enlargement and also enclosed a triangular section of the hilltop with sturdy town walls which still exist almost intact today. A violent earthquake in 1531 caused the collapse of the castle and part of the walls but everything was immediately repaired and the angles of the walls were reinforced by cylindrical towers. Unfortunately, in recent restoration work, the castle has been cement rendered which entirely destroys its ancient appearance. There is not much to see inside the castle, although vaulted rooms on all three floors are open, but it is worth the climb to the top for the extensive views which encompass both Évora and Estremoz. Near to the castle, in Rua Direita, stands a house marked by a plaque where a treaty was signed on 26 May 1834 to end the civil war known as the War of the Brothers, between Pedro and Miguel. Miguel was forced into abdication and exile but it paved the way for his niece, Maria, to become Queen of Portugal.

## Castles in Portugal

For a country which has been a battleground over millennia, castles are firmly woven into the fabric and history of this country. Social organisation in the form of *castros*, fortified hilltop settlements, appeared with the Celts around 700–600 BC and many of these have been discovered in the north, particularly around the Minho where excavations have revealed whole fortified villages, or *citânias*. The Romans too adopted and strengthened some of the *castros*. More conquerors in the form of the Visigoths and the Moors underlined the continual need for strongholds. By the 11th century Portugal was emerging as a nation and many of the earlier forts and castles, particularly those strategically placed near the country's borders and along the coast, were fortified to the best standards of the day. Spurred on by the fear of Castilian domination, the pace of castle renovation and rebuilding quickened with the arrival of Dom Dinis to the throne towards the end of the 13th century. Castle after castle was built or rebuilt and towns fortified in a broad defensive belt around borders most under threat and his son Dom Afonso IV carried on the same strategy. Modification and modernisation of castles carried on through to the 18th and 19th centuries.

Central to a castle was a principle defensive tower, a keep, which was the ultimate defensive position. It was also used as an emergency or even permanent residence and often contained the public treasury, placed there for safety. Military appointments sometimes went to a local nobleman who was appointed the *alcaide* (captain) which often became hereditary. If the nobleman was particularly powerful and landed then the appointment might become *acailde-mor* (captain major). The *alcaide* was responsible for the management and maintenance of this and other fortifications in the region, for enlisting men, collecting rent, taxes, and fines as well as paying a tribute to the king.

Outside the keep lay the garrison protected by the castle walls or ramparts, although ramparts now means the top of the wall or the path around the top encircling the enclosure. This was an essential element for providing sentries with a high and commanding viewpoint, allowing access to towers and offering a protected firing position down on the enemy. The thickness of the walls determined the width of the ramparts, but where good width was provided it allowed easy and quick access for archers to assume position and for the movement of defensive engines. Access was normally by stone steps set against the wall. Where the walls were thinner, the ramparts were often constructed of wood rather like a long platform. The introduction of cannons in the 16th century necessitated some changes in design leading to thicker walls and wider ramparts with access by wide ramps rather than steps.

Towers were also built into the castle walls as buttresses or simply as defence for long stretches of wall. From the 12th century, towers were predominantly square but prismatic angle towers offering a greater range of firing positions started to appear in the 14th century. Angled towers suffered a distinct weakness, destruction of a corner by the enemy led to the collapse of two adjacent walls seriously weakening defences. Recognition of this weakness led to the building of cylindrical corner towers around the 15th and 16th centuries. Walls were castellated for the protection of the sentries or archers but the battlements acquired various forms, typically square or chamfered in Portugal, and sometimes included arrow slits. From the 14th century onwards, the merlons were widened and the spaces between often made with a downward slope to assist the launching of stones or boiling liquid onto the enemy. Later, when cannons arrived, these spaces were adapted and shaped for guns or special embrasures were incorporated in the parapet.

Strongly constructed balconies were often used as an element of vertical defence and they are typically seen at a high position on the keep or sometimes on the castle walls. They were often provided with a hole in the floor through which boiling liquids could be poured.

Brackets (corbels) which supported the balconies themselves became a decorative element. A later development was the bartizan, a small enclosed tower built at the angle of the castle walls, although it was more frequently used on forts which lacked a keep or a tall tower. The bartizan provided a sheltered and protected lookout point for a sentry, usually just big enough to enclose a standing soldier. Architects had a field day with bartizans and many amongst the varied designs are decorative and attractive while still wholly practical.

Doors or gateways into the castle called for special defensive precautions often resulting in two offset entrances with a space or courtyard between them which could be used to trap and attack intruders. Ironwork, plate and bars were used to strengthen the doors against attack by battering rams and later an iron portcullis was introduced. Drawbridges, too. were part of the defensive system which was used from the Middle Ages onwards.

Gradually, when artillery had firmly replaced archers, the castle evolved into a fortress of simpler design which was more suited to modern weapons. The high tower was no longer appropriate. Now bastions were built into the angles of the fortress walls allowing fire to the flanks along the face of the main fortress wall.

> Southern Portugal is rich in castle remains, some still in good shape, others in sad decay, but all have experienced the thick of battle. Their mute stones could tell of heroic deeds, of death and starvation but, mute or not, they tell a tale of survival, of the emergence of a nation and their own redundancy.

# Estremoz

Estremoz, best known for its marble, is quickly reached from Évoramonte. It lies on chalky land containing zones of marble which is extracted from the ground in the style of open-cast mines creating deep pits which can be seen in areas just outside the town. This good quality marble, worked also by the Romans, provides the main source of wealth for the area. Local clay is available too which has created a strong tradition in pottery and the best place to buy it is on the main square, Rossio, in the lower town, especially at the Saturday market. When Estremoz finally returned to Portuguese hands after the Moorish occupation, Dom Dinis walled the town, enlarged the castle and built himself a residence, now a pousada. The imposing square keep is often called **Torre das Três Coroas**, Tower of the Three Crowns, since it is believed to have been built during the reigns of Afonso III, Dinis and Afonso IV. Rising to a height of 27m (88ft), it is crowned with Moorish battlements terminating in pyramids and fitted with Gothic angled balconies.

Rossio, the main square, lies at the heart of the lower town which straggles out to one side of the old walled town. Surrounded by cafés, restaurants, shops and two convents, the square is always full of atmosphere but comes fully to life on a Saturday when the market comes to town. There is always pottery on sale no matter which day for some of the pottery stalls seem to have taken up permanent residence here. Of the two convents, one is now the town hall and the other, once the Order of Malta with two cloisters and a church, became the Misericórdia in 1880. Next to this church, at No. 62, is located the **Museu Rural**, an excellent ethnographical museum with the life and lifestyle of the people depicted in miniature by models made in straw, cork, wood and metal with some of the genuine articles also on display.

The old upper town is reached along a steep rising alley out of Rossio square on the opposite side to the museum. Abutting the Tower of the Three Crowns is part of the palace where Dom Dinis and Rainha Isabel lived for much of their lives. It was damaged by explosion in 1698 but rebuilt by João V and further restored in 1970 to house the *Pousada Rainha Santa Isabel*. It has 30 rooms and three suites all luxuriously furnished in 12th and 13th century style but with a 20th century swimming pool! Isabel died here in 1336 and the room in which she died has been converted into a small chapel. She freely spent her husband's money helping the poor and needy and

*Colourful Estremoz pottery*

founding hospitals and orphanages. Dom Dinis was not altogether too pleased with his wife's largess at his expense and forbade her to continue. Seeing her walk out one evening on one of her mercy missions with some-thing beneath her cape which he knew to be bread, he challenged her to reveal it to him. 'It is only roses' she replied and opened her cloak to show him and sure enough the loaves had turned into roses. Through her good works and the 'Miracle of the Roses' she became a saint in her own lifetime. Ask at the reception to see the chapel which has walls lined with blue and white *azulejos* tiles depicting the miracle performed by the queen. Across the road, in the old Hospicio de Caridade, is the **municipal museum** housing a whole host of exhibits including stelae, a reconstructed kitchen, furniture and a collection of painted ceramic figures.

From Estremoz the route starts to circle around to the south to take in Borba, Vila Viçosa and Redondo. There is the possibility of a side trip from Borba out to **Elvas** which boasts an incredible **aqueduct** built between 1529 and 1622 on taxes raised from the people of the town. It carries water from Amoeira along 7.5km (4½ miles) of ducting, some underground, some at ground level but 1.24km (¾ mile) along some 371 main overhead arches with lots of supplementary arches too. As if that is not enough, this mighty frontier post has three well preserved forts.

Dazzling white **Borba** seems to be built of marble and has the ruins of a medieval castle to see and a collection of buildings from the 16th–18th centuries but none with the grandeur seen in the more illustrious towns in this area. Marble quarries dominate and there is no escape until Vila Viçosa is reached.

## *Vila Viçosa*

The peaceful broad streets lined with orange and lemon trees give no hint now of the drama which has unfolded here throughout the centuries both in the castle and in the Ducal Palace. Strongly favoured by the Dukes of Bragança, Vila Viçosa became home to Jaime, the fourth Duke of Bragança, after his father had been executed for conspiring against the king. He found the castle a bit draughty so, in 1501, he decided to build a new residence. It was here, in 1512, that Duke Jaime stabbed to death his Spanish wife Leonor in a fit of unfounded jealousy. Later, with the overthrow of King Philip IV of Spain, the eighth Duke of Bragança was reluctantly persuaded to leave his comfortable life of painting and hunting in Vila Viçosa to ascend to the throne in 1640 as Dom João IV. This was the start of the reign of the House of Bragança which lasted until Portugal became a republic in 1910. It was also the birthplace of Catherine of Bragança in 1638 and Dom Carlos spent his last night there before his assassination in Lisbon in 1908.

The somewhat austere three storey building of the **Ducal Palace** seems almost diminished by the huge expanse of the square in front which also dwarfs the statute of Dom João IV, the eighth duke, on his horse. Guided tours lasting about 45 minutes are laid on in various languages throughout the day, except for lunch time. Endless rooms contain a rich mixture of furnishings and paintings and one of the first to catch the eye is the painting on the marble staircase depicting the 15th century Battle of Ceuta in North Africa which started Portugal on a trail of discoveries and colonial expansion. English, Flemish and French tapestries hang in the tapestry room; the heady mix continues with Chinese porcelain and Brazilian ebony furniture, but it becomes less like a museum tour when the personal rooms of the artistic Dom Carlos and family are reached. Some of the king's paintings still adorn the walls, dresses and suits hang in the wardrobes and the table is still laid awaiting the return of the king and his son from that fatal last trip to Lisbon. The best is saved until the last, the massive kitchens with 2000kg of gleaming copper hanging there in the shape of pans of every description.

On the right of the palace, guarding the entrance to this massive estate, is the famous Manueline gate displaying the knots associated with the House of Bragança. The stables here house yet another museum, this time dedicated to coaches. Also in the grounds is a chase enclosed by 18km (11 miles) of walls reserved for royal hunting parties but overall the estate covers some 21,000 hectares of prime hunting ground.

A short walk up the road lined with orange trees opposite the palace leads to the **castle** which is not of special interest although it is possible to walk in the grounds and on the walls. The moated castle itself is entered from the far side across a drawbridge through the smaller gate into a courtyard which now houses a museum devoted to hunting.

# Alandroal

It is only a short drive from Vila Viçosa to Alandroal on the skirts of the hilly rather than mountainous Serra de Ossa. Alandroal, with its Moorish sounding name, has a coat of arms which proudly declares that it belongs to the house of Avis and the two together have written the main chapters in its history. In contrast to the electric blue and white used to decorate many houses in Alentejo, this is an ochre and white town, so painted as a protection against the plague. The proof of the pudding is that Alandroal has remained plague free. Blue and white is believed to ward off evil spirits and is probably a legacy of the Muslims who still believe the blue and white eye is a powerful symbol against evil. The old town, well shaded with orange trees and palm along the streets, is a pleasant place for strolling although there is not too much to see. A grand marble fountain, Fonte Monumental da Praça, has six heads but only the middle two spout water and beyond that the **castle** is the next point of call. Thanks to inscriptions left by the founder of the castle, Lourenço Afonso, 9th Master of the Order of São Bento de Avis, the work was started on the order of Dom Dinis in 1294 and finished in 1298. With the Arab Galvo as principal architect, it is not surprising to find Moorish elements, like the pyramidal capped battlements, in the structure. Inside the castle lies Igreja Nossa Senhora de Conceição which was built around the same time as the castle. Walking the battlement walls opens up good views of the town and the surrounding countryside.

From Alandroal the road divides, which leaves a choice of opting for a quieter life by visiting the small castle town of **Terena** located in rolling plains. This old town essentially consists of two narrow, cobbled streets and a castle but there is the added attraction of taking lunch on the terrace at *Migas*, perhaps trying the Alentejo pork speciality of *migas*. The other choice is to press on to Redondo. Both routes meet up again at Reguengos de Monsaraz.

## *Redondo*

Very much a pottery town, Redondo is fast expanding and gaining a reputation for its excellent wine. The road from Alandroal joins the EN254 before entering Redondo and this road leads conveniently into the main square, Praça da República, which is the location of Turismo. The town's claim to fame is that it was the headquarters of the intrepid Lusitanian shepherd turned warrior Viriathus, who caused the invading Romans so much trouble until he was eventually assassinated in 139 BC by three traitorous comrades bribed by the Romans. It is the pottery, the medieval walls and ruins of the castle which attract visitors. The town was fortified by that indefatigable castle builder Dom Dinis in 1319 but the castle was sacked by Edmund Earl of Cambridge in 1381 who also dealt out the same treatment at Monsaraz. The English at that time were invited to Portugal under the old Alliance to help defend the

*Monsaraz*

frontier during the wars between Dom Fernando and Henry II of Castile but the troops turned out to be the 14th century forerunners of the 20th century lager louts. Check the front gate of the castle, Porta do Sol, by all means but do not miss the rear gate, Porta da Ravessa, which gives its name to an excellent wine produced by the *Adega Co-operative de Redondo*. They produce some nine million litres of wine from 1200 hectares of vineyard in modern stainless steel equipment and by the latest techniques.

There is the sight of water at Barragem da Vigia on the road from Redondo to Reguengos de Monsaraz. Abandon ideas of stopping at this latter town, once a prominent wool town but now a leading wine producer, and instead look straight away for the road to the old town of Monsaraz. There is a chance to catch one of the megalithic sites, **Anta do Olival da Pega**, en route. Before Monsaraz is reached and just before the right turn to Horta da Moura, look for a small road off left marked with bollards which starts surfaced but immediately becomes track. Continue a short distance through the olive grove and park near the sign announcing '*Anta*'. This one is a burial chamber with a long corridor which yielded engraved slate and carved horn pieces when it was first explored.

## Monsaraz

Located on a jutting peak above the Guadiana river and firmly enclosed by stout walls, Monsaraz is one of those fairytale towns which is too good to miss. If time allows only one visit to the area then Monsaraz should be

*Cromlech near Monsaraz*

considered first. Dolmens and menhirs abound in the region telling of settlements as early as the megalithic and Iron ages; the Romans and Visigoths followed as did the Moors but leaving only faint footprints. Recovered from the Moors in 1167 by Geraldo sem Pavor, it was given to the Knights Templar by Dom Sancho II in 1232 as a reward for their help in recovering it, but it passed to the Order of Christ in 1319 when the Templars were extinguished. Dom Afonso and then Dom Dinis encouraged repopulation and ordered a castle to be built for their protection, which it was in 1310. When the English Earl of Cambridge took up residence after being invited by Dom Fernando, he and his merry band rebelled on not being paid and rewarded their host by sacking the castle in 1381 which probably made it easier for the Castilians to take it during the Castilian Wars of 1383–85. It was recovered from the Castilians almost immediately by Nuno Álvares Pereira, who later became known as the Sainted Constable.

Cobbled Rua Direita leads directly from the town gate to the castle past 16th and 17th century whitewashed houses all with square windows and doors. The parish church, Igreja Matriz, lies in the main square with the 18th century pillory part way along. Next to it is Turismo which has little to offer in the way of information except for a simple leaflet, but the town is so small it barely needs a plan. The former Paços de Audiência, also in the same square, houses an exhibition of sacred art which includes mainly vestments but is of limited appeal. At the end of Rua Direita is the compact granite **castle** looking as sturdy as the day it was built. Its battlements invite exploration. Climbing to the top of the keep is not too difficult and it is worth it for the views, not just of the houses clustered within the town walls but over the countryside including the Guadiana river. The upper floor in the keep was once the home of the *alcaidaria,* while the lower floor was earlier a prison then an armoury.

Signs from Monsaraz lead to Mourão which actually lies across the Guadiana river. There is the **Cromlech do Jerez** to visit en route which is found by turning down the track opposite the Quinta de Jerez. This one is a standing stone believed to be connected with fertility rights and the sacred area around is marked off by smaller stones.

## *Mourão*

Mourão is another fortified border town which was caught up in the some-times fierce battles along this frontier. Originally it was settled at Vila Velha nearer the river, probably by the Moors, but was deserted for some time after reconquest by the Christians. It was resettled on higher ground and the first fort was built under Prior Gonçalo Egas, Prior of the Order of St John of Jerusalem, in 1226, who is believed to have granted the first charter, confirmed by Dom Dinis in 1296. Further reconstruction and enlargement continued and by the time Dom Sebastião arrived to raise men for his North Africa campaign in the 16th century, the town was large enough to provide 400. The castle and town suffered heavy damage in 1657, during the Wars of Restoration, at the hands of an overwhelming force of Spaniards but the castle was again restored. Little remains now of even the 17th century rebuilding except for the walls.

Assuming that further megalithic sites in the area are not to be explored, it is a straight run from Mourão back to Évora through Reguengos de Monsaraz.

# Évora to São Cucufate

The prime purpose of the next tour is to visit the extensive Roman remains at São Cucufate, one of the best preserved Roman monuments in Portugal, but Portel, and Viana do Alentejo can also be visited en route. Set off by taking the Beja road out of Évora and enjoy some of Alentejo's scenery of rolling plains dotted with flat-topped ilex oak. The trees are pruned this way, to the delight of the pigs, to increase the yield of sweet acorns and the area of summer shade whilst the farmer delights in taking away wood which is ideal for converting into charcoal. Divert off the road for **Portel**, just awakening to tourism, to visit its robust castle. It is unusual in having massive cylindrical angle towers to give greater protection to the walls and most of these still stand. If the castle has no appeal, look in the handicraft shops for the miniatures of traditional Alentejo furniture which is a local speciality.

## São Cucufate

On reaching Vidigueira, take the Alvito road and look out shortly for signs to São Cucufate which lies just off the main road to the right. Remarkably, for one of the most impressive Roman sites in Portugal, it is unprotected. The substantial remains belong to a **Roman villa** built in the 4th century. Excavations have shown previous buildings existed starting with a villa built in the 1st century which was rebuilt early in the 2nd century around a peristyle but destroyed by the construction of the present building. The villa was used as a monastery until the 16th century, and may even have been used in Moorish times, which accounts for its remarkable state of preservation, although the monks destroyed certain outbuildings to use the ground as a cemetery.

The villa was a rectangular structure of two storeys with the lower vaulted floor used by the domestic servants and as a storeroom and the upper one to house the family. Just enough evidence remains upstairs to trace the room plan. The façade had a long terrace served by three stairways which opened on to a garden. Some of the original work stopped at foundation level. It is thought the building may never have been completed to plan and that the earlier 2nd century baths were adapted. On the edge of the villa is a temple very similar to the one found at Milreu outside Faro (see Chapter 5). Amazingly, the ruins stand to a considerable height and the brick work is still in remarkably good condition. Of the ground floor storage area, a crypto-porticus can be discerned, although the roof is missing and, unusually, there are no mosaics to be seen. It is thought to have belonged to some unknown family from Pax Julia (Beja).

## Viana do Alentejo

Leave São Cucufate to continue first to Alvito and then to Viana do Alentejo. Viana do Alentejo has a fine heritage in monuments built throughout the Middle Ages, and none more astonishing than the fortified and crenellated Gothic **Igreja Matriz** which stands within the castle walls and appears to merge with them. It is worth a stop just to see the church's Manueline doorway. Only the ramparts and battlements of the castle remain protected by a round turret at each corner. Just out of town to the east stands the sanctuary of **Nossa Senhora d'Aires** which has attracted pilgrims through the ages and still does on the fourth Sunday of September every year for which the town is authorised to hold a fair.

# Évora to Arraiolos

Other interesting trips out of Évora include the one to Arraiolos which is a relatively short distance, 22km (14miles), to the north. The main interest here is not so much the monuments, of which it has its fair share including the ruins of a medieval castle and some fine 16th century buildings, but its carpets. Making carpets and rugs is thought to have originated with the Moors but demand was stimulated amongst the nobility in the 16th and 17th centuries when the explorers brought back rugs from Persia and India. These were copied to such good effect in an expanding industry here in Arraiolos that the town has been famous ever since although now the original patterns have been replaced by local designs. Some of the 18th century work can be seen hanging on the walls of famous houses and palaces in Porgual, like Queluz Palace near Lisbon. Walking the main street will lead you to the carpet shops, some of which have workshops behind. But these colourful creations are expensive. If it is any consolation, they are cheaper to buy here than anywhere else in Portugal. Take a leaf out of William Beckford's book who, according to Rose Macaulay in *They went to Portugal*, on a visit to Arraiolos 'laid in a stock of bright carpets for his journey, lest he should find himself in an uncarpeted room; in the Estremoz pousada he spread them all around his bed, they made a flaming, exotic appearance and protected his feet from the damp brick floors'.

# Évora to Miróbriga

One final suggested excursion is to the **Roman site** of Miróbriga which is located right over in the west of the province, close to Santiago de Cacém. It could be combined with the São Cucufate tour (see p 189), particularly if just the two Roman sites were targeted and the town left for another day. From Évora it is a two hour rural drive with plenty of Alentejo scenery and no large towns to negotiate. The route starts out south to Viana do Alentejo, then Alvito, before heading west on the EN257 to join the road running south to Ferreira do Alentejo. From here it is a fairly straight run west on the EN121 with a short right then left dog leg to cross the major EN262. Just before entering Santiago de Cacém look for the sign left to Miróbriga.

## *Miróbriga*

This extensive site has been fairly well excavated and researched over the years. The first time in the 19th century was under the direction of the Bishop of Beja who used the artefacts to enrich his private collection. Further periods of research in 1940 and from 1958–78 culminated in an international project involving Portuguese and American archaeologists who carried out intensive studies from 1981–85. The site was occupied in the Iron Age and the Roman site was built on top which may explain some of the observed anomalies. It lacks a typical Roman urban layout and there is no other known site in close proximity. One view is that from the 3rd century the site was a sanctuary or large pilgrimage centre, with temples dedicated to Asklepius and Venus. It was also equipped with baths for use by visitors and a hippodrome to provide entertainment during religious festivals. A contrary view regards the temples simply as part of the forum as is the case with many Roman provincial towns. Unusually, no mosaics have been found on the site.

The site is well laid out with footpaths which lead systematically around the site past houses, the baths with hot and cold sections, through the hostel containing rooms with dining rooms to the forum or acropolis which was also an Iron Age settlement with a temple. The hippodrome is on a separate site about 1km south of the area and is the only one found in Portugal so far. Artefacts from Miróbriga can be seen in the Municipal Museum at Cacém.

# Practical Information

## Hotels and Restaurants

Much of the better accommodation in Alto Alentejo is in accommodation in manor houses of architectural merit in the TURIHAB (TH) scheme which are normally well outside town, or in rustic houses mostly within the town or close by and part of Turismo Rural (TR), or on an active farming estate in the Agroturismo (AT) scheme. See introduction for more details.

### ALANDROAL
**A Chaminé** (tel. 068 44 335). Frog's legs in tomato sauce does not turn up often on menus in Portugal, but here is your opportunity; otherwise stick to the grills which are good.

### ALVITO
**Pousada do Castelo de Alvito** (tel. 084 48 383). The 15th century fortress has been converted to provide 20 rooms, swimming pool, chapel garden and small amphitheatre.

### ELVAS
**Pousada de Santa Lucia** (tel. 068 622 194). Located in the town, this modern building is provided with 15 rooms and a suite.
**Hotel D. Luís**, Av. de Badajoz (tel. 068 622 756). Large three-star hotel with restaurant.

### ESTREMOZ
**Pousada Rainha Santa Isabel** (tel. 068 22 618). Built into the historic fortress, rooms furnished in 12th and 13th century style, swimming pool. Good restaurant.
**Monte dos Pensamentos**, Estrada da Estação do Ameixial (TR) (tel. 068 22 375). Splendid country house 2km (1¼ miles) outside Estremoz with four rooms.
**Restaurant Alentejano** (tel. 068 22 834). Wood panelled dining room above café, good on pork dishes, very reasonable.

### ÉVORA
**Pousada dos Lóios** (tel. 066 22 618). Opened in 1965 in a restored 15th century mansion, 32 rooms in a delightful setting with good restaurant.

**Évorahotel, Quinta do Cruzeiro** (tel. 066 734 800). A large three-star hotel with full facilities including restaurant, swimming pools and tennis.

**Hotel Ibis, Quinta da Tapada** (tel. 066 744 620). Well located by the old town walls, this is a new hotel in the Ibis chain. Plenty of parking, comfortable rooms and buffet breakfast, it makes an ideal base for exploring Évora.

**Estalagem Póquer, Quinta de Vale Vazios**, EN114 (tel. 066 31 473). Four-star hotel with just 15 rooms but with good facilities including restaurant, swimming pool and tennis.

**Albergaria Vitorias**, Rua Diana de Lis (tel. 066 27 174). Limited facilities in this four-star establishment, no restaurant, 48 rooms.

**Hotel Santa Clara**, Travessa da Milheira, 19 (tel. 066 24 141). Good standard two-star hotel with some facilities for disabled, restaurant.

**Casa de S. Tiago**, Largo Alexandre Herculano, 2 (TH) (tel. 066 22 686). Located in 16th-century house in the heart of Évora, six rooms.

**Casa de Sam Pedro, Quinta de Sam Pedro** (TH) (tel. 066 27 731). Converted 18th-century manor house 5km (3 miles) outside Évora with three rooms.

**Quinta da Nora**, Estrada dos Canaviais (TR) (tel. 066 29 810). Part of a farm 4km (2½ miles) outside Évora, five rooms.

**Quinta do Louredo**, Estrada do Igrejinha (TR) (tel. 066 22 813). Two rooms only in manor house just 5km (3 miles) outside Évora.

Eating in Évora is generally more expensive than in surrounding towns, and some of the overtly touristic restaurants are best avoided.

**O Fialho**, Travessa do Mascarenhas, 14 (tel. 066 23 079). Widely regarded as the best restaurant in town, serves traditional dishes to the Portuguese. Expect to pay a little more.

**A Muralha**, Rua Outubru, 21 (tel. 066 22 284). Fairly typical Portuguese restaurant, moderate cost.

**Cozina de St Humberto**, Rua da Moeda, 39 (tel. 066 24 251). A bit pretentious, avoid the house wine which is not as good as the food; moderate price.

**O Lampião**, Rua dos Mercadores, 72 (tel. 066 26 495). Award winning soups, plenty of good pork dishes at reasonable cost.

## ÉVORAMONTE

**Monte da Fazenda** (TR) (tel. 068 95 172). Rustic house on Alentejan farm producing olives and cork just outside Évoramonte. Five rooms with private sitting rooms.

**Restaurant A Convenção** (tel. 068 95 217). Next to castle, modern restaurant with good but limited range of dishes, on the expensive side.

## MONSARAZ

**Horta da Moura** (tel. 066 55 206). Rural hotel on agricultural property delightfully situated just 3km (2 miles) outside Monsaraz. 13 rooms and one apartment with good on site facilities including swimming and horse riding.

**Restaurant O Alcaide** (tel. 066 55 168). If the roast lamb has no appeal try the roast marinated snails, and very reasonable too.

**Zé Lumumba** (tel. 066 55 121). Plenty of game dishes in season, reasonable.

## MOURÃO
**Restaurant Adega Velha** (tel. 066 56 443). Old Adega, make wine on the premises, good atmosphere and reasonable.

## REDONDO
**Quinta da Talha**, Estrada do Freixo (AT) (tel. 066 999 468). Peacefully located 3km (2 miles) outside Redondo on farm estate, a group of houses offering four rooms.
**Vá Lá**, on Vila Viçosa road (tel. 066 99 521). Restaurant behind small café, unpretentious, good food and very reasonable.

## REGUENGOS DE MONSARAZ
**Restaurant Central** (tel. 066 52 219). On central square, has some interesting dishes on offer including baby shark soup, *sopa de cação*.

## TERENA
**Casa de Terena**, Rua Direita (TR) 45 (tel. 068 45 132). Restored 18th-century house in centre, six rooms and lounge available.
**Restaurant Migas** (tel. 068 45 188). A little more expensive than most but good regional specialities.

## VILA VIÇOSA
**Casa de Peixinhos** (TH) (tel. 068 98 472). 17th-century manor house forming part of a farm estate with six rooms.
**Casa dos Arcos**, Paça de Matim Afonso de Sousa (TH) (tel. 068 98 518). Situated in 18th-century Renaissance style manor house, with four rooms and two apartments.
**Restaurant Os Cuco**, Mata Municipal (tel. 068 988 806). New restaurant near market square offering good regional specialities, reasonable.
**Ouro Branco**, Campo da Restauração (tel. 068 98 556). Typical Portuguese restaurant.

## *Places of Interest*

## ESTREMOZ
**Museu Rural**, 62 Rossio. Open 10am–1pm and 3–5.30pm, closed Mondays and holidays.
**Museu Municipal**, main square inside castle walls. Open 10am–12 noon and 2–6pm.

## ÉVORA
**Museu Municipal**, near cathedral. Open 10am–12.30pm and 2–5pm, closed Monday and holidays.
**Museum of Sacred Art**, within cathedral. Open 9am–12pm and 2–5pm, closed Mondays and holidays.

## VILA VIÇOSA
**Ducal Palace**. Open 9.30am–1pm and 2–5pm, closed Mondays and holidays.

*Entrance to Évora Cathedral*

**Museu da Caça** (hunting) in castle. Open 9.30am–1pm and 2–5pm, closed Mondays and holidays.

## Tourist Offices

**Alandroal**: Câmera Municipal, Praça da República (tel. 068 44 150).
**Arraiolos**: Praça Lime de Brito (tel. 066 42 105).
**Borba**: Câmera Municipal, Praça da República (tel. 068 94 113).
**Estremoz**: Rossio Marquês de Pombal (tel. 068 332 071).
**Évora**: Praça do Giraldo (tel. 066 22 671).
**Mourão**: Câmera Municipal, Praça da República (tel. 066 56 113).
**Monsaraz**: Largo D. Nuno Álvares Pereira (tel. 066 55 136).
**Redondo**: Câmera Municipal, Praça da República (tel. 066 99 112).
**Reguengos de Monsaraz**: Rua 1 de Maio (tel. 066 51 315).
**Viana do Alentejo**: Câmera Municipal, Praça da República (tel. 066 93 106).
**Vila Viçosa**: Praça da República (tel. 068 98 305).

# INDEX